THE FUTURE WORKFORCE

The 21st-Century Transformation of Leaders, Managers, and Employees

Irving Buchen

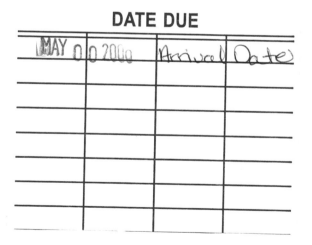
Rowman & Littlefield Education
Lanham, Maryland • Toronto • Oxford
2005

Published in the United States of America
by Rowman & Littlefield Education
A wholly owned subsidiary of The Rowman & Littlefield Publishing Group, Inc.
4501 Forbes Boulevard, Suite 200, Lanham, Maryland 20706
www.rowmaneducation.com

PO Box 317
Oxford
OX2 9RU, UK

British Library Cataloguing in Publication Information Available

Library of Congress Cataloging-in-Publication Data

Buchen, Irving H., 1930–
   The future workforce : the 21st-century transformation of leaders,
managers, and employees / Irving Buchen.
      p. cm.
   Includes bibliographical references and index.
   ISBN 1-57886-208-6 (pbk. : alk. paper)
   1. Work environment—United States—Forecasting. 2. Labor supply—
United States—Forecasting. 3. Industrial relations—United States—
Forecasting. I. Title.
   HD7654.B83 2005
   331.1'0973'01—dc22

                                                    2004023135

∞™ The paper used in this publication meets the minimum requirements of
American National Standard for Information Sciences—Permanence of Paper
for Printed Library Materials, ANSI/NISO Z39.48-1992.
Manufactured in the United States of America.

To
John Sobecki, Dave Gavin, and Lincoln Rowley of
COMWELL, Consultants to Management and to
Paul Zdrowowski of HR Partners

For providing me with the opportunities
to understand and train a diverse workforce,
and to be open to what those
employees, managers, and leaders
in turn had to teach all of us.

CONTENTS

SECTION III   THE FUTURE OF THE FUTURE

Future Work Issues

Future Workforce Impacts

INTRODUCTION

Many books and articles claim to be groundbreaking or far-reaching. They often fall short of being either because they are deficient in one major respect. They are present-bound. They stop short of crossing the threshold to the future. They remain safe on the other side because they cherish certainty over speculation, control over flow. In the process, they frequently offer yesterday's warmed-over rolls as tomorrow's panaceas. Worse, they insulate their presentation from the criticism and collaboration of the future. They prefer the certainty of the known to the unknown.

But the unknown is knowable. In fact, when past patterns and current statistics are extrapolated and linked with discernible trends, as much as two-thirds of the near-term future may be in hand. To be sure, there are always wild cards. And the future is never totally knowable. If it were, it would no longer be the future.

The downside, of course, is that the future is in fact often threatening, and always finally elusive. Thus, the title and scope of my work may invite and even deserve skepticism. But such misgivings always should accompany forecasts; they discipline presumption.

I am not totally convinced that all my projections are true or always on target. In fact, the advice I was once given by one of my wiser and older forecasting colleagues was to ensure that the time line I used exceeded my life expectancy. I thus would be spared the embarrassment of being around to be the object of criticism. But even here the future has been diabolically tricky. We are living longer and things are happening faster. But I am banking on another law of the future to be persuasive.

The law of crash is slip. The bridge that ultimately collapses has been falling apart little by little over time. In fact, we now require that such degrees of decay and risk as well as final collapse be factored into any projection. And to ensure that such programmed fallibility is honored, at least 50 percent of all strategic planning must now be devoted to monitoring.

Such invasive tracking has happily led to forecasts being not only more accountable and transparent, but also more evolving and malleable—more a process than a singular product or outcome. Above all, it has compelled future analysis always to back up to its present roots and then carve out a transitional intermediate stage. In the process, the future displays a developmental range that in fact is used here as this book's organizing structure.

Specifically three stages are presented: current, emerging, and futuristic. The first is synonymous with now, the second with the short term, the last with the long term. Each of the three sections in turn presents Work Issues followed by Workforce Impacts. The basic rhythm thus moves from the critical driving factors of the work environment to those who have to inhabit, endure, sustain, and even create the conditions of their working lives. Abstract issues always need to be finally rendered and tasked by actual people living and working in both real and future time.

But a few caveats. It would be incorrect to conclude that such a sequence is invariably progressive, or worse that each stage exists in a cause-and-effect relationship with what precedes or follows it and is inevitably predictive. The future is too much like its classical prototype, Proteus, and is nimble and quick like Jack and the artful dodger. Besides, the future may lie in the past. But if unheeded, precious resources are wasted. Expensive brick-and-mortar schools are now being built for an electronic age.

The value of beginning with the present and describing current practices is to benchmark where things are. For many professionals who are not even there yet, such portraits of the state of the art offer the immediate practical value of application. They exist in real time and are certain and useable. But they are only the easy pickings of the lower branches. Many avoid stretching higher. Immediate gratification sadly involves loss because although emerging and longer-term trends are more speculative and chancy, they may turn out to be more pivotal and transformative.

Another forewarning. Speculation inevitably involves theory. I am aware that for many hard-nosed realists that is anathema. But aside from its being an occupational hazard for all academics and some consultants—my image of the afterlife features endless theoretical discussions—theory has been maligned. To many it is self-indulgent, vague, and imprecise, and fundamentally distractive and irrelevant. Often true, but its exploratory options more than compensate.

Theory compels a return to square-one essentials. It challenges and brings to the level of examination unarticulated assumptions. It slips behind process to discern animating models. It often requires unlearning. It subjects the rapid and the trendy to slower, more philosophical review. It is a way of getting unstuck especially from the present. It thus can be the back and front of the future. Finally, it is never meek or timid. Indeed, theory can aggressively disturb the universe; or as Jean Baudrillard, the French semiologist, observed in an interview in the *New York Times* (August 12, 2003):

> It is not enough for theory to describe and analyze, it must itself be an event in the universe. In order to do this, theory must partake of and become the acceleration of this logic. It must tear itself from all referents and take pride only in the future. Theory must operate on time at the cost of a deliberate distortion of present reality.

Thus, each of the three stages of current, emerging, and future developments will be introduced, accompanied, and sustained by a fusion of driving change factors and their theoretical underpinnings. Although such a combination determines and shapes the specific applications of each stage, theory is ultimately my check-and-balance system. It is the way I control pie-in-the-sky indulgence. It is the way I put my projections on trial and give them the third degree. If they don't clear theory, they don't pass altogether.

One more caveat. Although a number of the examples and applications focus on business, almost all of the workforce projections apply equally to all sectors including government and education. Indeed, in some instances both education and government are ahead of the pack. The customary notion that education always needs to be saved by business therefore will be turned around to display applications to business. The three best-managed and future-oriented operations in my judgment are IRS, Medicare, and Social Security. (Many do not appreciate the last two until they are much older and hardly anyone has a kind word to say about IRS.) Indeed, one of the key theories and paradigm shifts of the future features the convergence rather than the separation of sectors.

If I am successful in persuading readers of the intimate and interoperable partnership between theory and the future on the one hand and of the knowability and tangibility of the future on the other hand, then even if some of my workforce projections are questioned, challenged, and even rejected, I at least can conclude that I have not written another one of those books that by promising little finally delivers less.

Irving H. Buchen
Ft. Myers, FL

I

THE NOW AND THE NEW

SPEED, BLUR, AND
FLUX MANAGEMENT

There ought to be a middle ground between the too hurried and the too slow.

—Akia Morita, *Made in Japan* (William Morrow, 1986)

SPEED AND BLUR

It is becoming increasingly fashionable to stampede organizations and intimidate audiences by invoking the litany of changing change. That is usually followed by striking fear into their trembling hearts and then exhorting them to adopt some new panacea that the speaker/writer is advocating and that like snake oil will cure all ills. And so in this way, different instant fixes and flavors of the month emerge from the womb of transformation.

It is thus almost a commonplace to recite such a litany of accelerated change. But few have noted what impacts it has had on leaders, managers, and workers; on their time and energy; on their working conditions and assignments; and even on their thinking and reflection. Whatever pressure the future is exerting, it is manifested in a present that is too much with us.

Workers are besieged by the now. To-do lists get longer and longer. There is no white space in calendars for the next three months. Paperwork is routinely taken home— to a home office where next to the computer are a fax machine and a shredder. The computer was supposed to make things easier but with laptops all it succeeded in doing is making the problems of work portable; and now the same has happened with cellphones. Since 9/11 even our language of numbers has been hurried. The most popular acronym for the age is ASAP.

Evidently, the promise of more leisure and a shorter work week disappeared with downsizing and stretch goals. No one is claiming that things will get better. Indeed, there is the veiled warning that they will get worse. In the meantime, help is offered in the form of better time management workshops, managers are urged to delegate more of their tasks, and teams are formed to be self-managing. It all has served as effective short-term Band-Aids dealing with symptoms, not causes. It has not addressed time-speed as the villain of the piece.

What workshops have not identified is the more profound impairment that comes with intense and relentless busyness. Executives have to make decisions, managers plans, workers priorities. But all that requires clearing the field of clutter and noise in order to focus. As a result, a new additional task now has emerged that has to precede all others: sorting out the wheat from the chaff. Now extra time has to be spent dealing with the debris of speed-time.

Ways and strategies have to be found to keep the busy and insistent present at bay and to clear space for setting up the short term (the long term may have been traded off long ago). The net result is endangering the capacity to discriminate between what is essential and what may be ephemeral. Here is a short list of warning questions that beset the current workforce:

- It is urgent, but is it also important?
- It is a good match, but is it a perfect fit?
- Does the solution mask a bigger problem?
- Type One Statistical Error: Did we get it wrong?
- Type Two Statistical Error: Did we get it as right as it can be?
- If it is broke, do we fix it so it won't break the same way?

- If it is wearing out, do we wait or replace it now?
- Even if it ain't broke, should we still try to improve on it?

The pressure of the present is blurring distinctions to such an extent that compromise becomes the standard. Routinely, work settles for the minimum, the marginal, and the manageable. Worse, halves are passed off as wholes. And when that regularly happens then the issue may be not so much that we are overwhelmed but that we are outclassed; and so perhaps are our products and services.

The key recognition, then, is that the impact of speed now applies to all levels: CEOs, senior vice presidents, middle-level managers, and workers. Such comprehensive inclusiveness is new. In all previous incarnations, the tension that routinely characterized the world of business basically involved the issue of leadership. The focus was on the CEO, and only later on all other senior levels. Tension functioned like a permanent overlay: top versus the bottom, managers versus workers, finance or engineering versus sales, corporate headquarters versus branch or satellite operations, and so on. But now every level of every company shares more than what it does not.

The common foci on productivity, profitability, and performance are unanimously held. No one disagrees about the commonality of alignment. In fact, precisely because that collective battle has already been fought and acknowledged can companywide solutions and new structures be recommended and discussed in the first place. We are thus at recurrent shared cross roads. Enlightenment may be born regularly of desperation, but moving on together from that special and inclusive commonality is still the way we have to go. In the process, flux needs to be not just confronted or dodged but managed.

But for that to take place and to hold, five preliminary steps are required: first, admitting collectively that we live in crazy times; second, acknowledging and describing its impacts on our sanity and the way we think and work; third, recognizing finally that we are not the cause and that our paranoia is normal and shared; fourth, identifying as the villain of the drama an intensive, invasive, and insistent future that does not have the common courtesy to wait until we come to it but insists on prematurely arriving regularly ahead of schedule; and fifth, engaging, analyzing, and finally managing blur so as to recover at least the illusion of focus, balance, and clarity.

FLUX MANAGEMENT

The panacea offered here is flux management applied to all levels of the company. It provides adjusted specific management models and techniques for change. Flux management is not new. But there is one crucial difference—there is now no attempt to still the turbulence.

No matter how difficult it may be, blur and busyness have to be accepted as a norm of work. In addition, flux management needs to be inclusive and include and hopefully integrate a number of other panaceas under one roof so that its impact is collectively reinforcing.

The situations to be explored here will be limited to three areas: forecasting and strategic planning, structural diversity, and professional development and training. But first there are five operating principles of flux management that need to be articulated here and that also serve as a précis of this book.

1. Temporary Fixes

    Nothing lasts and so nothing should be set in concrete. Solutions should be elastic and changeable. Connections should be Velcro so that they can easily and quickly be disconnected and reconfigured; in high-flux companies, hourly. Monitoring has to replace or constantly be ahead of planning. Adjustments can be programmed to be done automatically according to changing specs and parameters. Nor should this all mean fast and dirty. Quality can coexist with what is not permanent. The mind-set and the materials have to be altered.

2. Alternative Best Practices

    Best practices are a productive source of superior ways or systems of doing things. But it is often not used imaginatively or comprehensively. For example, there is not one but a number of best ways to change operations. Researching and exploring all the alternative versions hopefully will lead companies to select not only the best but also what best fits the operating culture.

In addition, the range of sources of best practices needs to be expanded to include all sectors and even all countries. Narrowing it to one's particular industry is shortsighted. Thus, one of the best-run organizations in the United States is the Social Security Administration. Some of the worst run are banks, where typically the right hand does not know what the left hand is doing. Banks might benefit by following the model of the social security agency rather than other banks that are as messed up as they are. Also, go global. Some of the best-run banks are in Europe.

3. Share, Share, Share until Breakthroughs Emerge

Knowledge sharing is the currency of knowledge management. The Internet, in fact, generates the model. The familiar starting point is: "Does anyone know of a way of doing or source for XYZ?" And then the flow starts. It moves like a search engine. And often serendipity operates and previously unconnected relationships surface and take hold. The process is one of constantly expanding circles of richness, often spectacular, sometimes overwhelming. And the search is never over. The solution is always temporary and unfinished. It carries an electronic date and a time.

4. The Priority of Talent

Spend at least 50 percent of your time hiring, orienting, and training new talent. There are two ways of taking care of the future: planning for what lies ahead and bringing on board those who relish the future. More important than background checks are long conversations and situational discussions: How does she think, how does she respond, how reflective and how fast is she, how creative and fearless, how smart and savvy and shrewd, how political, how does she see herself? And then, how will it be to work with her, how will all the other egos interact with what outcomes, what will the scenario be a year from now, will she stay or will we lose her, and so on?

That basic set of determinations having been made, there is more to do. Don't just send her to one of those often stupid and boring orientation sessions put on usually by HR. Require her to spend days with divisions she will not work with directly. Assign liaison persons in all the divisions she will visit. Have her meet and spend time with some of the oldest employees to learn about the origins and history of the company. Have her sit in on some upper-level meetings. Arrange for her to have breakfast with the CEO.

Set her on a professional development, lifelong learning course. Ask her what she thinks she could be better at and what additional training she could benefit from. Give her a book budget. Start her off with a selection of books and articles chosen by her supervisor and peers. Give her two subscriptions, one chosen by her supervisor, the other by the new employee. Invite her to attend a conference coming up that a few of her colleagues plan to attend. Make an appointment with a nutritionist and a personal trainer.

5. Be Future Driven

Managers and organizations generally fall into one of five time categories: past fixated, present focused, future oriented, future directed, or future driven. What are the essential characteristics of being future driven? The future becomes a constant companion and tutor. It is not a tabula rasa. It has an identity. It has a voice. It communicates. The future comes in three forms: stretch, strain, and shock. Crisis management is an oxymoron and needs to be replaced by flux management. The future is available. It is always whole. Innovation creates the future.

With these five principles in hand and with the goal of being future driven in mind, three applications of flux management can be offered.

Strategic Planning

Flux management needs to become central to strategic planning and forecasting. The first advantage it offers is repositioning planning from looking ahead to the future to standing already in the future and looking back. That way, flux is managed not by avoidance but by confrontation, absorption, and assimilation. The manager needs to be altered and startled by the future before he or she begins to tame it with planning.

Planning has to become intimate with the future. It must wine and dine the future and write scenarios like love letters. Fear of and distance from the future must be converted to participation by the future itself in present planning. The future is not a passive page on which forecasters arrogantly write whatever they want or hope. The future is a partner.

It contributes to our understanding and projections. It is not an enemy but an ally. Treated as a collaborator, it will make itself known, not totally but substantially. It needs to be given a voice and a script. Planning thus may become both less and more predictable

The most important lesson of the future is that transition is a norm. The conventional expectation of past-fixated and present-focused companies is that transition is a nasty temporary dislocation between what was initially stable and what will reemerge when the dust settles. But the operating assumption of flux management is that transition will give way to another transition and so on. The new metaphors of permanent transition and the new parameters of strategic planning stress circular rather than mechanical assumptions and systems.

Structural Diversity

Flux management must leave its stamp on structure. The conventional study of organizational structure assumes a fixed and steady object of examination. But that is less analysis and more autopsy. Recall Wordsworth's classic warning: "We murder to dissect."

What then are the true and vital characteristics of flux structures? There are at least two: variability and autonomy.

The days of the monolith are over. One single vertical wedding cake, solid and still, secure in its orderly arrangements and linkages, is a relic. Instead, it is gradually being replaced by flux structures that are incredibly varied. Incubators have been spawned, inhabiting sometimes the edges, sometimes the center. Whole new subsidiary companies have been created and launched with no umbilical cord. Selected divisions have been integrated, sometimes unexpectedly: R&D and finance. Branches or satellites have been put on a longer leash and given a declaration of independence to supplement their declaration of interdependence. Leadership and innovation have become distributed and written into everyone's job description. In short, structural diversity has arrived.

The visualization of new structure is the subject of position reports now more appropriately entitled positioning papers. Structure displays different shapes and rates of speed. It more resembles planets in the solar system than pyramids of permanence and dominance. But these new variations on a theme are not totally autonomous. They are separately set up financially as if each one were the child of venture capitalists. Their accountability is tyrannical: succeed or fold.

They run at their own speed, and in many cases there are no speed limits for them. They are frequently unsupervised from the top and from without. They select their own members and hire their own new people. No old-boy's network or baggage from the past. No comfort zones from old structures are welcome. There is no reigning guru. Everyone is equal, some more than others. All leaders are temporary. There are usually no bosses, they are intensely team driven; and they operate at work or at home. Like consultants or executive coaches, they are on call 24 hours a day, 7 days a week, 365 days a year.

Many of these new offspring appear as if they just emerged from gene splicing. They operate in a hothouse laboratory in which there is a no-holds-barred steady steam of ideas. Everyone is an entrepreneur. Everyone is innovative. The competition is intense. Everyone has a colossal ego and is also selfless. The pace is hectic, the communication hyper, the atmosphere manic depressive, the enthusiasm adolescent. The failure rate, similar to that of the Internet start-ups they resemble, is high. But their successes when they occur are spectacular, and their backers become very rich.

Professional Development and Training

Each new employee has two job descriptions, a present one and a future one. His or her career goal is to grow into that future role. Thus, each employee is set up with a lifelong learning and professional development plan that is both generic and individualistic. The generic version is generated by strategic planning.

Under the pressure of flux management, that becomes the standard for all. The assumption is that every employee like the organization itself is unfinished—has another life, skill, role, function, and commitment yet to be known, realized, and implemented. The unknown needs and demands of the future mandate individual growth. But flux management also requires that the opportunities and occasions for such development and training be always available. That brings into play total electronic access or flux training.

Distance education has become distance training. Providers like Ninth House offer a complete outsourcing training menu available any time online. There is no lost time at work, no scheduling obstacles to overcome. In addition, others taking the same course, even from different companies, are available for interaction. Indeed, such cross-fertilization might be a bonus. Thus, flux management needs to be matched with flux training.

One final, more collective version of flux training is the creation of an employee university. Training has to be focused on the present as well as on the future. Structural diversity ultimately leaves its mark on worker diversity. Each employee has to write his or her own mission statement, which is embedded in the present and which also reflects long-term development. Each employee has a dual loyalty: what he or she has committed to do not only in the next quarter and year, but also in the next two to three years. It is that flux document that provides the precise benchmarks for identifying training needs.

In some companies that has taken the exciting form of creating employee universities driven by employee development goals, which are both generic and individual, immediate and long term, always fully reflective of structural diversity. In a few brave instances where organizations are ruled more by competence than titles, employees also teach in the university. And thus gradually an employee-centered culture emerges.

In summary, then, flux management has significant framing and structural power. It touches all the bases. One foot is in the present, the other in the future. Its shapes combine the big and the small, the distant and up close, the solid and the chameleonlike.

Its coherence is always only partially available, even elusive like a river, dense like a rain forest. It is exciting and dizzying, terribly breathless and meditative, brilliant and exasperating. Often ruled by young new MBAs, these amorphous organizations function like comets. Although their spectacular light display and speed may be brilliant, their incredibly diverse and autonomous structures also may sputter, careen off course, and burn up. Tradition and wisdom are ignored or given token marginality.

The future alone beckons. And the future is always protean flux. The only difference is that it has now invaded and become the present. We are routinely living ahead of our time. We are managing not the present but ultimately the present edge of the future.

TECHNOLOGY: ROBOTIC AND HUMAN DEVELOPMENT AND THE MACHINE TEACHER

Two roads diverged in a wood, and I—
I took the one less traveled by,
And that has made all the difference.

—Robert Frost, Poems, Random House, 1984

There is little point to my describing and projecting what new technology and gadgetry will emerge. Others better qualified already are doing that. Besides, it is a losing battle. No one can keep up with the technological cornucopia. Instead, the focus here and in the next part is the human relationships with machines, especially as machines become smarter and humans more dispensable. The argument is that whatever philosophical issues this may raise, it is also a workplace issue.

The evolution of robots has a short but rapid history. It always has more of a future than a past and occupies the periphery of public attention more than the center stage. But the unequivocal symbol of its having arrived is its new marketing visibility and its sale as little people and household pets and vacuum cleaners.

Perceived perhaps as gimmicky, these midget machines that amaze and startle and invite naming already are making a young generation comfortable with mechanical companions, just as earlier the same acculturation occurred with computers. And yet, like all technology, whatever its popular applications, robotics has a more serious, even profound side that invites reflection and exploration. Indeed, robots offer a metaphorical history that may be more powerfully instructive than that of their mechanical development.

One of robotics' most revealing artifacts is Isaac Asimov's story "Bicentennial Man" that, although published first in 1947, was made into a popular film by the same name and released in 1999 to capture the millennium fever.

"Bicentennial Man" (BM) is a story set in the future about an android purchased to be a servant in an upper-middle-class household. Andrew arrives in an enormous mummylike box and obediently recites on command Asimov's famous three laws of robotics, which were first penned in a short story called "Roundabout" in 1942. The story covers three generations of the family whom Andrew serves faithfully with evolving intelligence. The story concludes with Andrew's gradually acquiring progressively human characteristics, falling in love and marrying the granddaughter of his original owner, and finally embracing mortality so that he can die like everyone else.

The film was reviewed positively and praised as one of the few warm, humorous, and kindly versions of sci-fi, although at times a little too moist. The humanizing of Andrew generally was perceived as an affirmation of the human condition. Indeed, a number of religious reviewers recommended it for family viewing (Jesus Christ Reviews, 1999).

To be sure, BM is a message film, almost a sermon celebrating obedience and the acceptance of human limitations and the ultimate limitation of death. Andrew plays out a number of human temptations including the ultimate superhuman one of immortality to persuade us all to accept and affirm our mortal lot. But that is the human message extracted from the story. There is also a robotic subplot that is powerful and even subversive but that is constantly deflected back into a more acceptable, nonthreatening moral fable. It is that story that needs to be coaxed out and examined.

Perhaps the best way to begin is with Asimov's by-now classic three laws of robotics, which launch and set the stage for the entire story: (a) A robot may not injure a human being or, through inaction, allow a human being to come to harm; (b) a robot must obey the orders given it by human beings except where such orders conflict with the First Law; (c) and finally, a robot must protect its own existence as long as such protection does not conflict with the First or Second Laws.

Clearly, Asimov's legalistic contract is designed to offer reassurance to humans, not robots. Control is vested in human masters. Androids clearly are subservient to the laws dedicated to protect their human owners. In fact, one early incident dramatizes how one-sided the arrangement is. The older daughter, who finds Andrew bothersome, orders him to open the window and to jump out. Fortunately, it is a one-story, short fall. Andrew returns a little dazed and with his language chip somewhat scattered, and the humor of the incident perhaps obscures the degree to which the android is an expendable plaything.

But things change rapidly after that. Andrew unexpectedly develops swiftly, thanks mostly to conversations with the father. In fact, what emerges is a pattern of development that consists of five principal stages or branch points: Andrew as learning machine, artistic fabricator, freeman/robot, bionic mate, and mechanical immortal.

1. The Learning Machine

Andrew asks questions or, more accurately, is encouraged to ask questions. The father of the family finds Andrew's responses intriguing, and often even amusing. An extensive Platonic dialogue flows regularly between them. Andrew learns quickly and in the process sets his master back on his heels by asking the kind of innocent and ethical questions used by satirists to critique contemporary society.

Sufficient space has been left in Andrew's program for him to become a sentient machine, displaying the rich and almost unlimited growth of artificial intelligence. At this point in the story and at this stage of Andrew's rapid development, there is no special application of this newly acquired intelligence. To be sure, he is no longer only a servant; he also has become a companion, often challenging and endlessly curious. But he is still an android. Then a pivotal incident happens.

Andrew accidentally drops and shatters Little Miss's glass horse. She is miserable and angry, and berates Andrew. Saddened, he goes to his basement room, studies the anatomy of animals in various books, and fashions a horse made of wood. Little Miss is enchanted and squeals that it is even better than the original (which it is). Andrew is delighted and returns to his basement workshop and begins experimenting with other designs and ultimately produces a number of fashionable clock sculptures.

2. Artistic Fabricator

This is a quantum leap for Andrew. For the first time he independently seeks out and acquires specific knowledge. He is focused and purposeful in his inquiries. But more important is what he does with it. He exceeds his original programming by creating something that never existed before. He fashions wood sculptures in a series of one-of-a kind artistic shapes that house mechanical or battery-operated electric clocks. He gives the first one to his master-owner who is amazed and exclaims, "This is unique. And so are you, Andrew!" His wife suggests that Andrew secure an agent to distribute his clock sculptures. Little Miss, who is now older, further recommends that Andrew have his own bank account. In fact, as it turns out, he becomes independently wealthy.

It is a fascinating stage because it both continues and adds new dimensions. On the one hand, Andrew extends his knowledge base through reading and analysis. He also begins to extract from his reading conceptual and artistic models. On the other hand, he fashions art that never existed before and in the process sets himself and his work apart as unique. But most important, Andrew achieves independence of thought and work. No longer is he solely tied to linguistic exchanges. He can travel anywhere intellectually and artistically through his reading, thinking, and creating. In fact, he fixes an old Victrola and listens in rapture to opera.

It is curious that Asimov in a sense used his own craft as a model for Andrew's development. The capacity to create or respond to art has fascinated science-fictionists. To prove that the aesthetic response is not acquired but innate in man, Mary Shelley in *Frankenstein* has the creature stop in his tracks one moonlit night on the moors and almost swoon with delight at the beauty of the sky. Vonnegut's favorite form of survival is the artful dodger. And all of Arthur C. Clarke's computer beings are adept at design. Thus, art functions, as it always has for humans, as the ultimate test of creativity and independence of thought and imagination; except, of course, that Andrew is an android. Nevertheless, art also serves as the threshold for Andrew's next stage of development: freedom.

3. The Freeman/Robot

Andrew pursues his reading further, especially in history. What he discovers is that although history is a sorry record of the pursuit of power and dominance, what emerges as the strongest desire of the oppressed is freedom. He then realizes that he is owned and that in effect he is a slave. He nervously goes to see his master and tells him of his reading and concludes by asking for his freedom. His master is hurt. He takes it as a personal affront. He dismisses Andrew and tells him he will think about it and make a decision in a few days.

Why the shock? The master in many ways has in fact brought Andrew to this stage. But perhaps that is just the point. The master recognizes that granting freedom means that he is no longer the master. In turn, Andrew is no longer a servant but has become his equal. That Andrew in a condition of freedom still decides to stay with the family and serve them only means that now that role is chosen, not imposed or programmed. Andrew in short seeks to acquire free will. The master reluctantly agrees to grant Andrew his freedom. Sadly, he begins to contemplate the almost inevitable lamentation: "What have I created?"

Indeed, what? A unique, thinking, learning, and creating machine. Pretty impressive achievement. So why so sad? Because Andrew no longer needs him for growth. He has become self-sufficient, autonomous, and independent. But perhaps the deepest concern is that Andrew, who up to now has followed a human model and path may now pursue another direction. We thus come upon the pivotal point of this moral fable.

"Two roads diverged in a wood and I—I took the one less traveled by." The drama has become one of choice. The fear is that Andrew will choose a path that diverges from that of all humans. Just as the three laws of robotics were self-serving and human centered, so here the question is whether Andrew will move off into science fiction, will become something in excess of the human, a mechanical God, a superior Einstein, a greater Leonardo da Vinci.

That such prospects are seen as lamentable or fearful is essentially a reflection of human earth-bound egotism. It is stirred by the fear that future history will record the acquisition of power by machines and lead to the dominance of the human race by what it fact it has created. Nowhere in Asimov's drama is there any recognition that man basically has gone as far as he can go from an evolutionary point of view; and that if he aspires further it will have to be symbiotically through his creations. Indeed, once again art is the midwife, only this time not just in the creation of a work of art but in a quantum leap for humankind.

Ironically, it is human beings who turn out to be more programmed than Andrew. We cannot imagine intelligence superior and different not just in degree but in kind from our own; a brain that combines both hardware and software in one; and an artistic capacity that can essentially produce designs never imagined and that in fact could extend life. The occasional critiques of society are nothing compared to the critique of human imagination and the ultimate failure to accept the prospect of creatures greater than we are, extending and enhancing us in ways that exceed our capacity.

In short, humans cannot accept an inferior position. Faced by the prospect of disobedience or independence, we behave like Greek gods furious with Prometheus and determined to punish him. Unlike Andrew, we are not big enough to use our freedom to choose traveling an alternative evolutionary path. We cannot surrender mastery. If we have to choose between ruling and serving, even though the path is noble and stirring, we will choose to remain in charge of our limitations.

It is this archetypal fear and choice that contributes much to technophobia and probably is the main reason there is little integration of technology into the curriculum. Teachers fear that machines will replace them. And we have lied to them and given them the same kind of false assurance as Asimov's three laws have. The truth is teaching machines, can, have, and will replace the teacher as the source of direct instruction. But Andrew ultimately surprises everyone by making three decisions: to remain as servant, to build his own house to live in, and to search everywhere for an android companion like him.

4. Bionic Mate

Andrew secures the addresses of all the androids made with the same specs that he has. He journeys all over the world to try to find a mate. He is down to the last one and discovers a lively girl robot shopping. He follows her home and meets her master who happens to be the son of the original manufacturer of androids and who has set up a shop to experiment with androids. He quickly and sadly discovers that the android's liveliness is the result of a personality chip and that she, unlike him, is nothing special.

Once again, Andrew comes to a branch point. Which way will he choose? He can choose to perfect himself, become even more intelligent and artistic, create other androids—a mate in fact—and endow them with higher states of knowledge and conceptual power, and finally live forever. Or, as it turns out, he can remain, but improve the model—an android who remains a giving servant and helps to sustain the superiority of humans.

And so he embarks on an elaborate, intricate, and brilliant series of bionic designs of android-human interchangeable organs and parts. To be sure, Andrew is the first recipient because his goal clearly now is to become totally and recognizably human. In fact, he acquires a human face, begins to wear clothes, and later acquires sexual organs so that he can enjoy physical love with the granddaughter of his original master.

So desperate is Andrew's desire to become totally human and to marry and to erase all signs of his android self that he appears before the world court to plead his case for being designated as a human. They decline, claiming that what precludes him from being declared a human is his immortality. Saddened, Andrew contemplates his future decision.

5. Mechanical Immortal

Andrew chooses to join his beloved on her death bed so they will be together. As he is about to expire, the notice comes from the world court that he has been accepted as a human. But it is perhaps this last triumph that dramatizes the extent to which the dice are loaded against Andrew. In effect, he never had real choices, given his author's determination and that of all the other humans in the story not to disturb the universe and to keep Andrew in his place. Indeed, the story can be reconceived from Andrew's point of view as a violation of the three traditional historical human taboos: Thou shalt not eat of the tree of knowledge of good and evil—in short, thou shalt not be as smart as your creator; thou shalt not be male and female, hermaphroditic and reproduce your own kind by yourself; and thou shalt not live forever.

The supreme masters of the universe establish the pecking order. Divine beings set the standards and conditions for dominance. The gods limit humans and the humans in turn limit others, including androids. But in this case, the hidden laws of the universe and history are exposed. There is always a top over a bottom, a master over a slave. And so what humans cannot do, Andrew, although he can, is persuaded or programmed not to do.

No human creation can be allowed to exceed its creators, just as man, Faust, and others notwithstanding cannot exceed God's. Andrew is potentially an embarrassment. He is as smart or smarter than humans. He even can achieve in his lab super intelligence because he would be free to create on a higher level than his human fabricators. He could reproduce one of his own kind as a mate and companion, an Andria. And of course he is immortal.

In short, he already is poised to demonstrate his total difference and even uniqueness from his human creators by having survived all the three taboos. But that won't do. He must not exceed. He must choose mortality.

The threat of Andrew is real because Andrew is involved in perfecting the body of man and potentially enabling him to live forever. Occupying the laboratory of bionic futures, mechanical as well as intellectual, Andrew stands on the threshold of violating not only the three laws of robotics, but also the three laws of human limitations. But lest this overreaching emerge as a strong threat, it is softened and curved back to earth. A sad, weepy sentimentality ends the story and its potential subversion, and allows viewers and readers to leave undisturbed and reassured.

Clearly, it is Asimov's intent to write not only good fiction but also equally good theology. Neither is allowed to rise to the level of the heroic or tragic. Overreaching is cut short and the road less traveled by ultimately reads like the one everyone takes. In the process, however, the various branch points of Andrew dramatize the choices not made and illustrate the need for an additional law for robots: Thou shalt not expose the ultimate limits of your masters and above all their omissions and uncreated prospects of excessive mastery.

Asimov's story thus is ultimately one of human intellectual and artistic imperialism. But the powerful parable gets through: Robots may not only surpass us; they may also be embarrassingly more human. Above all, technology is the constant and insistent agent of a sly future that offers servants and playmates that later may become our masters. But an intermediate position absent from the story is future symbiosis: the human-machine creature capable of traveling an evolutionary road previously closed to us—not just less but untraveled.

THE MACHINE TEACHER

Technology in the workplace is not always welcomed. Indeed, sometimes it is resisted to the point of sabotage. But when such paranoia rules, it is not always irrelevant or uninsightful, especially when it is collective. It thus pays to proceed under the assumption that acknowledging the existence of a persecution complex may be instructive. Thus, the lack of integration and even use of technology as a learning tool in public education are rapidly approaching the dimensions of an enigma. Here are just a few factors that add to the bewilderment. (a) It is available. Indeed, many schools already have extraordinarily rich technology environments and equipment that are minimally used. (b) It is steadily improving. Hardware and software are improving at rapid rates and are being routinely tried and tested as a daily staple of most home schooling arrangements (*Ed Week*, May 10, 2002, p. 34). (c) It is welcomed. Students generally are becoming increasingly technologically proficient, although often in wayward ways and badly in need of the kind of redirection that learning experts and schooling alone can provide. (d) It is getting cheaper. Technological costs are steadily becoming an ally, not an enemy of budget crunches. (e) It is powerful. Technologically centered learning has become increasingly synonymous with student-centered learning. Indeed, both are on a convergence course toward symbiotic human-machine hybrids (Kurzweil, Ray, *The Age of Spiritual Machines*. NY: Penguin, 1999).

And yet we seem to be moving up a down escalator. Larry Cuban describes the near total failure of faculty at Stanford University to make curricular use of the extensive technology lavished upon them. Two years after having been provided extensive training, hardware, and software, a handful of professors have made minor adjustments in their courses. Most have restricted the use to outside classroom activities—e-mail, Internet searches, and word processing.

If one were to compile a wish list of what education currently needs and what might be viable alternative technological equivalents, what would that list include?

CURRENTLY NEEDED ALTERNATIVES

1. Quality Teachers versus Quality Teaching Machines
2. Student-Centered Learning versus Student-Partnered Learning
3. Teacher Shortages versus Technology Abundance
4. Teaching to the Test versus Drill Sergeants Plus Test Design
5. High Cost (salaries and benefits) versus Lower Costs, No Benefits Paid
6. Construction of New Schools versus Use of Less-Expensive Cyber Space

Another way of exploring equivalents in the most basic terms is to identify the essentials needed for optimized learning. There are three: teacher quality, students as learning partners, and supportive environment.

Now let us complicate, extend, and add a dash of reality to each as follows: teacher quality: limited availability and high cost; learning partners: finding and facilitating appropriate curricula; and supportive environment: cost of administration, calendar, school size, class size.

When technology is factored in and added on to each of the three areas, the following emerges: learning machine quality; individualized and group relationships, class size becomes less relevant; and environment: 365 days, 24 hours a day, limited new school construction.

Was technology oversold? Did it promise too much too soon? Actually, the expectation generally was for gradual accommodation. Technology would obediently wait in the wings to be summoned incrementally. Its use would be gradualized and customized. It might ease the teacher shortage and help minimize the teacher quality problem. It would engage students as coproducers of learning. It even would transform operations and evaluation by providing monitoring and tracking databases. But generally it has not happened. Why? Because significant change generally requires four future conditions for it to happen: desperation, accountability of testing, documentation/demonstration, and vision.

1. Desperation
    Education will begin to sag under the weight of its costs. The shortage of quality teachers and administrators will drive up budgets. One-time hiring incentives will create problems of equity within existing ranks and jeopardize retention. Expenditures for brick and mortar in an increasingly electronic age will be routinely challenged and frequently rejected.
2. Accountability of Testing
    That will force the fast fix. The most attractive fruit on the lower branches will be plucked by enterprising for-profit education management companies.
3. Documentation /Demonstration
    Technology universities and commercial developers will set up lab schools to demonstrate that it can be done. One already operated by Stevens Institute of Technology Research is studying the use of technology in home schooling. Promising results may in fact significantly result in an increase in home schooling.
4. Vision
    A national vision of education that refuses to accept the constant loss of quality on the one hand and the corresponding loss of workforce talent on the other hand will increasingly take shape and hold. Economic pressures will compel a search for solutions outside the box, and technology will likely emerge to occupy center stage. What will be the principal stages of implementation? Gradual, accelerated, and radical.

- Gradual

    Technologically amplified and leveraged teachers will appear and serve to bridge the traditional and the technological. They will not champion one curriculum but many and in the process demonstrate that technology is not a prisoner or favorite of any one approach. Their task will be aided by parents pushing for relevant career applications for their children. The school district that places a high value on teachers being technologically amplified as part of the overall definition of quality will have an easier time attracting and retaining quality teachers. In effect, such schools will become the alternative many ex-teachers seek to go to.

- Accelerated

    This arrangement will facilitate bringing together regular and home schooling, face-to-face and distance learning. Schoolwork and homework will become the same with different venues. This arrangement will drastically affect school calendars and places of instruction. Cost-benefit analysis will persuasively argue for its acceptance and enlargement.

- Radical

    This calls for a leap into the future. It will appear (already has) increasingly in the creation of separate cyber schools and in the designation of lab schools or beta sites created by technology-driven vendors and universities. In some cases they will essentially be K–12 versions or adaptations of corporate universities. But in all instances they will be actual, not drawing-board plans of what is to come. In the next twenty years all three plus the traditional version will coexist.

What should be done now and for the next few years to bring more light than heat, more debate than acrimony to the exchange of differences? There are at least three issues that need to be explored: the economics of education, the fears of educators, and the critique of technophiles.

Each of these could be the subject of a separate article or even a book (and have been). So what will be given here is the proverbial tip of the iceberg in order not to lose the focus of the argument presented so far.

1. The Economics of Education

Until recently, hardly anyone considered education as a way of making money. Teachers and educational administrators gave up on that a long time ago. Then things changed. Virtually every new university created in the last twenty-five years has been for-profit and proprietary. Many in fact are listed on the stock market. Some have been purchased from their original owners by venture capitalists seeking to diversify their portfolios. A few have been purchased by major corporations. Sylvan Learning Systems recently bought Walden University for $80 million dollars.

Because many of these education businesses maintain their nonprofit status through creative bookkeeping, not unlike what most universities have been doing for years, the image generated was that education is generally inept and therefore always needed grants, gifts, and alumni contributions. Imagine what would happen to alumni solicitation if the profit and loss statement showed a profit?

Similarly, the image generated by public education is that it always has to be on the dole. A number of years ago a popular bumper sticker read: "You know things have changed when the military has to run a bake sale." Teachers routinely spend their own money annually to purchase school supplies. That sad situation is now a tax deduction. Suddenly, in parallel fashion to the appearance of for-profit school management companies like Edison, that has been compounded and hastened by the decision in 1991 in Minnesota to allow charter schools to operate under the old arrangement of the farm collective.

The enemy was no longer outside but also inside the gates. New schools were set up that teachers not only led but also owned. But the dramatic difference was that it was possible to operate charter schools and still pay district-level salaries on the per capita contribution of each student. Talk about students being customers; if they were not, the school would soon close.

As public education lost its monopolistic status and entered the world of competition, the pressure of accountability took on an additional focus. If Edison and other private companies who do not use substandard people or pay substandard wages can operate schools within budget, and sometimes even show a profit, why can't all the others? What charter schools demonstrated economically and intellectually to teachers is that they do not have to leave the profession altogether to find more meaningful educational alternatives and governance options and still get paid at district-level salaries.

Still, the image persists that education needs subsidizing and constant bailout. Private companies and charter schools in effect have challenged public education to operate within the same budgetary constraints they have to. Of course to do so would compel a reexamination of the way they operate, which is precisely what competition requires every organization to do. But the economic leverage to change is even more demanding than just changing accounting or operational procedures.

An enormous disservice has been done to education. It has been insulated from economic and market forces and allowed to drift in la-la land. Pereleman is not reciting the standard litany about education being a business and the need to have it managed like one, at which teachers and especially professors of education predictably and in knee-jerk fashion take umbrage. No, it is more serious and substantive than that. What Pereleman and others are pointing to are the economic and market factors that have changed learning and knowledge acquisition altogether; altered especially graduate-level education and training to distance and online education; and created a powerful, sophisticated, and flexible teaching and learning technology beyond anything possessed earlier. Pereleman is describing the almost global context of information and knowledge transformations that education should be at the center of but has been excluded from by its insulation from economic and market forces. In short, the forces driving educational change are economic and futuristic and increasingly they are one and the same.

2. The Fears of Educators

We have not been honest with teachers. We have given them the false impression that technology is docile, nonthreatening, and respectful. It is none of those things. Rather it is ubiquitous, invasive, and substitutive. But teachers intuitively knew that they were being lied to. Although they did not become Luddites, they became retaliatory—they became passive-aggressive.

They ignored technology, offered it token roles, limited more acquisitions, or turned it over to students during free periods (knowing full well that they would spend all their time playing games). And it is not expected to get better. Almost all undergraduate and graduate business curricula now are labeled and extended as e-courses. Even a staple like economics is now e-economics. Finally, a split seems to be appearing in the teaching ranks. One group of teachers (usually smaller) attends the technology sessions at conferences; the rest of the teachers don't.

The truth is that machines can and probably will replace teachers. They will be able to do so because they are, in fact, teaching machines and can provide solid and competent instruction. But their creators and programmers will not be content with basics and with passive androids. They will offer creatively interactive invitations to player-learners. They will offer "hard fun." They will display a wide menu of design and simulation challenges—of ecological systems, of political elections, of mass-transportation systems, and so on. And so on and so on. And that is what teachers intuitively know and fear. Why should they conspire to accelerate their own demise?

It should not be forgotten that for most teachers, just like for most hand weavers in England in the nineteenth century, the prospect of a mechanical replacement was inconceivable. Why? Because nothing could match the variety and subtlety of human activity. Nothing could preserve and enrich developmental stages and rites of passage. Nothing could enliven and occasionally inspire students. No computer program could beat a chess master; and when it happened, it was ascribed to mechanical not mental superiority.

In short, teacher objections and fears are profound, the number of converts few, and the prospects for new mind-sets dim. That is why progress across the board, if it occurs at all may require the passing away of a current generation for new perspectives to emerge. The conventional consolation of not living long enough to see that happening has been dealt a double blow; it is happening faster and people are living longer.

3. The Critique of Technophiles

When computer scientists design a program or create a robot with mental acumen and self-learning capacity, they first have to learn a great deal about brain cognition. Similarly, when the impacts of technology are added, that immediately broadens the base of inquiry to the ways society and the economy work. Neil Postman, in *Building a Bridge to the 18th Century*, (New York: Knopf, 1999) has raised five basic questions about technology, ideally to be asked before, or concurrently with, going ahead with its development: What is the problem to which this technology is a solution? Whose problem is it? Which people and what institutions might be most seriously harmed by a technological solution? What new problems might be created because we have solved this problem? What sort of people and institutions might acquire special economic and political power because of technological changes?

These questions are not unlike the rigors employed by the EPA to examine the multiple orders of impact of a proposed environmental change or the Japanese business and engineering systems of asking why, when something fails, what the root cause was. Postman elaborates his rationale:

Wisdom means knowing what questions to ask about knowledge. I do not mean technical questions which are easy. I mean questions that come from a world other than the world from which the knowledge comes. And no where is this kind of wisdom needed more than in the story of technology. (p. 96)

Sadly, if teachers were more technologically literate and if they were threatened less by learning machines, the level of debate could be significantly raised and the above generic and substantive questions would be reformulated as challenges to both technophiles and teachers. Indeed, preparing the current and next generations to live in and to question an increasingly technological society is the major task of education. In fact, it is precisely that futuristic prospect that will enable education to recover and affirm its own traditional role and also to find its own future.

Literature has been defined as a critique of society. The same definition applies to education. But not petty or petulant criticism, not driven by self-serving fears and motives, but by tapping that aspect of critical thinking that has always been penetrating: anticipatory thinking. And if reframing of the debate takes place, we will have the best of both worlds: education as questioner and technology as performer. But if that partnership falters or fails, there is little doubt that technology will fill the vacuum and appear as both educator and performer.

But neither role, let alone its combination, will be as good as it can be without the loyal opposition to task it. When such exchanges are either absent or fearful, both machines and teachers are short-changed.

3

GLOBALITY: THE INTERNATIONAL BRAVE NEW WORLD

It finally has happened. Global competition, which has long been touted as beneficial, is now retaliatory. No longer abstract or distant, it has reached in and directly affected the American workplace. It has eliminated U.S. jobs internally, and jobs are also now being externally shipped abroad. Sadly and strangely, American jobs have become a major U.S. export except that they are now sold not to the highest but to the lowest bidder.

Americans generally have never had a historical love affair with the world. Certainly, it never approached the constant interest and involvement of the Europeans whose roots were still deeply set in the infrastructure of empires. The United States also was a latecomer to the manipulative process of butter following guns. Protected and insulated by enormous oceans on both sides, and enjoying a self-sufficiency few nations possessed, the United States remained politically and economically isolationist. Even after WWII when national companies increasingly went multinational and shipped their managers abroad, we did not fare well. We were not able to sink the kind of take-hold roots that other foreign nationals could with greater ease. Our general inability to be transplanted was covered up by the democratic gesture of training and turning over overseas operations to the native nationals.

But shipping American jobs overseas was a wake-up call. Whether or not the political outcry results in restrictive legislation, now of jobs as well as goods, what is clear is that global competition is real, invasive, and job threatening. The standard threat of a punitive environment—"If you can't do the job I will get some one who can!"—now has overseas implications and applications.

What has also upped the ante and made the situation not occasional but congenital is that we did it to ourselves. It recalls the classic formulation of Pogo: "We have met the enemy and he is us." CEOs were just doing their job as good capitalists. Partnering with enterprising overseas facilitating companies, U.S. companies just were seeking to increase productivity, reduce costs, and preserve profitability and ROI. In short, the American workplace has been jolted into the twenty-first-century reality of globality as a new and permanent context of the workplace and the workforce.

What that new perspective minimally involves is the acceptance by the American workforce no matter how reluctantly of the new borderless traffic of global exchange. In turn, organizations and organizational thinking also have to become boundaryless and permeable. Outsourcing already has broken down barriers and normalized exchange and flow. It will not stop especially as other factors propelled by technology and electronic connectivity are added to the mix and reinforce international interoperability. It is in short a brave new world with all the gains and losses attendant thereto. Once again, American workers have to work not only harder, but also smarter. And the first item on the agenda is global competition.

Although overseas outsourcing has been going on since the 1990s, the pace has increased significantly in the last decade and especially in this century. To be sure, there are some signs that the extent of overseas comparative advantage may lessen. Already computer programmers in India are demanding initial hiring bonuses and higher wages. The law of supply and demand may thus have its way and even out the playing field.

But perhaps a greater drain is the new trend of attracting mid- and upper-level managers. The demand for American managerial ability may lead many MBAs in the United States to consider relocating abroad. That should not be surprising. After all, managers routinely seek and accept jobs anywhere in the United States. This is but a logical and global extension. Besides, many of these jobs are more like the positions of years ago when strong managers were highly desirable.

Global employment has been enormously strengthened by electronic connectivity. Its obvious application is in call and cost centers. Customer and technical service are easily rerouted to India, Ireland, Philippines, Guam, and the like wherever English is spoken and wherever the British or the United States had prior culture and linguistic presence. But less acknowledged is the extent to which the global Internet has also leveled the commercial playing field of the big and the small.

Two older Scottish ladies who produce excellent and warm lamb's wool sweaters from their sheep are now able to compete with and sell their products worldwide. The profit margin is sufficient to absorb both the cost of the electronics and the shipping. Similarly, the Internet can leverage advantage to the less wealthy. Thus, although Germany spends only one-fifth of what the United States does on educational technology, it has the highest percentage among the top ten countries—86.1 percent—of 15-year-olds who have at least one computer at home. Little Iceland, which is determined to end its isolation electronically, beats Germany with 93.8 percent of 15-year-olds with at last one computer at home (*Ed Week*, May 6, 2004, pp. 9–10).

Increasingly, worldwide electronic networks are not only linking countries, but also generating global best practices especially in business and education. Routinely, the state of the art in teaching and management is now a comparative inquiry. Even U.S. Amazon.com has a UK Amazon .com counterpart. Equally as important, organizations are researching and developing international electronic relations and in the process setting up a global database. The recent report "Technology, Innovation, and Educational Change: A Global Perspective" employed 174 case studies in 28 countries.

In the process, three levels of comparison have appeared. First, there will be the obvious diversity of range reflected in expenditures and degree of connectivity. Second, the content and applications will also vary but be increasingly driven by innovation or creative solutions, thus generating global best practices; and that often will be independent of size and wealth. Third, electronic interconnectivity already has established a new global lingua franca and protocol that cuts across all countries and cultures. In other words, a global mind-set is gradually evolving, being shaped and providing a cultural parallel to global business and trade. Just as mathematics possesses its own language, so global networks and links will have the same function and prepare the way for an increasingly closely knit wired world.

The basic obstacle in the path of such understanding is no small matter. What makes this general shift difficult for Americans to accept is its total reversal. Traditionally and even currently those abroad struggled to come here, sometimes even illegally, to live and work. The United States was where the jobs and opportunities were. Now, in effect, we have partially given away one of the historical major incentives for immigration.

Generally, Americans are not used to perceiving themselves as a dependent nation. Except for a few natural resources, we have everything we needed here, even oil for most of the time. Unemployment never reached or politically was allowed to reach the enormously high levels of underdeveloped countries. Underemployment also was a unique overseas phenomenon that never reached these shores. All we worried about perennially were inflation rates, especially by certain sectors of the economy like health, medications, and energy, and higher education, whose increases were out of all proportion to others in the economy.

To be sure, we occasionally recognized that we were perceived from abroad as an incredible market especially for foreign cars and electronics. Jobs began to be lost in the automobile industry and fearful of the imposition of trade restrictions, Japanese car manufacturers located their plants in the United States. You can't restrict what is already here.

But unlike outsourcing, this clever Japanese maneuver neither eliminated jobs nor replaced American workers. But when U.S. companies went abroad, we created jobs where there were none before. Thus, the paranoia of Catch-22 may become normal for many Americans. Immigrants seek their jobs on the one hand and their jobs are also being shipped abroad on the other. It is a double whammy. Indeed, the outsourcing of American jobs has now become in turn a major business.

Free trade has always been advocated by classic capitalists. It was supposed to grant two benefits: lower-cost goods and a healthy competitive incentive for American businesses. Thus, the trade agreements of NAFTA with Mexico and Canada were negotiated with those two aims in mind. So Volkswagens and Mazdas were assembled in Mexico and shipped to and sold in the United States. To be sure, dealers would often warn customers only to buy the models made directly in Germany or Japan. That confirmed and reassured Americans that superior products still needed a superior workforce being well paid to manufacture quality products. But that traditional consolation is fast disappearing. China now dominates not only the plastic industry, but also complex computer parts. They even make BOSE audio and visual equipment.

Free-trade policy failed to anticipate a paradigm shift from goods to services, from products to jobs. Of course, being good capitalists and determined to be productive and profitable, CEOs first downsized and when that was exhausted, they looked abroad to maintain their competitive advantage. Actually, outsourcing has turned out to be another form of downsizing. But what generally been overlooked is the cumulative effect of all these individual decisions.

It is not unlike the parable of the English commons, which served as the collective grazing ground of the village. It worked as long as each villager limited the number of sheep. But when prices suddenly went up, everyone became greedy and each family added just one extra sheep to their herd. The net cumulative result was the overgrazing and ultimately the death of the commons.

Economics encounters ecology. In rural areas, the rule of thumb for emptying waste into a stream was one mile of clear water between you and your neighbor. But introduce one extra dumping from someone new and that meant that the neighbor down the stream inherited partially polluted water.

The spoilage of what is held in common also translates into income. If downsizing here and abroad continues, American may not have the means to purchase even cheaper goods. The basic way the middle class has been able to sustain its standard of living is to opt for the two-income family. That has also been accompanied by having fewer children. It has even created a new category called DINC (Double Income No Children) that also includes the unacknowledged single-sex unions. In short, the United States may be encountering the law of diminishing returns.

CEOs regard themselves as good capitalists with an obligation to their stockholders to deliver returns on investment; and if that involves shipping jobs overseas, so be it. The outcry of workers and their unions made outsourcing a political issue calling for legislative restraint of such practices on the one hand, and more extensive training programs of workers on the other hand.

The political outrage and promises notwithstanding is mostly hype. American companies cannot be artificially constrained from acting in their best interests. Besides, the economic gains are already in hand; and once the cow is out of the barn, it makes no difference whether you close the door or not.

In addition, the superiority of education and training may be losing its competitive advantage. American workers are already some of the most trained employees in the world. The problem is not skill but salary. The $45,000 American computer programmer can't compete with or offset his or her $25,000 counterpart in India. All the training in the world cannot eliminate a $20,000 differential. The American worker increasingly may be going up a down escalator.

Doomsayers already are surfacing and proclaiming the rise and fall of the United States and hailing China and a united Europe as the new dominant markets and producers. That shift to Asia and to a unified Europe already is happening; China buys from both Boeing and Airbus. But three different developments and responses need to be considered.

The first requires a leap of the imagination. The world in effect and over time may become one increasingly interconnected and inoperable total economic network. Companies and workers will be part of global commerce without sacrificing their individual culture and historical identity. The model already exists in the painstaking process of putting together the European Union with one currency and one passport between all member countries. The Germans still speak German, the French still speak French, and all preserve their own cultural identities. But it is as if they have a double citizenship now: one for their country of birth, the other of the European union.

Second, globality also has made possible joint ventures in which instead of competing with each other, talent can be pooled for collaborative enterprises. Airbus is a Euro company. China and Russia have proven that communism current or recent are no obstacles to capitalistic opportunities. Third, finally, imagine the boon that such a collectivized world would bring to global ecology, which does not recognize national boundaries. In short, as always, crisis needs vision, and in this case the foresight of a global heterogeneous and integrated network of countries and economies not abusing but optimizing the commons.

Meanwhile, while that is slowly and gradually happening piece by piece, and while self-interest and shared purpose begin to learn to negotiate with each other, what happens here in the United States? The basic response is to continue doing what we already have been doing. While this global redistribution of gain and loss is taking place, American workers, managers, and leaders have produced one of the most impressive records of productivity, profitability, and quality of any economy and workforce.

But that achievement is not only overlooked, it is also unexamined. The story of how the American workforce has been able to rack up major economic gains in the face even of radical downsizing has not been told. What is particularly lamentable about that sin of analytical omission is that it has obscured the emergence of major transformations of the entire workforce—at all levels, in all sectors. No group has been left unaltered.

Moreover, when those changes are fully analyzed, what emerges not only is a series of explanations of why and how the total American workforce has successfully maintained the economy, but also profiles the future performance of the most productive workforce the United States and perhaps the world has ever produced, rivaling even the vaunted Japanese. Indeed, this country may develop and provide the global training and learning model that may become our next major export.

4

DYSFUNCTIONAL WORKPLACES AND DREADFUL BOSSES: THE ORGANIZATIONAL PAIN. BLAME, SHAME, AND GOTCHA GAME

There are many companies—perhaps too many—that are unhappy places to work. And yet most are unaware of the condition; or if they are, little or nothing is done about it. When consultants are invited in, they are asked to tackle only the big questions. Things are too urgent and critical to go after small potatoes like happiness or fulfillment. The next thing you know, every employee will want his or her own therapist. But aside from jeopardizing productivity and innovation, unhappy employees are not so much personally as institutionally unhappy. In other words, the problem is not personal—it is organizational. The problems are not self-inflicted; they are structural or endemic. They are created. The enterprise is culpable. Here are just three examples.

1. Organizational Pain

    Many employees are pained by the organization they work for. They are not proud of where they work or what they produce. They do not think top management is smart or savvy. They do not regard middle-level managers as particularly bright or competent. They believe many decisions are dumb and even embarrassing. They endure the cheap and empty cheerleading meetings and messages. They do not respect the ability of the new hires. And there is virtually no trust. . . . It's all been recycled endlessly into obedience or used up.

2. Organizational Dependency

This is the destructive drama of bossism and subordination. Many managers cannot function unless they boss people and push paper around. The lesson they seek to communicate is subordination and to make employees dependent. Thus, a twisted relationship is set up. Those who want to be always on top need a bottom to be on top of. In fact, that need is greater than the need to be productive and innovative. Ironically, both goals are impossible with a dependent workforce. If one wants to estimate the future of any organization, examine the need for top dog, because underneath there will be protesting whelps.

3. Organizational Inertia

The pains of stasis occur when the number of promotable professionals exceeds the number of available opportunities for advancement. All entreaties for continuous development, attending graduate school, going to conferences, and so on fall on deaf ears. Worse, when promotions occur that are filled by questionable in competents, then morale suffers immediate decline and the rumor mill has another occasion for grinding out a new cynicism.

When any or all of these conditions prevail, and employees have no other job alternatives, then organization blues take hold and workers moan and groan that old tune that their soul belongs to the company store. Even downsizing might be welcome. Anything to break the cycle of being trapped. Well, is there anything that can be done? There are a few happier tunes that might be played.

1. Organizational Pride and Smarts

No one wants to work for a dumb company. If you are not such a company, find out why that perception exists. Whatever the reason, find ways to demonstrate and communicate smarts. What's more, make that the task of the CEO and the senior vice presidents. And if they fail, then maybe they really are dumb and should be replaced.

2. Organizational Declaration of Independence and Interdependence

    End bossism once and for all. If some of your managers have problems with that, ask them to head up teams and be accountable for the results or lack of them. Make it clear that the days of dependency are over and that what is needed and valued is independence and, above all, interdependence. Wherever possible, write it into your mission statement and job descriptions.

3. Organizational Opportunities and Innovation

    Establish as a policy that leadership and innovation are no longer tied to specific positions that traditionally have had a lock or monopoly on leading and creating. But that won't work unless the opportunities are accompanied by the creation of both a recognition and reward system. That way the acknowledgment of the leadership of those who are not officially leaders and the innovations of those who are not part of R&D become routine and known. And the bonuses for either or both should match what is given to the official leaders and innovators.

    Isn't it surprising or at least interesting how these small, niggling, apparently self-indulgent issues have a way of working themselves up companywide and becoming as important or even more so than the big issues the consultants were asked to tackle? Actually, good consultants would turn to the blues first because they know that God is in the details. And where God is so is the future.

DREADFUL BOSSES: TAMING THE BULLIES AND BRUTES

> The kind of people we are looking for in our management ranks is someone who can be persuasive and who can make people cooperate with them. Management is not dictatorship.
>
> —Akio Morita (1986)

According to research cited by CareerBuilder's website (January 2001), 25 percent of employees would be happy to fire their bosses. Actually, based on my experience as a consultant and trainer, I would put the number higher, as much as 50 percent. That's dreadful, especially when one considers that a boss is really half the job. Indeed, a lousy boss equals a lousy job. Indeed, Talentkeepers, an organization that specializes in retaining talent, claims that the primary reason for losing good people is a lousy boss. Moreover, with the greater emphasis on achieving the stretch goals of increased productivity, profitability, and performance, an organization with such managers jeopardizes its present survival as well as its future growth.

Long ago Edward Deming claimed that 85 percent of all problems were the fault of managers. For better or worse, they were supposed to model the right behaviors. But evidently now when we need good managers more than ever, we have many of the worst examples possible. If training dollars ever had to be optimally focused now, it should be on reinventing and reengineering managers (Champy, 1996).

What would that training include? At least three subjects: a list of the crimes of bullying bosses, the structure and culture that shape and support bossism, and some possible ways of taming the beast.

The list below is mostly self-explanatory and sadly familiar.

A List of the Crimes of Bullying Bosses

1. Managerial Crimes and Excesses

    This includes creating a precarious environment, breeding uneasiness so that everyone is walking around on eggshells, sowing seeds of insecurity about the ax falling and cutbacks.

2. Blame, Shame, and Gotcha Games

    Accusations of ineptitude, finger pointing, rallying group disapproval, being poised to catch errors or lapses, the public humiliation of dressing employees down loudly so that it can be overheard, attacking individuals at meetings, summoning employees to be chastised by a higher-level boss, and menacing warnings, verbal lashings, and actual threats.

3. Stealing Ideas

    Appropriating suggestions earlier ignored or rejected; borrowing language from a report, memo, or e-mail; taking credit for employee accomplishments.

4. Never Saying Thanks

Seemingly incapable of being grateful, unable or unwilling to acknowledge superior performance, taking for granted extra special effort or accomplishment as just part of the job.

5. Halo of Managerial Indispensability

Projecting an image of a savior, a model of perfection, a paternal protector—in short, the only one who holds this wretched group together and regularly saves their proverbial butt.

6. Two-faced Hypocrisy

Dreadful to you, fawning to superiors. Duplicity is a norm. Unofficially, a bully; officially, the perfect embodiment of participatory democracy. Putting on a show to superiors of crediting all to employees so as to be overruled and praised for his selfless efficiency and management. Often may play the role of bully of humility.

7. Extremes of Abandonment or Micromanagement

Either suffocating or abandoning the employee on his or her own. Assignments are sink or swim. Hovers incessantly. Wants to see early drafts, checks in constantly, asks for daily, even hourly, updates.

The Structure and Culture That Shape and Support Bossism

Bullies may be born or made, but what is clear is that they are also created and supported by certain organizational values, cultures, and structures. Bossism is in fact sometimes a reward for higher levels of education, work experience, and professional development. Being on top is always sought after. The pyramidal organizational chart enshrines ascent. The transformational or charismatic leader who saves or turns around a failing organization is a recurrent and supreme model of emulation.

But there cannot be a top without a bottom. Managers are always over those they supervise. Being superior is where the power comes from. And power is definition. That is what sets supervisors apart from employees. Preserving that distance and difference is what bosses are determined never to relinquish and have employees forget.

So in a very strong and real sense, bossism is endemic. It is built into vertical structures. It also taps the American dream of Horatio Alger pulling himself up by his bootstraps and reaching the pinnacle of final success. Indeed, often it is a one-shot experience. Fired CEOs seldom are able to find another high-level position. Evidently, leaders only get one chance to catch the brass ring. And they hang on tenaciously, never willing to let go or share. In general, the myth of leadership celebrates the incandescent moment rather than the long, steady, and deliberate climb to higher levels. The day-to-day details are neglected. Only the power and glory are featured. Thus, structure and mythology traditionally favor strong bosses and leaders who are in charge and increasingly indispensable. Breaking free of that historical and cultural pattern is difficult. Indeed, many MBA executive programs only reinforce the stereotypes.

To comprehend that kind of difference and preference requires understanding the psychology of dominance. Clearly, it goes back to individual experiences within the family, and masculine or feminine role models. We know, for example, that if parents fail to give their kids opportunities to independently complete tasks but instead always do it for them, that they later evidence a chronic inability to complete things. In fact, it is described as completion deficiency syndrome. Research also has indicated how codependent relationships in childhood frequently create codependent managers. But clearly such deep-rooted matters are beyond access and maybe beyond correction. However, what is available, accessible, and changeable are behaviors and attitudes, especially toward work, employee performance, and team performance.

Less disguised and more available are the personality biases we all have. Those who work hard like to work with people who work hard. Those who are detail oriented have the same work preferences as do those who cherish meeting deadlines. On top of that, there is the unfortunate tendency to hire people from the same background. (Talk about academic programming, observe the same thinking of graduates from the same MBA program.) So in addition to structure and culture externally feeding into bossism, there are all the internal pressures and biases. In the interview situation, what is called *chemistry* is really the commonality and camaraderie of the good-old-boys club and tie.

Clearly, then, there are many formidable factors that shape the manager as dictator. Although many of the deep-rooted psychological factors may be unavailable or unusable, many leverage points are accessible and changeable and can have an effect on taming the beasts.

Taming the Beasts

1. Change the Culture

    Changing the culture is admittedly a big order and requires time (it is estimated it takes twenty-five years or another generation to do so), but the significant advantage is that such change alters much. It corrects not just one boss or bully but hopefully many as a new paradigm of management emerges.

    Moreover, two factors, one immediate and the other long term, function as allies. The immediate is crisis, the second is a generation of new hires. Crisis has made possible the kind of total changes in configuration championed by Hammer and Champy (1993) and total evaluation systems of the balanced score card put forward by Kaplan (1997). The prospect of baby boomers beginning to retire soon opens up the possibility of an entire new generation of managers, shaped during the years of empowerment, coming on board. But to ensure eliminating throwbacks, devote a year of orientation training to the new recruits. In short, time—immediate and long term—is on the side of change.

2. Embrace Diversity

    No longer limited to race, gender, and ethnicity, although all those are crucial ingredients, total diversity requires hiring graduates from many different colleges and universities, from distance education programs, and from home schooling, and above all from different industries and even sectors. The ritual of the fit is myopic and often predictably confining. The same kind of people are regularly hired and then everyone wonders why there is no change.

    Diversity also involves creating and sustaining alternative work structures, ranging from small incubators to large divisions, from autonomous teams to interdependent horizontal organizational units. Criss-cross divisional lines so as to produce heterogeneity and cross-disciplinary interactions rather than homogeneous sameness. Experiment with distributed leadership in which leadership is included in everyone's job description just as innovation is also comprehensively distributed. Even team leadership needs to be employee centered.

The cumulative effect of implementing all or many of these ideas mentioned here would function the same way an obstacle course does for a runner. He would not have an unencumbered or unobstructed straight shot at his goal. He would be forced to shift and dodge around hurdles. He would wear himself down and out. He would not to be able to find one hill above all that he could claim to be king of. That has already happened, especially in manufacturing with team management. Supervisors and engineers have become increasingly marginal.

3. Focus on Behaviors and Performance, Not on Personalities

Much of bossism comes from bias and subjectivity, pitting people against each other, characterizing employees as lazy, dumb, slow, thick, obstinate, and the like. These epithets increasingly are no-nos and the basis of lawsuits. The two standards of performance appraisal are objectivity and documentation. Characterization of motives and description of personality traits are not the appropriate language of evaluation. If HR does its job, such characterizations would be sent back as unacceptable and require that they be rewritten in situational and performance terms. The focus is on the job and the way it gets done or does not, and how well or poorly, as measured by objective standards. With such focus and discipline, bosses would be hard pressed to be self-indulgent.

4. Employee Productivity and Coaching

In the last ten years the emphasis has been on supplementing technological with employee productivity. And it has been working when bossy managers are transformed into persuasive coaches. The reason coaching has been so productive has nothing to do with the image of the coach as a nice guy replacing the familiar brute but with a transfer of power from supervisor to employee and granting the worker the opportunity to solve problems. Indeed, what many supervisors have discovered is that by backing off and giving space for worker input, the range of solutions is often greater and more productive and innovative than any single supervisor could conceive. Restraining the ego and self-importance of the boss can produce minor miracles.

5. Collective Covenants

All indications are that the next stage of management development will be self-management by employees. Firms are already involved in encouraging employee mission statements as a way of recognizing and encouraging intellectual capital to find and express its own voice. There is also some evidence that the example of Motorola University, Ford University, McDonald Academy, and others will be generally and generically extended to the shaping of employee universities, replete with the prospect of some employees also serving as instructors. The steady inclusiveness of collaboration by employees is in the form of workers covenants. That in turn has led to the expansion of job satisfaction to include providing satisfaction to others. In short, all signs point to the fact that we are steadily moving toward an increasingly employee-centered organization in which tyrannical bosses will be dinosaurs.

Although there are a number of individual actions employees can take, they are generally ineffective. Bullies usually hold all the cards and know how to play them. In fact, that is why and how they have lasted so long. The only thing one can do is quit and let them know that it was because of a lousy boss. But their days are numbered. Companies cannot afford managers who tamper with and fail to tap productivity, profitability, and performance. Such recognition, coupled with the increasing centrality of workers, spells the end of bossism. As the head of Sony noted, management is not dictatorship. The American version should be management as democracy.

REFERENCES

Champy, James. *Reengineering Management*. New York: HarperCollins, 1995.
Hammer, Michael & James Champy, *Reengineering the Corporation: A Manifesto for Business Revolution*, New York: HarperCollins, 1993.

KNOWLEDGE ACQUISITION AND MANAGEMENT A LA TOFFLER AND SENGE: KNOWLEDGE WORKERS AND LEARNING ORGANIZATIONS

Ever since Alvin Toffler predicted that the successful professionals of the future would have to be knowledge workers, that phrase has stirred and tyrannized us. It appears now in virtually all job descriptions and advertisements as a catch-all. It is also an unavoidable area of questioning during interviews and the current hot training topic (now called *knowledge management*).

I have no quarrel with the prediction or with the phrase but two nagging matters plague me. The first I admit is somewhat defensive: what were we before we were told we had to be knowledge workers? Ignoramuses, incompetent, ignorant? The second is more philosophical and structural: What is it that a knowledge worker is supposed to know to qualify? Both questions can be folded into each other and answered together.

Clearly, we have always been knowledge workers. Being designated that did not change us. What did change was the speed, the sources, and configurations of information and knowledge we acquired. Calculations that were only dreamed about could now be done. Pie-in-the-sky scenarios finally could be indulged: Global simulation systems models could be launched. The old world of manual monitoring and even record keeping disappeared. Accountants could process hundreds of tax

returns in the time it took to do twenty and then file returns electronically. Information technology generated a new acronym: IT; and when
integrated across the board, IT evolved into the more comprehensive
MIS (management information systems). Knowledge processing and
storage even became a black box enabling us to speak in different languages. The list is almost endless and constantly impressive.

It also was reciprocal. Knowledge workers created knowledge systems
that in turn extended and created knowledge workers. Software was designed to create better software. It increasingly became impossible to
conceive of work and workers apart from their machines and systems.
The symbiotic relationship between human and machine was no longer
science fiction; it had become science fact. In the process, all the
changes were so immediate and total that discontinuities were rapidly
established not just between old and new ways of doing things, but between age groups—hence the notion of a new generation of knowledge
workers.

But here is precisely where we perhaps have become too glib and
rapid. The transition did not include or acknowledge that there was another more serious, even threatening transition. Initially, information
technology was a servant. It did our bidding. It was our gopher. Our increasing dependency required that the technology be a handmaiden, a
servant still, but favored. But as the knowledge worker came into his
own, the relationship changed to that of a partner, even collaborator.
Unknowingly, that evolved into the role of an autonomous designer.

The increasingly symbiotic relationship between humans and technology has reached the point where in some cases the human half has been
reduced to a quarter and finally to zero, as the intelligent machine of
knowledge technology has taken over. Even in the academic world where
change is measured in glacial time, new definitions of basic courses
emerged. Basic economics is now information or e-economics; sociology,
information or e-sociology; education, information or e-education. Research references and bibliographies now routinely include websites.

In recognition of the power of knowledge to transform and even reconfigure traditional content, MBA courses were paired off initially with
matching e-versions. Eventually, they became their equivalents. It is
now inconceivable to envision marketing as other than e-marketing. In

short, it might be more accurate to speak about the knowledge worker in more "chicken/egg terms." Which came first, the worker or the machine? And which is now the top dog, the worker or the machine? And to what extent is the workplace now the e-place?

Perhaps, its major evolutionary development is increasing employee portability. With laptop and cell phone, an employee is constantly connected by an electronic umbilical cord to the mother ship. Increasingly, he or she can telecommute to his or her job. New homes are being designed and prewired to accommodate working from home. It even has spawned an entire industry of home-based businesses.

The forecasters stopped too soon. What understandably was beyond Toffler and the others who hopped on the bandwagon was its evolution—of how information and knowledge technology would develop and how those transformations would change the relationships of those who used and directed those knowledge engines and, surprisingly, how they in turn ultimately would both be used and directed.

They also did not fully anticipate that as knowledge workers became the norm of corporations, education, and government, they also would emerge as home-business entrepreneurs, support home schooling, and provide sources and platforms for citizens.

Equally as important was the recognition that current standard job descriptions were inadequate. They either omitted the inclusion of knowledge worker or generalized it to the point where it had no specific content. Although such a definition is a work in progress and varies from industry to industry and job to job, here is a generic job description of a knowledge worker that may serve to define not only the worker but also the workplace.

Knowledge workers are supplementers, amplifying linear-sequential with systemic thinking. They are preeminently brokers, routinely establishing linkages and alignments between information paths. They are extenders, constantly stretching systems so that they are ever more inclusive and interdivisional. They are prioritizers, altering individual and divisional goals to align vertically with company objectives. They are assessors, monitoring and evaluating priorities and making just-in-time corrections. They are symbiotically amplifiers, invasively embedding information technology to make more informed decisions and plans, sometimes hourly.

What is thus finally revelatory is not the catchphrase of being a knowledge worker but knowing what knowledge workers do, can do, and above all will be doing in the future. Because such a worker was created by the future, that is also where his evolving definition will take place. In fact, his development in the future constitutes the current agenda for in-house training and for MBA curricula.

A postscript. There is another dimension about being a knowledge worker that is also generally unexamined. We are often so busy focusing on the content that we minimize the context. To be a genuine knowledge worker means not only knowing one's job, one's profession, or even one's industry, extensive though that may be, but also knowing the global context. The search for best practices is no longer confined to one sector of the economy or one country or one theory. Online MBAs are offered in Europe, Hong Kong, South Africa, and China. And shocking as it may be to an American sense of superiority, they are not all versions of the Harvard MBA or case study approach.

Similarly, the knowledge worker must know future trends, especially those that may not directly impact one's industry or field but may occur later and from an unexpected direction. It also requires understanding new formulations and theories about knowledge, immunology, genetics, chaos theory, and the like. It should include extensive understanding about invention science and the many, often intuitive ways in which innovation comes into being. Finally, there is a need to wean oneself away from the tried and test solution systems that ironically can imprison and limit by their very success and find ways to unlearn the learning that has programmed the basic problem-solving methodologies in the first place.

In other words, uniquely perhaps, we have reached a point in the history and evolution of knowledge systems where there is no limit to what the knowledge workers can and perhaps must know, just as they are no longer limited by their particular jobs as to what they can know. In effect, each knowledge worker can be and sometimes is a CEO, CIO, CFO, and COO all in one. Being an executive or a visionary is no longer the monopoly of top management. The knowledge worker can become what was reserved for a few—a student of the business, the total business, the future of the enterprise. But that also means, surprise of all surprises, the return to hierarchy. Namely, there are knowledge workers and there are the knowledge workers. The machine may be egalitarian, but not so those who use it to the max. Indeed, perhaps, the most ambitious stage is reserved for those enrolling in doctoral programs and becoming researchers—not just a knowledge worker but a knowledge producer—the ultimate version of the knowledge worker. And that is more a European than an American tradition.

6

SIZE: LIMITS TO BIGNESS, STRUCTURES, AND PERSONNEL

In the past, hardly anyone questioned that big was better. It was proof of growth, market share, stability. The business giants were so secure and generous that like universities they could grant managers the largesse of tenure. But when things changed radically and competition took hold of the jugular, such excesses were difficult to correct, largely because such practices were no longer the problem. The issue had become not what the companies were but what they were not. They were not quick, agile, swift. They were obedient, predictable, cocksure.

Scale and structure became mirror images. Size compelled distance, from the top and from what was on the right or left. Everything was boxed and boxed in. Accountability to stockholders was high but inventiveness was low. Coasting became the norm. People were busy but energy was always contained. Underperforming became routine. Then, because desperation not enlightenment is often the mother of invention, what was considerable immutable—scale and structure—became variables, and experimentation with small-scale structures began to take place.

Big corporations created smaller businesses within the larger business. Profit centers consisting of 100 to 200 employees were cobbled together. In manufacturing, the singularity of the production line gave way to the manufacturing cell. In many companies, teaming and cross-training became a new way of doing business. Other organizations opted for distributed leadership based on contribution rather than title. Other groups created future teams of 100 or so professionals within an organization charged with engaging the territory ahead. And so on.

Scale and structure combined to create miniatures of the whole, little worlds made close. When these new forms prospered it was because they were given their own way and budget. They were not forced to reflect or obey the culture of their offspring. But when the umbilical cord was tenaciously maintained so that when they were asked to run their legs in effect were tied, they faltered and failed.

If one examines the characteristics and qualities of the most successful experimental smaller versions of their parental forms, one finds at least five essential factors.

1. Communication

     Small groups or structures up the ante on communications. In fact, that is what holds the group together. They constantly talk things out. They discover ignorance or arrogance that way, and search for the cause of either or both. The job, the problems, the obstacles, are constantly discussed; consciousness raising is made possible by communications raising.

2. Identity

     Small groups are always in search of their identity, of what they should be called, how they should be described, and how they should be explained to those outside the group. As the search goes on for that elusive identity, there is the recognition that when and if found, it will still remain fluid and a work in progress. It has to be that way because the final shape of the group overlaps the future and is therefore permanently unfinished. The groups will stubbornly not jettison evolution for premature clarity. And yet, for all the uncertainty and the temporariness of its identity, their difference is clear to everyone involved. And so no one is frantic.

3. Questioning

     The dominant mode of conversation and conducting business is inquiry. Questioning is the norm. Challenging assumptions becomes second nature. Everything is up for grabs. Nothing is sacred. Members regularly unlearn as their version of the learning organization. Innovation is pursued relentlessly; and the sign of its visiting the group is the sense that the future has visited the present.

4. Autonomy

The group is self-possessed. It is capable of functioning primarily in an open rather than a closed system. Such a system requires that processes constantly be repaired and altered. All design, no matter initially how good and serviceable, is temporary. Unlike mechanical closed systems that seek perfection because they were designed never to require transformation, the group is constantly self-organizing, self-learning, and self-developing. Autonomy is a group's version of freedom.

5. Consensual Culture

Unlike the other items in the list, this is newly minted. It never existed before in precisely the way it does for each group. It is a group's signature. It is its modus operandi. It is the way the group develops, how the members evolve to work together with each other as individuals and as a group. Consensual culture also subsumes all the above. It is created and maintained by communication. The nature of the consensuality constitutes the group's identity and diversity. It evolves and is shaped by the questioning mode. And it is inconceivable without self-organizing systems. In fact, one can claim that consensual cultures are in fact the unique creations of such autonomous open systems.

In summary, then, small is better only if it is intelligently so, designed and crafted with the right dynamics that make scale and structure the servant of a special fusion of independence and interdependence. Granted freedom and autonomy, such heterogeneous cohorts can optimally tap the unlimited potential of diversity and innovation. Freed of the structure and culture of bigness, they can create and nourish their own systems organically from within, not imposed from without. If salvation requires passing through the eye of a needle, then the small shall inherit the earth and its future.

The decade of the 1990s witnessed an enormous burst of organizational reengineering of all kinds, at all levels, across the board, from top to bottom, often at a furious pace. Now that the dust has settled, assessment of the impact is beginning to appear.

Evidently, it did not work in many cases. According to Smith (2002) one third of all overhauls were successful and met the expectations of their sponsors. Equally as fascinating is why so many panaceas fell far short. Moreover, it was not so much the change involved as how it was managed. Above all, it faltered because of various myths of change management, which range from the limits of charismatic leaders, the inertia of company cultures, and the failure to remove barriers to behavioral change.

Although other failure points could be added ad infinitum, a recent *USA Today* survey (October 2002, p. 1) of 1,400 CEOs of small to midsize companies indicates that their two top-linked priorities (48 percent and 46 percent, respectively) were restructuring and personnel. Evidently it is not easy to join the two and to align the aspirations of organizations with the aspirations of employees, and vice versa. On the one hand, the operational environment must be shaped to accommodate change and stir initiative and innovation. On the other hand, it also must provide employee comfort, security, and satisfaction while encouraging rank and file not to perform obediently in lockstep fashion. How can the two halves be brought together?

What follows below are a series of principles for reviewing and reconfiguring current structures and personnel practices to optimize the interface between environment and relationships. It is not so much a template as an overlay of what should guide and drive the design of environment- and worker-interaction models. To facilitate the ultimate pairing of structure and personnel, the principles of each half need to be stated separately but always proximate and parallel to each other.

STRUCTURAL PRINCIPLES

1. Horizontal

   Increasing pressure for greater autonomy from the satellites of global or large organizations has compelled a shift of focus from control to coordination. Traditionally, the home office or corporate center maintained its centrality not because it was effective but titular. CEOs always sought to be at the flagship corporate office and reign over all. But when effective structure becomes more important than executive ego, dispersion replaces hierarchy (Cox and Walker, 1990). The predominant direction of repositioning is thus always horizontal (Thompson, 1993; Kurzweil, 1999).

2. Communication Flow

The litmus test of effective internal and external communications is diffusion, not concentration (Argyris, 1990). It routinely has to be disseminated throughout the company and not hoarded exclusively as the only currency of the realm in the hands of a few. If power is knowledge, then the content of communication is leveraged intelligence. If the customer is data, then when shared, personnel can customize customer service (Bethanis, 1993).

3. Capitalism as Sociology

Organizations are communities, not properties. The perpetual preoccupation with satisfying stockholders as owners compels the compulsive and shortsighted concentration on the short term. As communities, organizations need rules of governance not of ownership (Brown, 1992). Sociological not commercial practice should apply (Carroll, 1993). Organizational charts need to be reconfigured as neighborhoods, work contracts as work covenants (Champy, 1995).

4. The Political Science of Capitalism

Traditional structures worship central government, which like God is distant, omnipotent, and unchallenged (Argyris, 1994). The chain of command is exactly that—a rigid series of links tyrannically and unilaterally directed upward. And then we wonder why innovation does not happen, why the emperor regularly appears without any clothes, and why truth telling requires the extraordinary act of whistle blowing. The center has to be dispersed. It has to become more a series of nexi rather than a singular monolith, more a network than a place (Diehl, 1992).

5. Power Plays

Authority is the power to make something happen. But often it is the means to stop things from happening. Such negative power, of course, is never called that. Instead, it is characterized as a necessary and ultimately indispensable series of checking and rechecking things before they happen to ensure that they do. But in the process it provides hundreds of people with the license to approve something before it happens. If too many approvals are required, nothing happens. The net result is that either it does not survive the gauntlet, or if it does, it finally appears as such an exhausted, transformed, and limp version of the original that it may not be worth implementing (Isaacs, 1993). Bureaucracies stifle. Energy is power. Positive power is the energy to make changes, to create, and to initiate. Negative power is not allowing any of that to happen, and to hide behind rules and procedures and even policies that reign supreme. After all, it is tempting to be paid for not working, for not exercising the power. Downsizing should take place in good, not hard times so that enlightenment, not desperation can discover and stop the drainage of energy and power.

6. Both Big and Small or Twin Hierarchies

Paradox simplifies and facilitates duality, choice, and contradiction (Drucker, 1994). Small structures want to be big. Size confers protection. Big wants to be bigger. Monopoly is the ultimate form of dominance. The trick is how to be both big and small at the same time—how to enjoy the economies of scale without incurring the paralysis of bureaucracy—how, in short, to preserve neighborhoods in large cities. The answer is that structure regularly has to apply size to process. Big companies become smaller when focus is extended along many decision points and is not the sole prerogative of the top; and when divisions are not exclusively places of singular expertise but miniaturize the whole. In short, if access and comfort zones can be structurally accommodated, big and small can comfortably and paradoxically coexist.

In the process, such coexistence also may help honor and reconfigure the traditional two hierarchies of all companies that often are sadly in conflict (Handy, 1996). One is the status hierarchy, the other the task hierarchy. The first acknowledges and rewards seniority. Older employees are paid more. They also are respected and deferred to for their knowledge, experience, past performance, and proven stability. Traditionally, they are called upon to lead a task force or head up a new project. The problem that often occurs, however, and if unanticipated invites not just objections but mutiny, is competence. If the project requires skills and expertise that exceed that of the senior leader, then the task hierarchy asserts its claim to leadership. The resolution of this inevitable conflict has been typically left to a senior-level employee playing the role of Solomon. But when interdependence and coexistence become the goals of structure not diplomacy, then deference and competence are built into all leadership opportunities (Mulgan, 1997).

7. Structural Codependency

Most current structures support the recurrent drama of boss, subordination, and routine. Central to that ritual is organizational dependency. Supervisors manage by having people and papers to push around; and employees in that environment don't know what to do without being pushed around. Psychologically, that is codependence. Each one enables the other to remain intact. But when the structure that supports and even sustains such mutual inertia is altered from prescribed to self-determined opportunities for defining work and work relationships, autonomy not dependence reigns.

In general, then—and with this conclusion we cross over to principles of personnel—employees should be encouraged to do things in their own way as long as it is in the common interest; they need to be well informed and well trained to discern and interpret that common purpose; and finally they do more and give more when they are led not managed, better still when they lead. The key to high-performing organizations is energy. Arthritic, angry, and punitive structures bottle up, deflect, and drain energy away. What releases it is autonomy—freeing the slaves and taking them out of Egypt. Examining organizational energy flow or the lack of it not only will determine, but also predict performance.

PERSONNEL PRINCIPLES

1. Reverse Delegation

To delegate or not is no longer the question. It is to whom or better still in what direction (Barfield, 1993). If the dominant direction of restructuring is horizontal, the key direction of delegating like communication is downward. The principle is that power belongs to the lowest possible point of the organization (Handy, 1996). The decisions of employees should not be appropriated or stolen. The state should not legislate or do what parents can do better. In turn, parents should not appropriate or steal the decisions of children growing up. The Catholic Church works on the holistic premise that every priest is a pope in his parish. Similarly, Judaism asserts the local rabbi is the sole and absolute interpreter of liturgy and ritual.

Robert Galvin of Motorola does the same when he informs Motorola's sales force that they have the authority of the CEO with customers. Employees of Ritz Carlton, no matter what their level, have the power to solve the problems of guests, up to $10,000 per guest. Like information flow, reverse delegation enervates from the bottom up not the top down (Habbel, 2002).

2. Raising the Accountability Bar

Effective personnel policies always engage expectations, which rightly are now called stretch goals (Bakken, 1993). This finds a parallel in statistics (Handy, 1996): type one error means simply not getting it right, but type two error means not getting it as right as it could have been. Typically, we have focused personnel practices on type one accountability: trying to ensure that no mistakes are made and then stopping there, smugly satisfied. But like reverse delegation, we should up the ante to type two accountability, seizing every opportunity to make every improvement possible and imaginable. But that, too, cannot be stolen or appropriated by the top or the efficiency experts and consultants (Pfeiffer, 1998).

3. A New Productivity Formula

Handy's definition of corporate fitness offers a productivity ideal: ? by 2 by 3. Half as many on the payroll, paid twice as well, producing three times as much. This goes way beyond Pareto's famous dictum of 20 percent of the people doing 80 percent of the work. How can that ideal be realized? In three ways. First, review all jobs that are essentially mechanical or repetitive and can be done as well or better by technology or robotics. Second, define core competencies and delete or outsource what is not. Third, hire heads not hands, the best not the average, the most entrepreneurial not the most obedient. Employ the overqualified. Shrink the center and the workforce to the least and the best within their sphere. Cross-train not to exchange jobs but to exchange perspectives of the whole. And then implement the changes in structure and personnel presented here as the means to get out of their way.

4. Distributed Leadership

Every job description should include a leadership component (Elmore, 2000, 2002). That should send a clear-cut message that leadership is not a monopoly of the top or of managers. That would immediately eliminate or reduce the refusal to do something because that is not part of their job description. The definition of a leader is one who does whatever it takes to get the job done. Therefore, make everyone a leader. Distributing rather than hoarding leadership invariably also produces ownership. It is like signing what one produces. It energizes not only the organization but also paradoxically the CEO who now can function as a company coach counseling many on what he knows best (Block, 1993).

5. Planned Disruption

Complacency kills and routine stifles. Often challenge comes from without. The economy is lax, competition increases, technology regularly threatens continuity and may hasten obsolescence. But such external pressures are not purposeful, designed, or focused. They scatter rather than concentrate energy. Strategic planning and HR should band together to plan intelligent and calculated disruption. Too many major companies collapsed from always being the dominant winners. Unlike Germany and Japan, they did not lose the war and find their past disrupted. It is often better to rebuild a factory from the ground up than to retrofit constantly an old relic. But lest this process of planned disruption be capricious, it must be informed by the next (and the last) personnel restructuring focus—the future.

6. Engaging the Future

Once again the base is the source. Reconfiguring job descriptions so that they include leadership options has to be expanded further to factor in the future. Employees need to be encouraged to speculate how their job may change two to three years ahead, and what new knowledge or skills company training will be required to offer.

The fusion of structure and personnel may best be expressed and summarized as an interfacing matrix. Here are the highlights:

Restructuring Options	Personnel Initiatives
Horizontals	Reverse Delegation
Communication Flow	Mutual Job Satisfaction Sociological Capitalism Accountability
Political Science Capitalism	Productivity Formula
Power Plays	Distributed Leadership
Big and Small and Twin Hierarchies	Planned Disruption

Although discussed separately, convergence should rule. It is not enough to change the environment and leave untouched the relationships between employees any more than it makes sense to talk about company goals apart from and without aligning worker goals. Indeed, one could argue that what regularly jeopardizes organizational change is passing off a half as whole. Excellence is holistics. Only then is there a chance for the whole to be greater than the sum of its parts.

REFERENCES

Abrahamson, E. "Managerial Fads and Fashions: The Diffusion and Rejection of Innovation." *Academy of Management Review* 16, no. 3 (1991).

Alexander, C., and Langer, E. *Higher Stages of Human Development.* New York: Oxford University Press, 1990.

Argyris, C. *Overcoming Organizational Defenses.* Needham, Mass.: Allyn & Bacon, 1990.

Argyris, Chris (1994). "Good Communication that Blocks Learning." *Harvard Business Review*, July–August, pp. 77–85.

Bakken, B. "Dynamic Decisions Environments." Diss., MIT, 1993.

Barfield, L. *User Interface.* Reading, Mass.: Addison-Wesley, 1993.

Bethanis, S. "Transforming Organizations." Diss., University of San Francisco, 1993.

Block. P. *Stewardship.* San Francisco: Berrett-Koehler, 1993.

Bohm, D. *On Dialogue*. Ojai, Calif.: Ojai Institute, 1989.

Brown, J. "Corporation as Community." In *New Traditions for Business*, ed. J. Renesch. San Francisco: Berrett-Koehler, 1992, pp. 32–46.

Carroll, G. R. "A Sociological View of Why Firms Differ." *Strategic Management Journal* 14, no. 4 (1993).

Champy, James. *Reengineering Management*. New York: HarperCollins, 1995.

Cox, K., and Walker, D. *User Interface Design*. New York: Prentice Hall, 1990.

de Geus, A. "Planning As Learning." *Harvard Business Review*, March/April (1988).

Diehl, E. "Effects of Feedback Mechanisms on Decision Making." Diss., MIT, 1992.

Drucker, Peter. *Post-Capitalist Society*, New York: Harper Business, 1994.

Elmore, Richard. (2000). *Building a New Structure for School Leadership*. Washington, DC: Albert Shanker Institute.

Elmore, Richard. (2002). *Bridging the Gap Between Standards and Achievement*. Washington, DC: The Albert Shanker Institute.

Greenleaf, R. *Teacher as Servant*. Indianapolis, Ind.: Paulist Press, 1987.

Habbel, R. *The Human Factor*. New York: Booz, Allen, Hamilton, 2002.

Hammer, M., and Champy, J. *Reengineering the Corporation*. New York: HarperCollins, 1993.

Handy, Charles. *Beyond Certainty*. Harvard Business School Press, 1996.

Isaacs, W. *The Systems Thinker*. Cambridge, Mass.: Pegasus Communications, 1993.

James, B. Q. *Strategies for Change*. Homewood, Ill.: Richard D. Irwin, Inc., 1980.

Korten, J. *Getting to the 21st Century*. West Hartford, Conn.: Kumarian Press, 1990.

Kuhn, T. *The Structure of Scientific Revolutions*. Chicago: University of Chicago Press, 1970.

Kurzweil, R. *The Age of Spiritual Machines*. New York: Viking, 1999.

Miller, L. M. *American Spirit: Visions of a New Corporate Culture*. New York: Warner Books, 1984.

Mulgan, Geoff. *Connexity*. London: Chatto & Windus, 1997.

Rosen, R., and Berger, L. *The Healthy Company*. New York: Putnam Publishing Group, 1993.

Thompson, J. W. *The Human Factor*. Farmdale, NY: Coleman, 1993.

Wheatley, M. *Leadership and the New Science*. San Francisco: Berrett-Koehler, 1992.

7

TEAMS: EDUCATION LEADERS AND BUSINESS SWAT TEAMS

Shortly after the Russian Revolution, communist agricultural experts sought to persuade individual farmers to farm collectively. In the next two years, thousands starved until the change took hold. Nearly seventy years later as the warm winds of capitalism began to thaw proletarian collective rigidity, experts went out calling for the new ideology of individual entrepreneurship. Again failure followed until a new competence was developed.

The point? Cultures change reluctantly and slowly. In the process, there is inevitable fallout, but still progress occurs, and occasionally it is stirring and even startling. Such is perhaps the case in Minnesota where some dozen charter schools under the collective name of Ed/Visions have forged a series of governance structures and collaborative teams of teacher leaders.

First, a profile of the Ed/Visions schools: They are all charter schools chartered by the state of Minnesota. (There are currently 2,431 charter schools in the United States serving 580,000 students.) Charter schools are public schools and thus receive per capita funds for each student enrolled. They have to find and operate their own educational plant. They are all small, averaging about 150 students, grades 7–12. What they do, how they do it, and how they evaluate are essentially design options.

Those design decisions are submitted with the original petition to the state. There are some state-mandated requirements: meeting graduation subject standards, employing certified teachers, acceptable pass rates on state tests, and so on. There are no administrators. Teachers run the school. The school board is made up mostly of elected teachers.

Although there are differences among the schools, some substantial, there is no pressure for uniformity. The association of the schools is a loose confederation done mostly to achieve common political ends, to employ specialists like grant writers working for many schools, and to enjoy economic savings through collective purchasing. Other than these few common benefits, each school is basically autonomous. Each school is allowed, even encouraged, to develop its own vision and mission statements, hire and fire staff, set salary and benefits levels for all personnel, and generally run its own shop. But what is fascinating is how in all cases the challenge of creating a school from scratch produced such strong commonalities. In effect, the twelve variations on a theme produced a generic artifact worthy of examination and perhaps replication.

GOVERNANCE AND MISSION STATEMENTS

A core staff spent the first year finding a site, hiring other staff members, designing the curriculum, and developing a governance process. It is the last task that is the focus of the examination here. In that connection, the first matter to be addressed was developing collectively a vision and mission statement. Unknowingly, that also turned out to be the first team assignment and test.

Initially, the members failed to function well as a team. Everything took an inordinate amount of time and energy. It was extremely difficult to break free of past models, even past language. But finally a draft emerged that housed a number of key assumptions that could be extracted and used as the agenda for planning the first year. Unexpectedly, the need to vent was so strong that it had to be encouraged in order to clear the field and the air for constructive discussion. But it left its mark. All that the planning team was against was compiled. Here are five of their "thou shalt nots": Thou shalt not use or invoke old models. Thou shalt not revert back to systems that preclude change from happening. Thou shalt not create or recreate authority figures as power sources. Thou shalt not have classrooms with doors that close. Thou shall not call the learning staff teachers.

That was enough to get things started and to clear the field for further discussion. What then emerged were several overriding questions and issues. How shall we organize ourselves? Against what goals? And who does what? What curriculum and learning process best minister to the talents and interests of each student? How do we measure students' development? Who orders supplies and pays bills? Who compiles the data for required state reports? Who maintains the delicate political relationships with the board, the district, and the state? How do we allocate our resources? Who manages the budget?

Concentrating and limiting the focus to structure will provide a profile of the governance process that evolved. But it should be noted that there would be strong dissent from the group about such a separation of parts from the whole. Indeed, holistics characterizes the entire collaborative process and even defined the first major issues that were addressed.

Gaps Identified and Bridged and Operating Conclusions Drawn

The group members preferred to use a problem-solving format. So they started with a number of the gaps that existed in traditional systems. First, there was the gap between administration and the classroom. Most principals did not teach; and even if they decided to, they were not current. Besides, their subject-matter competence was limited to their original specialization, and they could not lead where their credibility would preclude followers. Above all, learning and reform has to occur in classrooms. If not there, nowhere. First conclusion: Close the gap and solve the problem of the relationship of administration to instruction.

The other gap that was immediately visible was that between the learning staff and other-than-classroom evaluations. These had to do with schoolwide performance data, state-mandated test scores, aggregated curriculum assessments, and so on. Typically, teachers do not think outside the box of their classroom. They seldom even know what grades other teachers of other subjects have given their students. Many never know or even inquire how they are doing two years later. Both externally and internally, evaluation was at best a scattered affair, at worst piecemeal and fragmented.

The core team was enormously disturbed by what they discovered. This was of a different order than the first gap. This was personal and professional. All concluded that if they not had to create an entire school, they would not have realized how limited and even counterproductive their training in general and their understanding of evaluation in particular had been. They found their practiced ignorance and circumscribed perspective painfully unprofessional. Evaluation thus assumed an importance it had never had. Vows were taken never to allow it to become again a sin of omission. It was to become equal to curriculum in priority and even be the equal object of creativity. Second conclusion: Close and eliminate the external and internal gaps between instruction and evaluation.

In a rage of perfection, the team then turned to the gaps that exist within instruction—between staff and staff, staff and students, and staff and parents. Teachers sharing the same student often do not talk to each other let alone undertake common planning and coordination. Students occupy the receiving center of the wheel but their input is not sought. Parents know a great deal about their kids and especially their histories and habits, but their observations and insights are not made part of the instructional process and noted in the file. What emerged dramatically is that a great deal about schooling and learning is about relationships and behaviors. Nor does that exist apart from learning relationships and behaviors. Again the holistic emerged to rule. Two resolutions emerged. Third conclusion: The school is a community of learning and personal relationships and behaviors. Modeling caring and sharing interpersonal exchanges carries over into searching out and integrating multidisciplinary relationships. Living and learning are one and together support a principled and purposeful community.

Fourth conclusion: The same standards for everything apply equally to everyone, every time, everywhere. Accountability is total. We enroll not just kids but families; and the staff acts in loco parentis.

Mission of Integration

The convergence of all four conclusions led to a rewriting of the mission statement. The charge of the entire school became the integration of administration, instruction, and evaluation into one seamless, reinforcing whole. Achieving that end became the responsibility of everyone. It was the equivalent in industry of every employee being committed to quality. In particular, everyone was an administrator. Everything had to be managed so that it served instruction. Instructional opportunities exist everywhere. They were the monopoly neither of the classroom nor of the certified. Everything has to be planned and coordinated. All staff members must plan instruction together so that it is internally interactive and bridges administration and evaluation. Evaluation must be of a piece with instruction and should be as much of a classroom experience as subject matter. Measurement should not be a stepchild but subject to the same high level of importance and creativity as curriculum. One staff member obsessed with acronyms noted that this should be called project AIM: the integration of Administration, Instruction, and Measurement.

Those familiar with traditional structures in any organization know that such a total commitment to integration is the exception rather than the rule. In many ways, by perpetuating hierarchies and division of labor, the system itself precludes wholeness. Thus, the structure compels the principal to stand outside and apart from the dynamics of the classroom he or she is asked to administer. He or she is always an outsider, never an insider. The teachers often are not much better. They are sealed within their classroom; indeed, many treasure that isolation. There are no or limited external or internal interfaces with evaluation so that they really do not know comprehensively how well or poorly their students are doing. Or the disconnect is quickly picked up by administrators within and outside the district as an opportunity for accountability. Passing off a half as a whole, they become indignant judges or extravagant cheerleaders.

Under the aegis or pressure of integration, administrators generally emerge as powerless. They are too far removed from the classroom by the separatist nature of the structure and too distant in terms of competence to intervene with credibility. Solutions thus elude them and so they turn to the end of the process, the results of evaluation, to secure leverage. But by then it is frequently accusatory or punitive or, if desperation is high enough, offers bonus incentives to instructors to raise test scores. Thus, teaching to the test becomes the moral model of the school. In short, failure endemically accompanies a system that separates what it should bring together.

The three essential areas to be integrated are Administration, Instruction, and Measurement. It was not only a proactive, but also a diagnostic trinity. It served as a holistic x-ray on the entire situation. In addition, the commitment to AIM determined the nature and goals of all teams. In effect, each one had to be a miniature of the whole. It constantly had to address the interrelationships between the three essential parts. But that immediately raised an issue of competence. Suppose the particular problem to be addressed was essentially beyond the competence of the team leader? Perhaps it was more suited to the experience of another member of the team? What happened in that case? The conclusion was that competence determined rotation and who would take the point position. It was based solely on a match between ability and need. Students queried, "Did that mean that students on the team might be designated as first?" In fact, they often were.

And thus the school developed a team-centered, collaborative structure that operated by consensus and focused on the integration of AIM. The consortium arrangement with all the other schools in the confederation was welcome as long as it did not add another layer of administration or involve additional meetings. The teams were given different foci: curriculum, finance, student court, personnel, and the like but learning staff, students, and parents served on all and all focused always on integration of services. When the integration problem between different teams was particularly thorny or tough, the teams met as a larger group to resolve the issue.

And everybody lived happily ever after? Not by a long shot. In the first two years, especially, there were serious problems. Many if not all emanated from creating a new and different culture. In fact, most of the difficulties were throwbacks. Indeed, solving these turned out to be as difficult and liberating as all the basic conclusions. What were the essential difficulties? Basically, there were three.

1. The Problem of Team Dynamics

   The group quickly discovered that teams and committees are not synonymous. Committees make recommendations, not decisions and exist in a dependent status. Teams make decisions and exist as independent and interdependent. The carryover from a previous life was thus downright counterindicated. In short, teams are not born but made. The solution was to hold workshops on teaming facilitated by team trainers. That turned out to be so beneficial that the workshop became a staple of the start of every year, involving now not only staff, but also all students and parents.

2. The Law of Diminishing Ideology and Competence

   The launching vision required that everyone do everything. But even the collective brilliance of the group failed to turn up an expert in finance and budgets. An ex-principal among the group had done that but did not want to. That was not why he joined the school. He wanted to teach. He would serve on the finance team but that was as far as he would go.

   Reluctantly, all agreed that they could not remain pure in this important area. Besides, nobody wanted to do it and nobody was competent to do it. A retired accountant was hired part time who promptly recommended that many financial matters, including payroll and benefit deductions, be outsourced. A number of purists experienced great pain but agreed. It worked so well that subsequently purchasing and procuring were added. All were consoled that they had not given away their soul or birthright for a bowl of cabbage by reminding everyone that the basic money decisions were still being made by the finance team and the board.

3. Agreement by Exhaustion

   The school was student intensive. When staff members were not involved in direct instruction, they served as tutors, resource persons, and facilitators to students on research projects or community assignments. They also met with parents. In addition, they were all heavily involved in teams whose meetings after school seem to go on interminably. Staff members were worn out by the length of the meetings. And they were not sure that when consensus finally prevailed it was not really agreement by exhaustion rather than by enlightenment. Once again, the general dilemma was how not to throw out the baby with the bathwater. The particular predicament was how to rescue consensus and collaboration from excessive wrangling. Above all, how much of this problem was remedial? How much was bad management of meetings, agendas, and discussion? How much was the result of flawed or inept decision-making processes? Most delicate of all, how much was the result of certain participants who recurrently and compulsively seem to make everyone else's collective and team life just plain difficult if not annoying?

Two solutions emerged. One was fast and dirty, the other reflective and brooding. Quickly, expert trainers were brought in to offer team time management, conducting meetings, moving agendas along, facilitating decision trees, developing negotiating and conflict resolution skills, and so on. The effects were immediate and long lasting, and once again they were made a permanent part of the orientation process at the beginning of the year. But there was still a nagging feeling that the problem was more deep-seated than the quick fix could resolve. It had to do with the consensus process itself, or rather, with how that process can become encumbered and embattled by accommodating everyone, every time, without limit. Above all, a minority can rule especially if they were perfectionists, malcontents, letter-of-the-law types, sermonizers, interrupters, and so on. In short, how do you deal with people of principle who are capable of holding consensus hostage? Everyone refused to touch that with a ten-foot pole. But unexpectedly, humor came to the rescue.

The school routinely maintained up front two big lists. One was the Gripe List and the other was the Laugh List. Not surprisingly, both lists were originally student ideas. The lists were usually independent of each other and there was little if any crossover. The subject of a gripe seldom appeared as the object of humor. But then something unique occurred. There was not just crossover. There was simultaneous appearance. The subject of meetings appeared on both lists. Under gripes appeared such items as When does talk become baloney? Is consensus a fancy word for filibuster? Analysis, analysis; paralysis, paralysis. Who ever erected a monument to a team? New 11th Commandment: Thou Shalt Not Meet!

Under humor appeared a series of portraits: Who is Chief Big Talk? Who is his sidekick, Big Foot in the Mouth? Yes, but. Yes but. Yes but. Want short meetings? Don't provide chairs.

The issue of consensus was too much an integral part of the governance structure on the one hand and too basic an assumption of operations on the other hand to become merely the focus of another workshop. Everyone knew how serious it was because of its double appearance on both lists, and because particular individuals were being singled out for criticism. Just or unjust, such disrespect could not be allowed to continue. The decision was to fight fire with fire. Meetings were scheduled on the subject of meetings, except they took place in the form of a retreat offsite at the Moose Lodge.

Three topics were announced: Consensus: Definition and Alternatives, Completeness: When Is Enough Enough? and Constraints: What Are the Legitimate Limits of Self-Restraint? What took place could be the subject of a separate piece. But the essentials that emerged were clear and shared.

The first was that consensus was affirmed. The conclusion was that like democracy and capitalism it was the best we could have. However, a compromise was effected: the use of intermediate straw votes to see which way the wind was blowing. A second issue required group acceptance of working within the limitations of time and data. Because we never will have enough time or information, the team has to operate within parameters. If the team seems to be going too far or taking too long, anyone can stop the process by calling out "Reality Check!" That immediately requires a return to square one. Third, and finally, each team member was asked to develop an identity tag that reflected his or her role at meetings; and an assigned buddy was asked to develop one as well. The final results of the negotiation were displayed. The range went from perfectionist to yes, but we have not taken enough into account, to troublemaker, peacemaker, noncombatant, and so on. Curiously, bringing such epithets to the surface calmed everyone down, especially each individual. What emerged was the full recognition and acceptance of the diversity of the group and that everyone had a part to play. The problem occurs when we play the part too vigorously or compete with other people's parts and above all at the expense of the process of consensus and collaboration that hold us all together in the first place. Many wore their tags to all team meetings.

In summary, then, what stands out? Much. First, team management has become team governance. This is not semantics. It is a miniature of the whole. As such, it is inevitably and productively interfacing. Integration and alignment at all levels are the structural goals. It is mostly horizontal and nonhierarchical because there is no top or bottom. Continuous development and growth occur routinely because of the constantly expanding range of the competence and expertise required. Genuine community exists because of the inclusion and active participation of all staff, students, and parents and because of the commitment to create a caring community of humane values. Accountability is ensured because it is common to all. The same standards apply across the board.

Perhaps the last word should be given to an ex-principal, now member of the staff : "When I was a principal my major task was getting them to come to school. Now it is to persuade them to leave and to go home."

CREATING BUSINESS SWAT TEAMS

In the drive for increasing productivity and innovation, HR has had to develop methods, mechanisms, and managers able to reengineer operations, stir creativity, and distribute leadership. But a new and different wrinkle of late is to put together ad hoc teams of troubleshooters—employees who in a climate of uncertainty seek to identify and to minimize, not necessarily always solve, the impact of problems. Invariably, HR frequently turns to consultants for help since preeminently they are in the troubleshooting business.

Clearly, what is driving this preventive approach is increasing unpredictability. The conventional wisdom is if you keep doing what you have always done, do not be surprised if you always get what you have always gotten. But now uncertainty has upped the ante. Now if you do what you have always done, you may not even get what you have always gotten. Not only have the rules shifted; the game itself has changed.

The result is that CEOs and senior managers find themselves unnerved by all the shifting sands around them. So alongside all the familiar creative and proactive initiatives, they are asking that HR provide them with something new—trouble-avoidance insurance. And HR, generally inexperienced in this realm, is calling upon consultants to help them out. Here is a typical case in point.

The "specs" of the challenge include the following: selecting a team of troubleshooters for which no criteria have been provided, limiting the members exclusively to existing employees, providing no additional budget for financial incentives, and operating on short-term assignments that are temporary and when concluded the members return to their regular jobs.

Typically, here are the questions, thoughts, and misgivings of our consultant. Limiting the members of the team to internal talent, even the best available, may be inadequate. Selecting the most effective SWAT team will still have to be followed by training. Then, too, why would any employee volunteer? What would motivate them? There is no extra hazard pay. They are not singled out for special praise or distinction. With no fanfare they silently slip back into their regular jobs. In fact, they may have to play catch-up for the first few days on workload and e-mails. And if team cohesion and spirit were forged, which would be a lovely side benefit, that would just fade away. Clearly, the consultant has his work cut out for him in this assignment.

He decides to take the bull by the horns and wade in and find out whether there will be any takers. He meets with a number of groups, averaging twenty in each. He introduces the topic of risk avoidance and then proceeds to give a short lecture on the history of risk analysis and its methodology. Most find the topic fascinating and even familiar, claiming that is what they do under different names: total maintenance systems, quality control, ISO 9000, Baldrige criteria, Six Sigma, and the like. Sidestepping the issue whether all these really are part of risk analysis, our consultant welcomes their enthusiastic buy-in and goes to the next step. "If we were to put together an internal team of troubleshooters from our own employees, what would be their principal goals or activities?"

Small group vigorous exchange finally produced the following five basic avoidance tasks for the troubleshooting team: They help you get out of trouble, they can prevent more trouble from happening, they anticipate trouble before it becomes trouble, they keep the company and top management out of trouble, and they keep others from getting into trouble.

"OK. That is quite an impressive list. How many of you would be will-ing to try your hand at these tasks? Remember, no extra pay and if you are captured by the enemy, we don't even acknowledge that we know you." The majority raised their hands. (We learned later that those who did not were not really against it; they just were not sure at this point or were involved in key projects that they could not leave.)

"Great response. No wonder we won the war. Now here is the hard part. What qualities should we be looking in selecting members for this team?" The consultant paused because he wanted to drive home a spe-cial point. "The reason this is difficult is that in many ways it is the op-posite of those qualities the company was looking for when it initially hired you. The emphasis was on the positive not the negative. The focus was on growth not survival. There was never any question that you would be provided with the resources to do your job. But in these cases those resources may be sparse or nonexistent. In other words, you may have to turn everything on its head. You have to think outside the box. You have to think about trouble creatively and as a norm. Do you think you can do that? Let's break into groups again but with new members and see what you can come up with as the essential qualities we should be looking for in the members of a troubleshooting team."

Again by consensus, they came up with five. First, they must be fail-ure oriented. They must operate on the assumption that if something can go wrong, it will. They must be chronic worriers. Second, they also must be anticipatory. The future has to be viewed as the enemy. In ad-dition, the group cannot wait for anything to unfold. They must be time travelers who visit the future before it arrives to threaten the present. Third, they must be caretakers. They are almost parental in their capac-ity to offer protection. They all behave like secret service agents sur-rounding the president. Fourth, they must be rescuers. They always have an emergency kits and supplies. They know where all the exits are. Fifth and finally, they must be survivalists. They are basic minimalists. They use string, spit, scraps of wire. No high tech. Fast, essential, portable problem solving. Nothing fancy or dazzling. Square-one stuff. Quick and safe ways in and out. Escape to survive.

Our consultant at this point, having successfully launched the project, secured extensive volunteerism, and elicited from within the goals and qualifications of the team, shifted his role to that of trainer. He ordered copies of the various survival simulations (crashing in the Arctic, desert scenarios, boating disasters, etc.). Of course, the side benefits were in building teams and trust that is always welcome. The troubleshooting volunteers eagerly took to the exercises, although many were initially disheartened when they "died" or failed. But that demonstrated that the stakes were high. In any case, within three weeks, the consultant comfortably could name the participants of at least two troubleshooting teams.

Everything had gone as far as it could go. Simulation was one thing. But real trouble could not be manufactured. Two issues nagged at our enterprising consultant. The first is that he requested he be called in when the team was activated to evaluate the work done and the dynamics of their troubleshooting. That was quickly agreed to. And then he dropped the other shoe.

What is the chain of command? Who do they report to? Not accidentally, that generated considerable debate. The strongest position was that they report first and sometimes only to the CEO and senior management. Indeed, the troubleshooting team was to function essentially as a temporary and separate advisory arm of the executive level. In that capacity, the team was instructed never to write anything down. When instructed to do so, it is for executive eyes only.

But when the members of the team received the above marching orders, they were not happy campers. It was one thing to work undercover with no tangible rewards or recognition. It was another to be almost invisible. But what really irked the team was that in the process of troubleshooting they might come up with matters that pointed clearly to certain individuals, divisions, or systemic flaws that were at the heart of the problem. They were fearful that these would be swept under the carpet. Even more serious was the prospect that some or all of these factors, if uncorrected or unidentified might spawn other even more serious problems.

The consultant found himself on the proverbial horns of a dilemma. Top management hired and paid him. They come up with the need for a risk-avoidance or risk-reduction strategy in the first place. They gave the task of making it happen internally to HR but with no budget except for a consultant because they believed that current employees would be the best troubleshooters. They knew the company. They were preeminent problem solvers. They would rise to the occasion of saving the company and their jobs from disaster.

But the teams were not happy with the proposed arrangement and told the consultant in no uncertain terms that if this was the way things were to happen they would not volunteer. Suddenly, it looked like all the hard work of building confidence and teams was set to go down the drain. And what made it particularly difficult and frustrating is that both sides were right. Indeed, the classic dilemma requiring the wisdom of Solomon is trying to resolve not a conflict between right and wrong but a conflict between equal rights.

The solution came from the employees themselves, not the executive side. Employing their troubleshooting skills, they recommended that each troubleshooting team have a member of the senior staff as an equally participating member, not a leader. When and if the trouble was resolved, and the reasons for it known, then the team would negotiate with the member of the senior staff as to the next steps of the communication and implementation process. If the causative factors involved individual mangers or employees, that would be left in the hands of senior staff to handle openly or confidentially. But if the fault finding was found to be structural or systemic, that was to be communicated along with any proposed remedies by the troubleshooting team to the entire organization. Both sides accepted the compromise. All admiring eyes turned to the consultant who wisely just beamed and said nothing.

POSTSCRIPT

Our consultant was invited back three times within the next year to evaluate the performance of the troubleshooting teams and the effectiveness of the compromise. The first was an unqualified success, the second problematical.

Sometimes, the findings were like a hot potato that no one wanted to handle. Or the problem disappeared by being turned over from one department to another so that it disappeared under many rugs. Occasionally, it was farmed out and subjected to other kinds of analysis by other specialists: attorneys, risk managers, communication specialists, and the like. But in general, the suggested compromise did hold.

Although one senior staff member served as a part of the team, negotiation with that individual was often so intense and adversarial that the senior executive did not volunteer again or soon. But the teams made final peace with not having them at all. They accepted that when matters fall between the cracks, they would soon be called back again to confront a variation of the problem.

Our consultant stepped back to view the entire experience and to reflect on its value. His overall conclusion in spite of the difficulties and imperfections was affirmative. Whatever the problems of follow-up, the need to create special forces and intelligence-gathering teams, sometimes clandestine, as support units was demonstrably clear. But adjustments in mind-sets and strategies had to be made. The principal one was that troubleshooting teams were temporary in three senses.

First, the special units are called into action only as needed and for short durations. Second, all the members have regular jobs to which they return when the task is completed. Third, the subject of the inquiry varies to such an extent that it may never be repeated again.

Competition and risk may be driving corporations to internally tap their own people rather than traditionally turn to consultants. The obvious challenge is that consultants have to change their role and help employees become consultants. Above all, they have to become advocates of such internal resourcefulness and embrace the need for employees to save their own company and jobs. In other words, to survive and to flourish, both a visible and an invisible strategy may have to coexist. Productivity may be the public slogan, but the private version is failure avoidance.

A troubleshooting team may have to serve as an advanced early warning system of senior management. If the organization turns right, the team may have to go left. They are officially charged with deviant thinking: ambiguity and even alternatives. In the past, troubleshooting teams were consultants. Now they are internal consultants often trained for a hefty fee by outside consultants to be autonomous and available.

At any given moment they can be quickly assembled to put out fires and restore equanimity. Although the expertise of the original consultant thus has to be transferred, the blend of the two still provides the best of both worlds. In the final analysis, the ultimate model of the artful and resourceful dodger still remains the collaborative troubleshooter.

8

CHALLENGING THE SACRED ORDER: ROCKING THE BOAT AND UPSETTING THE STATUS QUO

Conventional wisdom warns: Don't rock the boat, call attention to yourself, volunteer or above all, suggest changes. The rationale is that if one is obedient, invisible, or harmless, one will be rewarded over time, probably even be protected and promoted, and escape downsizing. But promotion does not guarantee retention, and downsizing is basically statistical, not individual.

The different advice offered here, therefore, is not for the faint of heart, for those who always play it safe, or for those who worship political correctness. Rather, it is recommended for those willing to take some calculated risks, who have a mind of their own, and are intelligent and sometimes creative enough to discover and point out better ways of doing things—in short, for about one-third of the typical workforce. But lest any conclude that this is the siren call of a Pied Piper urging those to jump off a cliff, some safety nets are provided.

Two issues need to be conjoined at the outset. The first is determining the qualifications of those who undertake quixotic adventure. The second is to describe in detail the process of rocking the boat. Each feeds into and illustrates the other. Five qualifications and five rethinking or unlearning exercises have been linked together.

First, as an introduction, see table 8.1 for a short qualifying quiz for identifying rockers.

Second, there are at least five ways of rocking the boat: embracing paradox, using the third degree, revealing that the emperor has no clothes, insisting on going back to square one, and invoking the cause of the bleeding heart.

1. Embracing Paradox

Rocking the boat requires a nimble, thoughtful, and often mischievous mind. The world is perceived through the other end of the telescope or at a tilt. A certain perversity tips the scales so that the answer is both unexpected and profoundly complicated. Matters become interesting and unsettled. Unfortunately, successful rocking of the boat often is greeted with annoyance and impatience.

The orderly and ongoing nature of business is forced to pause or deflect from its designated path. Things are stalled, while everyone tries to figure out whether this odd way of thinking means that business as usual cannot continue to operate. Sometimes, there is in fact great anger at this trouble-making intrusion and intruder. A determination to persist even at the expense of truth surfaces and bulldozes the troublesome obstacle out of the way. Indeed, if no one speaks up, the opportunity for greater understanding and development is lost, and the one who cried wolf is treated as a troublemaker and an outcast.

That unfortunately is a regular occurrence in many organizations. Whether or not the one so pilloried enjoys or resents his or her martyrdom, the truth is that in order for the act of paradox to benefit both the rocker and the boat, there must be other rockers. In short, the process must take place in a company-supported en-

Table 8.1. Quiz for Identifying the Boat Rockers

Questions	Safe Answers	Rocking the Boat Responses
1. Things are either right or wrong	Yes	Yes, No, and Maybe
2. Technology is good or bad	True	Both, but it is also never neutral
3. Teams are always smarter	Generally so	But often tyrannical and myopic
4. Information sharing is good	Of course	But who owns the data?
5. The customer is always right	Absolutely	No, but that is the challenge

vironment so that there is some chance of creating a substantial minority and loyal opposition. Learning organizations require not only many predictable, incremental learners, but also deviant and discontinuous unlearners. A loner who is not joined by a few other solitaries does not stand a chance of change, and everybody loses the edge.

2. The Third Degree

The second kind of eligibility and intervention is sometimes attention getting and even sensational. It is not unlike the performer who stops the show to thunderous applause. Curiously, it may happen with a little question that disturbs the universe. Thus, one of the best ways of rocking the boat is to encourage the art of inquiry. Many are familiar with the powerful Japanese ritual of asking why at least five times in order to get at the root cause. This second exercise builds upon the power of constant inquiry and Platonic "noodgery" and echoes the wisdom of Louis B. Mayer's classic remark, "For your information, let me ask you a question."

The basic kind of inquiry is epistemological—how do we come to know what we know? Such introspection has been invested with greater sophistication and precision with the advent of extensive brain research. It even has helped by extending the question of what we know to what we don't know. All of this can become somewhat convoluted and even paralyzing but its value is that it creates sufficient uncertainty to stop matters in their track, which is as good a definition of rocking the boat as one can find.

A less philosophical but no less important set of questions has to do with what the current research shows. Why always reinvent the wheel? This is not a favorite subject in business because the prejudice is that the practitioner has it all over the researcher, and further that case study is superior to survey. Besides, one's learning days are over. That is all behind the holders of the MBA. But even the *Harvard Business Review* has adopted a new, more popular format and style so that it more resembles *Fortune* and *Forbes* and makes research more available. Then, too, the pursuit of a doctoral degree in business, which used to be exclusively a European tradition, has increasingly attracted many contemporary managers, especially through distance education or weekend programs. The

PhD is a research degree and what is being called for here is to be involved in original company research. Indeed, many companies have expanded their tuition remission programs to include doctoral study so that they secure the benefit of a trained researcher and a dissertation that researched practices in their own company.

Another different set of questions centers on where things are going, what directions the company is taking, where the market is, where the customers are, where the competition is heading. It is also here where the scenarios challenging the status quo have to surface, where all the assumptions of continuance have to be raised to the surface and questioned, and where nothing is sacred or out of bounds. Once again the one rocking this boat may meet with impatience and resistance. William Blake defined friendship as opposition.

Finally, adopting the questioning and thinking of ecology there is a need for a rigorous examination of the second, third, and fourth order of impacts of products, services, and decisions that, like the proverbial rock thrown into a pool, send out ever-widening circles. It resembles the classic case of the tragedy of the commons. Each neighbor innocently added one additional sheep to the grazing. The cumulative effect of overpopulation resulted in the end of the commons. In other words, questions regularly have been asked about what lies ahead, especially about the life expectancy of current success.

3. The Emperor Has No Clothes

A third approach to rocking the boat considers the mystery of the herd instinct applied to intelligence. Why do so many Broadway plays fail? Why are so many jerky movies made and lose money? Why are so many short-lived products or questionable services ever offered? The answer is the emperor has no clothes and nobody tells him, or anyone else for that matter. There is often an incredible lack of truth telling in business. Worse, when it is offered and not heeded, one understands why the truth is not told in the first place. What supervisors regularly seek and encourage is the heavenly choir, the sex exhalation of yes. Observe the face and body language of a typical supervisor when one of his favorite projects is challenged, or when she is the martyred enforcer of a new and unpopular policy or procedure and encounters criticism.

The failure of not exposing an emperor without clothes is that it feeds into the obscuration of unarticulated and unacknowledged assumptions that drive decisions and strategies to their doom. If the Platonic notion that the unexamined life is not worth living is worth heeding, then what shall be said about the unexamined assumptions of an organization's existence? Rocking the boat in these instances is really saving the boat. Consider the fallout of morale when a company blunders its way into the future by acting on reassuring but unquestioned stereotypical scenarios and regularly fails. Who wants to work for a dumb company? Or worse, who wants to work for a company that has successfully intimidated and persuaded its employees to play dumb?

4. Square-One Methodology

A fourth way of rocking the boat is the square-one approach. It raises multiple issues: What is our core business? How did we start? What was our original vision and mission? What did we originally think our future was? The value of questioning and returning to first principles is that it backs a company up to the source of its momentum and what drives it forward. Square one argues for a time out—a pause in ongoingness to deliberate about origins and ends. It is essentially both an introspective and anticipatory process. As such, it generates Janerian benchmarks. Rocking the boat aligns retrospect and prospect and makes them seamlessly one.

When encouraged in organizations, this Janerian nexus accommodates and creates a recurrent focus on reframing, repositioning, reengineering, reconstructing, and above all refocusing. Information sharing becomes who owns the data. Team leadership is not an oxymoron if the leader is designated as primus inter pares—first among equals—and the position is rotational. The learning organization becomes also an unlearning organization. Leadership is no longer a monopoly at the top but distributed throughout the company. In short, all kinds of paradoxical reconfigurations are possible by returning to a double source—the past and the future—and in the process making them one.

5. The Bleeding Heart

Finally, there is the cause of what some negatively call the bleeding heart: the entreaty that the company adhere to ethical and humane standards, that in effect it go beyond what is required by law and regulation to behave as the model of a good corporate citizen. Research tells us that companies that establish a caring and even spiritual environment experience higher levels of retention and productivity; and companies that consciously value the environment enjoy higher than average levels of profitability. Why? Because it goes beyond what is required to what is needed, because it exceeds profit as a sole determiner and instead is committed to an ennobling end. Employees and customers respect that. Indeed, that creates immediately a bond between them.

In summary, then, when employees rock the boat by asking their companies not only to be smart, but also humane they should be heeded. And when they are, as in all the aforementioned examples, watch for the emergence of a more assertive, innovative, and challenging truth squad and problem-solving professionals. Rockers of the boat will reveal not only that the emperor has no clothes, but also what he needs to wear in the future. As you sow, so shall you reap. The way the problem is posed sets up the innovative solution.

Going against the grain creates finally a unique company or at least one that is set far apart from all the others with their assumptions buried in the sand. And best of all it does not require massive exhortation or training. Just suggest to managers a different way of managing. Encourage paradox, loyal opposition, and minority positions: Invoke the rule of the devil's advocate. Instead of giving orders or promulgating official policy, pursue inquiry. Pay more attention to the questions than the answers.

And when solutions come forth, treat them as problems—subject them to the same five questions directed at finding the root cause. Establish the company's double source—its Janerian identity in the past and the future. Return always to Square One but create a Square Alpha as well to stretch the present. Finally—and this may be the most difficult— lure managers away from that hard-nosed, heartless, and often cynical behaviors that they have wrongly been persuaded to take in order to be successful and efficient. An incompetent individual can still be fired without being treated inhumanely. Caring companies generally succeed. When they also encourage rocking the boat and challenging the status quo, then they will have demonstrated that, as e. e. cummings noted, "tomorrow is our permanent address."

⑨

NEW ASSESSMENTS: 360-DEGREE HOLISTICS, BALANCED SCORE CARD, AND BARRETT'S SPIRITUAL AUDIT

As the focus on productivity increases and as downsizing scatters balance, there is a need to develop and apply more rigorous and comprehensive forms of measurement. Many emerged but three in particular were significant: 360 degree, balanced score card, and spiritual audit.

360-DEGREE HOLISTICS

The use of 360-degree holistics, also called all-around, multisource, multirater assessment, is increasing. According to the survey of the *BNN Bulletin* (1997), 29 percent of employers are already using it and another 11 percent had plans to implement it. In addition, Nowack (1993) has found that it is also increasingly being used to identify training needs. Although Romano (1993) has examined the general fear of feedback that 360-degree assessment does not totally eliminate, it is nevertheless viewed with more confidence by employees than the traditional singular appraisal. Budman (1994) provides the most comprehensive review of the problems associated with the process, especially the time delays caused by its complexity. But he also notes steady improvement especially in the capacity of computers to handle the number of variables and to speedily process data. Since Budman's piece appeared, a number of firms who specialize in 360-degree assessments for a fee have come into being. In effect, companies, especially those that have reduced their HR staff, outsource the task to professionals who can accomplish it faster and at lower cost. Finally, the most extensive and longest use of the methodology has been by the military—the so-called TAPES program (Total Army Performance Evaluation System).

To appreciate the difference of 360-degree from conventional assessment, the chart in figure 9.1 may be helpful. The downside of the 360-degree system is obvious. It is more complicated and slower. It requires more sophistication to review the comprehensive data and to assign the appropriate weights. It is often resisted and even resented by supervisors because their centrality is reduced and because it generally takes more time to do. But all in all, it has been favored by employees and by HR professionals in general. It thus would appear that the figure 9.1 provides a sufficient number of reasons to adopt this new system of evaluation.

BALANCED SCORE CARD (BSC)

There are at least five benefits of employing the balanced score card.

1. Clarity

    Like an x-ray, BSC cuts through the surface to essentials and offers transparency of internal operations, trade-offs, habitual behaviors, deal making, and so on. Every process becomes highly visible and open to inspection, review, and reformulation.

2. Simplicity

    BSC serves as a single summary of four main complex operations. Aggregated into one main frame, it is also portable and can be carried by managers from one operation to another.

3. Consensus

    BSC compels shared understanding of vision and mission but also identifies, sometimes for the first time, areas of disagreement, divergence, and difference of point of view and philosophy, especially because of unarticulated assumptions.

Traditional System vs. 360-Degree System

1. Single rater vs. Multiple raters
2. Singular focus vs. Perspectival
3. Subjective vs. Objective
4. Imposed vs. Negotiated
5. Isolated focus vs. Alignment
6. Hand tally vs. Computerized
7. Secretive vs. Shared
8. Limited to evaluation vs. Recruitment and training
9. Past and present focus vs. Future career pathing
10. Many complaints vs. Fewer objections, Greater acceptance

Figure 9.1.   Assessment Characteristics and Foci

As well, it compels commonality of definitions. For example, twenty-five executives agreed that superior service and targeted customers were excellent objectives. But when pressed by the score card to define what they meant by each objective, there were twenty-five different definitions.

4. Measurement and Management

BSC forces an alliance between the management of measurement and the measurement of management. All managers have to develop their own divisional and appropriate list of critical indicators of performance, not provided unilaterally from on high.

In the process, managers operationalize and translate the vision and mission into divisional processes, now subject to appropriate measurements. At the same time, managers can use the same approach to test the goals and projections of the strategic business plan.

5. Multiple Linkages

BSC always employs multiple perspectives (customers, financial, etc.), multiple measures, and multiple managerial approaches, and generates multiple alignments of vision and mission, senior- and middle-level managers, managers and employees, and the present and the future.

The rationale for using BSC as the primary mode of assessment involves the following reasons.

1. Big Picture

   BSC replicates the total business in miniature. At a single glance, all the essential parts can be framed and summarized. That is, it provides the focal point for discussion and definition of integration. It also accommodates new initiatives but prevents them from being favored or becoming pet lone ranger projects by insisting from the outset that they fit in and support the big picture with everything else.

2. Multiple Measures

   No single measure can sum up the whole. Multiple measures constitute a check-and-balance system. Multiple measures compel interaction, integration, and consensus.

3. Harmonizer

   BSC brings together under one roof all that is going on: customer focus, shortening response time, improving quality, reducing launch time, cutting costs, teamwork, and so on. It corrals all initiatives in a one-stop-shopping mode to determine to what degree they reinforce or oppose each other. It compels recognition of and interaction between disparate parts of the business, many of which do not ordinarily dialogue with each other.

   Harmony positioning requires short-term goals to be supportive, stepping-stones to long-term strategies; and vice versa—forcing long-term strategies to check and if necessary correct the positioning of short-term steps to reach the long term.

4. Reallocation Decisions

   Putting everything together in one big picture, single frame does not obscure separate still shots of individual divisions and individuals. If financial measures only are used to add up results, then often divisions that are doing well are lumped with divisions that are not. The result is an averaging process that is distortive or lopsided. But if each division is evaluated as an independent profit center, then performance and market share determine allocation of resources. Above all, BSC alerts senior- and middle-level management to suboptimization by any one unit at the expense of another.

5. Alignments/Linkages

The compilation of BSC cannot be accomplished by any one person or group. It is a collective effort. In the process it aligns managers with each other: It thus helps to foster a culture of consensus and commonality of vision and goals.

6. Strategy Driven

BSC puts strategy, not control in the driver's seat. The problem with using exclusive financial measures is that such measures are primarily limiting and controlling. For the short term, that is acceptable but control is not possible in the long term. Control also tends to pit divisions and teams against each other in unbridled competition for resources and recognition, and thus inhibits or deflects away from the creation of a consensual and cooperative environment.

7. Fusion of Management and Measurement

BSC is both a measurement and a management system. In fact, it manages through measurement. The process is both gradual and localized. The goals and measurements to achieve those goals are developed in tandem.

8. Future Driven

Unlike the focus of financial measures, BSC, especially because of the separate emphasis on innovation and creativity, is involved in future considerations. In fact, BSC is in many ways a strategic business plan, except that it is more dynamic—a performance business plan.

9. Questioning Culture

BSC inculcates a questioning form of inquiry. In addition, the questions stem from the perceptions of others so that managers are forced to think in terms of company performance and image rather than in personal achievement. Four questions address four areas: customer, income, strategy, and innovation.

10. Adaptability

BSC is a form, not prescribed content. It can be adjusted to virtually every organization and sector. Indeed, it would be more accurate to claim that there are as many different BSCs as there are companies.

BARRETT'S VALUES AUDIT

This unusual assessment is based on Richard Barrett's book *Liberating Your Soul and Your Company's Soul* (Fulfilling Books, 1995). Its focus is on unearthing gaps, especially between employees and their companies and among employees. It is Barrett's contention that these are essentially little-recognized values gaps and when identified, they can lead to closer alignment between employees and their organizations and to improve working relationships between coworkers.

The key to undertaking such assessments is developing a taxonomy of value descriptors that is sufficiently universal to be applied to most if not all organizations and employees. Barrett turned to Maslow because of his general familiarity and acceptance on the one hand, and his emphasis on different levels and an aspirational and progressive hierarchy on the other hand. In the process, Barrett expanded Maslow's five levels to seven, as noted in the following list:

Barrett's Values Version of Maslow

Values Levels
7. Service Ethics/Vision
6. Making a Difference Stewardship/Employee Fulfillment
5. Meaning Commonweal/Generosity
4. Transformation Empowerment/Learning
3. Self-esteem Pride/Quality
2. Relationship Respect/Communication
1. Survival Safety/Self-Discipline

One of the unexpected benefits of applying the Barrett–Maslow taxonomy is that in order to determine, for example, any values discrepancy between employees and their companies, the values of the company have to be defined. In most cases, that had not been done. The typical response was to offer up the mission statement as the equivalent. But although later some companies mined their mission statements for buried values, companies, especially senior-level executives, had to engage, often for the first time, in extensive soul searching. The net result was a clarification and articulation of their foundational values. That led in many cases to a revision of their mission statement.

Two other applications are worth noting. In the first application, strategic plans were reviewed to determine to what extent they embodied company values. Because often there were gaps, many companies required that not one but a number of plans be developed, each one articulating the values driving its design. That way, the search for optimum coincidence could occur. The version finally selected exhibited the highest congruence. The second application focused on

---

1. Work Relationship Audit. Identify two fellow employees with whom you regularly work, one whom you like and get along with, the other whom you don't.

    A. Like
    B. Don't

2. Briefly describe your work relationship with each, especially in terms of what you like and don't like respectively. Give a few specific examples or samples of conversation.

    A. What makes it easy and pleasant?
    B. What makes it hard and unpleasant?

3. Project what you believe are the operating values of each.

    A. Likable values
    B. Unlikable values

4. What, if anything, does your preference for one and not for the other tell you about yourself and your own values?

    A. My likable values

5. Review your own behavior and conversations with the individual you don't like. Suppose your own success and capacity for change was contingent on your greater ability to get along with people you don't like or whose values you do not share.
    What would you do to bring about a change in the work relations with the one you do not like according to the following levels of escalation?

    A. Gradual (trial balloons)
    B. Indirect suggestions/comments/gestures
    C. Direct exchanges
    D. After-work activities

6. Finally, speculate on what would be the work outcomes of your change in relationships. For yourself personally? For your division? For the company?

Figure 9.2.   Sample Values Audit

changing and improving work relations through a values audit (see figure 9.2).

In summary then, current assessment tools are not passive but invasive. As such, they not only measure change, but also serve as change agents in their own right. Although they represent cutting-edge efforts developed to best match changing workplace conditions now, other techniques are being developed to meet emerging and future challenges.

REFERENCES

Budman, S. H. *Treating Time Effectively*. New York: Guilford, 1994.

10

NEW EMPLOYEE PROFILES: JOB SATISFACTION AS THE COMPETITIVE EDGE AND EMPLOYEE MISSION STATEMENTS

What are the three most pressing problems facing human resources directors today and in the future? Hiring good people, keeping them, and optimizing and aligning their performance. But that is nothing new. That has been the traditional and familiar goal of HR. True, but the rules have changed; and even more important, so has the game itself.

1. The Pool of Candidates

    The selection process involves an increasingly limited and competitive pool. The increase in the number and intensity of recruiters and headhunters is a sure indication of the shortage and expectations of professionals.

2. The Issue of Company Loyalty

    Organizations have convincingly demonstrated through downsizing, mergers, and acquisitions that company loyalty is no longer a way of ensuring job security or retention. Applicants are rightly wary and focused on numero uno.

3. Job Satisfaction

    Many businesses have inadvertently contributed to less-than-stellar employee performance by focusing almost exclusively on definitions of job satisfaction, which are primarily self-centered.

It thus may be time to go back to square one and think anew and through the whole issue of job satisfaction. Indeed, current and future pressures compel a total reexamination of all the assumptions of contemporary employment. Here is a short list of some of the current operating assumptions of employees.

Money is not an initial or final arbiter of selection or retention. (Actually, it never was; besides, the economics of supply and demand takes care of the basics anyhow.) Every new employee is a temp. Primary loyalty is to self. Retention is more important and difficult than selection. The match is more important and chancier than ever before. Prospective employees are researchers. They may know more about the company than those who interview them. They may even expect to meet and talk with the CEO. Culture match or mismatch: The chemistry has to work both ways.

Performance appraisal systems are given greater weight. The clumsy, old-fashioned, buddy-buddy system will drive people out faster than any single factor. It is amazing how many progressive organizations have changed everything except the way they evaluate employees, and in the process failed to see that system as a major motivator or disincentive. The new employee sees himself or herself as a miniature of the whole, not some incidental cog as part of a huge machine. The new employee values his or her centrality and hopes that his or her bosses will similarly understand the significance of his or her contribution. If they don't, then they may be getting less than the employee can give; and he or she may go somewhere else where his or her contribution will be more appreciated and valued. New employees are impressed by company challenges, especially those involving interpersonal expectations.

The problem with working with and for organizations who are not open to rethinking the complex and multiple processes of hiring, retaining, and evaluating is that even when they are willing to go forward, there is no or little focus. They are either all over the place trying desperately to hold together a number of different evaluation fragments put together over the years or obsessively fixated on one part of the whole.

In addition, everyone involved believes he or she has the key to the puzzle. That usually takes the form of identifying the one big factor that determines everything. Moreover, if one can just take care of that—offering big salaries, bonuses, gain-sharing, stock options, and so on—everything else will fall into place. But that is deflective.

The key is to be inclusive and integrative—to find the missing links that hold the entire new chain together. The recommendation is to revisit and perhaps reconceive what satisfies employees. A good place to start is with current expectations.

Most evaluations of job satisfaction are self-evaluations. Employees are asked to what extent they are generally satisfied with their job. That is often then followed with a series of subheads from which to choose: salary, benefits, work environment, vacations, promotional possibilities, and the like. The aggregate generates a score of job satisfaction that is essentially less job focused and more self-focused.

Moreover, a number of critical questions are not asked: Are you happy or content? Do you see yourself being here next year? Are you pleased with your boss? Do you feel significantly involved in decisions that may affect the future of your job? The future of the company? Do you believe the business is well run? Proactive? Innovative? How would you rank its standing in the industry? What would you change?

Many would argue that these are not appropriate questions to ask employees. Others would maintain that they do not relate to job satisfaction.

Such disclaimers may be just the problem. They are important questions. They are empowered questions. And if they are not asked at all or ever and if they are not made part of job satisfaction, then what is lost is the focus on the basic balanced partnership between the company and its employees.

You can't get unless you give. Employees are always hungry for the big picture. They see themselves as intelligent and knowledgeable enough to judge whether the CEO has made the right decision or not. They also want spelled out the implications of that decision in terms of their job and their job future. If they are valued in their field and have been approached by headhunters, they usually have an excellent sense of what is going on in the industry. In fact, knowledge about the cutting edge has become one of the increasing responsibilities of recruiters and is a key part of the Q&A of the conversation. In short, job satisfaction has to include two-way work communication. Being ignored or bypassed will not sit well with any employee who has a sense of his or her value and what he or she can contribute to the company.

If such responsiveness is provided to employees, what does the company have a right to expect in return? There are two additional yields to the definition of job satisfaction, each one larger than the one before and both significantly more comprehensive than the traditional self-centered focus.

No one is an island unto himself or herself. Even the Lone Ranger had Tonto. Individual workers have to be defined not only in terms of themselves but also in terms of interacting with others. In addition, workers should recognize as part of their job responsibility the extent to which they contribute to the job satisfaction of others. The old political guide of the supervisor—"It is your job to make me look good"—is not without considerable truth.

Two additional developments have intensified the need to develop an expanded definition of job satisfaction. One is teaming, the other is intra- and interdivisional evaluations of productivity.

The team approach has mandated not only the acknowledgment but also the negotiation of group satisfaction. Many teams also rotate who heads up the team. Indeed, that arrangement compels employees to take their turn at satisfying and unifying the group. Studies of productivity have shown that the greatest gains are secured not so much from increasing individual output as group productivity, especially among and between groups or divisions. In short, employees need to be increasingly aware and asked to factor in the degree to which they provide satisfaction to those they work with, not just what they in turn receive from others. Such stretch will be welcomed by employees who may regard such shared satisfaction as a collective form of job security as well.

But even more can be expected. The payback for an organization that constantly communicates the big picture and its future is alignment. The horizontal extension of the individual into the group can also be intersected by the vertical extension of the individual into the company vision, mission, and strategic objectives. Thus, job satisfaction is always double. It measures the degree to which the individual finds his or her work aligned with achieving companywide objectives and with his or her fellow workers in his or her division.

Increasingly, companies are willing to go far to find and implement other ways to create the basis of alignment. For example, customer satisfaction is often made an absolute priority. But a number of professionals who are critical to the successful achievement of that objective never routinely engage or are even proximate to customers. Instead of lamenting the difficulty of closing that gap, the company can be resourceful and make customer satisfaction part of the give-and-take of job satisfaction.

With that blend as the driving factor, many ways can be found. For example, on a rotating basis, invite employees to the president's annual meeting with distributors. Similarly, when customers or vendors come to the office or plant, arrange time to meet them. Provide e-mail addresses of some customers so that communication can take place and relationships can be established. Invite employees to meetings of sales and marketing to listen to how they talk about customers. Develop a customer profile database that among others things spells out internally how what the company does directly or indirectly impacts on that customer.

In other words, if a company really wants alignment, it has to work at it. The employer has to put aside empty slogans and aspirational pictures on training walls and above all provide a cheer leading call for everyone to get behind the push toward customer service. It requires special effort and intelligence. The company has to put itself out in order to have employees put themselves out; and it has to do that by always asking for more and raising the bar of performance expectations.

In summary, then, the challenge is clear: Job satisfaction should be properly expanded to include supporting satisfaction for others; extended to involve aligning individual contributions to meeting company objectives; and finally made to empower employees to assume leadership, innovative, and futuristic roles. Job satisfaction becomes job security for the individual and provides a competitive edge for the business.

EMPLOYEE MISSION STATEMENTS

Who usually decides on training topics? Top management often, occasionally HR. Who assigns priorities? Ditto. Occasionally, employees may be asked, but if so, it is usually from a predetermined list. And with that input in hand, or without it, decisions are made and the company frequently then claims it is a learning organization. Or it links together a number of training offerings and occasionally some e-mail linkages and describes itself as a corporate university.

In most organizations the selection of training topics is determined by one of three factors or a combination thereof:

1. Inefficiency or Ineffectiveness
    Something needs to be fixed. For example, the way employees are evaluated or judged as to who receives incentive bonuses has serious flaws. A better performance-appraisal system is required and needs to be installed and explained.
2. Ignorance and/or Updating
    Incremental needs require catch-up, mostly technological. Highly technical updates dominate the offerings of most corporate universities and e-businesses.
3. Big-Picture Correction or Amplification
    Paradigm shifts occur that require revising training: reengineering the corporation, balanced score card, teaming, learning organization, and so on.

When all three factors are operative, the list is at least representative and respectable. But it is far from ideal for a number of reasons. It is essentially external and depersonalized. It may tinker with what is needed, but it does not touch who the employees are or better still what they can become. In addition, because the selection process is not broad based enough to generate comprehensive input, the final results, although beneficial may when applied be partial, fragmented, or ill-fitting.

When training becomes scattered or piecemeal, it lacks coherence. It also may not be ambitious or profound enough in its reach or depth. It does not rest on the fundamental bedrock of self-directed and focused learning and unlearning. It may fail to define in visionary and specific terms what a knowledge worker really is and knows. Finally, it falls short of profiling a model of the employee as a contributing and developing lifelong partner of the business.

Creating an employee-centered organization is based on employee self-definition. Each member of each division has to craft an employee mission statement. In fact, he or she needs to write two pairs: One pair should summarize who the company is now and who it wants to be; the other pair should describe what the member's division is and what it seeks to be.

These overarching statements can be aggregated both horizontally and vertically to generate both divisional and company performance goals. They also collectively shape the future training agenda: What instruction will be required to reach those future performance goals, who shall offer it, and what preferable forms might it take? Above all, employee mission statements can become either supplements to job descriptions or, better still, a more dynamic, authentic, and owned replacement.

What are the building blocks of an employee mission statement (EMS)? The standard mission statement is organizational. It speaks to the business of the company and its values. Employees are seldom mentioned. They are assumed. If they are explicitly identified, they are given an aggregated identity as teams or the workforce. But empowerment has raced far ahead of such traditional and impoverishing descriptions. In many cases, it has fundamentally altered organizational structures, cultures, and charts. It has intensified the importance of interpersonal and teaming relationships.

Capital is now defined as human capital as well. Above all, it has required CEOs to be leaders of workers, not just organizations because without their focused efforts, the five major goals of productivity, profitability, quality, customer service, and innovation can never be accomplished. Thus, the notion of an employee mission statement comes as a natural new outcome of an evolutionary process. It is an equity step.

One way to help the process along is to identify the major areas or essentials that minimally an EMS should address. The temptation is to use managerial categories that in fact dominate most traditional mission statements of organizations. But the need is to personalize the process, to align it as much as possible with everyday conversation, to have it express the genuine voice of employees, and to get it to flow so as to reach down and articulate true feelings and even deep doubts. The last is important because two paired mission statements are to be written. The first addresses the present, the second the future. Although a number of topics can be chosen as guidelines for discussion, the following five minimally have been found to be engaging: attitudes, expectations, learning, relationships, and standards.

The discussion of each of these can be aided and preceded by a brief questionnaire of multiple-choice answers. The choices in turn can be structured so that the last one is always an "ideal" one and thus sets up the key descriptors for the second or future-oriented EMS. Here then are some examples in each category.

1. Attitudes—Toward Work

Four choices generally cover the field: Generally OK, Sometimes Strong, Committed, and Passionate.

Typically, the first two items are chosen. Discussion between members then usually is centered on definitions. What do we mean by committed? By passionate? One or two who have selected either may gingerly begin to describe their choice. They may be greeted by sarcasm: "You expect me to be passionate about filling out forms, patiently listening to some stupid customer's complaints, sitting through all those dumb meetings we have to attend, and so on." Quickly, the rubber hits the road and reality rears its truthful head.

After venting, the new question becomes, "What will it take to change our attitude to being at least committed if not passionate?" The quick consensus response is "A lot." A list then is prepared to serve as the conditions for a change in attitude. But the change is noted in the future version of the EMS as the stretch goal and the conditional list is sent upstairs. In short, the future is negotiated.

And so is everything else in each category, including the relationships between categories. Inevitably, trade-offs are required for change. But the process has just started. Other areas of change have to be similarly explored. The final results then are related to each other. The interaction may result in revisions. Thus, each EMS is a draft.

The process is not linear but circular, cumulative rather than sequential. The final point is revisiting all the stages and asking, "What kind of training do we need, who will be the instructors, and so on to help us reach our future stretch goals?"

2. Expectations—Of Performance

The basic discussion here is open-ended. It addresses three basic issues: What are our performance goals? Who sets them? How often do we meet or exceed them?

The value of the initial discussion is to get everybody on board the same train. It is often surprising how many are not. The second issue may result in some spirited exchanges. But here too the gap is between extremes: one advocating no leash at all, the others some leash hopefully long. Again compromise comes to the rescue: a medium-size leash. Next is to arrive at some common ground: "At least let us have collaborative determination of performance goals."

The future EMS statement puts the two pieces together and attests to the following: "All mutually defined performance goals will be minimally met and at least half exceeded." Before leaving this topic, one member of the group notes that it will take a committed, passionate attitude to exceed goals. Everyone nods in agreement at the emergence of the first linkage.

3. Learning—Knowing Not Just the Job but Also the Business

This issue regularly generates complaints and surfacing of some past baggage. But such venting should be encouraged because it clears the air and the field and thus prepares for a discussion that turns directly on the employees themselves as knowledge workers. "How smart are we? How important is it that we be smart? Work smarter not harder? Sharpen the saw? How often are we self-analytical about our job? How do we it? Is there another and better way to do it? Do we routinely pursue root cause? Or opt for the easy way of the fast and the dirty? Of blame and shame? Do we ask 'why' five times when something goes wrong? Do we ever do research or ask for it? Are any of us students of the business? Do we want finally to get rid of the culture of blame and shame?"

Unlike the first two sessions, which by comparison were always vigorous, easy, and fluid, this one stops many employees in their tracks. They become increasingly reflective and introspective. They are a bit shocked to find how mechanical, unthinking, and unquestioning they have been about their work. Many acknowledge, often for the first time that they have operated with a number of unarticulated assumptions that need to be examined. Curiously, all find it relatively easy to quickly agree that the future statement should focus on the model of knowing not just the job but the total business.

Finally, they perceive that being a student of the total business is incrementally beyond being a knowledge worker, and that an employee university is superior to a learning organization. In fact, they designate both knowledge worker and learning organization as belonging to the present, and student of the business and employee university to the future.

4. Relationships—Aligning Linkages

The focus here is on work relationships and job satisfaction. The goal is to determine the strengths and weaknesses of interpersonal relations, how that affects, positively and negatively, performance. If teams are already operative, the assessment is both individual and group. If not, then the exercise serves the diagnostic function of indicating what strengths can be tapped and what areas need improvement if teams are in the future. Above all, because again the stress is on present benchmarks and future growth, unhappy current work relationships that may jeopardize performance can be changed with some helpful coaching. Indeed, that becomes a future EMS statement. But perhaps the most dramatic change in this arena has to do with present and future definitions of job satisfaction that have just been examined and now need to be folded into the EMS.

5. Standards—The Practice of Quality

Quality embraces all. It is what holds everything together. It is both quantitative and qualitative. It can be measured in terms of zero defects, minimum spoilage, total customer retention, and the like. It has its data.

But it also constitutes the culture of the enterprise. It is how we do things around here, and above all what we do not do. It is about integrity of relationships so that every employee is treated like a customer. In short, every goal, action, relationship, outcome, and so on will carry the overlay of quality. And where there are current limitations, the future EMS will project quality goals to be achieved.

Those may include the end to bossism, to blame and shame, to manipulation, to coercion, insecurity, and so on. And in their place will appear a commitment to persuasion and consensuality. Not pie in the sky but all reachable because what is aspired to is trainable. Indeed, one of the final comments in this session is that one cannot be a student of the business without being a student of quality.

It might be helpful at this point to offer a draft of the two composite versions of an employee mission statement.

1. Current

    We are a dedicated workforce with high expectations of ourselves and our products and services. We are committed to constantly improving what and how we do our job. We also value learning about and creating best practices and insisting on quality operations throughout the organization.

2. Future

    We aspire to be a cohesive and passionate workforce committed to the highest quality standards of customer satisfaction. We seek to become students of the business so that we can meet and even exceed our stretch goals of constant and continuous improvement. We aim to set the standard for the industry.

Although the creation of an employee mission statement is justified in its own right, it does offer and needs to serve as a powerful supplement to the organizational version and thus acquire the same official status that the traditional one always has enjoyed. In addition, it reflects an organization that values the centrality of its employees and provides them with a forum for their own voice. It thus says to customers that when they choose this company they are fundamentally choosing its people. And when employees believe that they make such a difference, they frequently do.

MANAGER RANGE: MANAGERIAL HOLISTICS, REFLECTION AND TRANSITION, AND THE MULTIPLE MANAGER

Most of the values that undergird organizations are unknown, unacknowledged, or unexamined. In other words, we generally do not know what is deeply driving us. As a result organizations, CEOs, and managers go about their business without often fully understanding the wellsprings of their operations. To be sure, they can fall back on vision or mission statements but those tend to be uniformly uninformative and sound like everyone else's. In short, organizations need to be more aware of their core knowledge center of guiding principles that should be thoughtful, deliberative, and comprehensive.

But the principles cannot be generalized or float free of specifics. Instead, they should always be proximate to operational situations so that when an organization decides to do something, why and how it makes and carries out that decision should be all of a piece. The net result is that the business elicits pride and inspires respect because it makes sense, internally and externally. It knows what it is doing. It is conscious.

A key discipline for finding a company's animating definition is holistics. Why is holistics so adept at this deep task? Does it perform as an organizational psychiatrist or archaeologist? What is it? Holistics is a process of comprehensive inquiry. It encircles a subject, taps the full reach of its implications, and reaches beyond the predictably known. It delays analysis, often viewing it as prematurely reductive. It is not disdainful of data but is not driven by it either. It assumes that what is being searched for is not yet available for quantification. In short, it is a mode of inquiry, a process of organizational soul searching.

Nor is it done once and for all time and then memorialized in a vision statement. It is up for grabs daily whenever problems have to be solved and a future action has to be chosen. In a real and active sense it is the threshold for planning, innovation, and reinvention. It must always obey a basic law. It must never become too theoretical or removed from daily operations.

The method to its macroreach is invariably circular and entwining and involves three steps. The first involves stepping back, the second stepping aside, and the third stepping ahead. The holistic process is the art of seeing things whole—stepping back to see the forest as well as the trees. It is also the art of seeing things that are directly threatening or compromising—stepping aside to see dangers. And finally it is the art of anticipating the future—stepping ahead to see the unforeseeable.

The three-step system is tyrannical in that it requires that the three steps be completed every time the holistic process is invoked. Although the order is not sacred, there can't be any fast-and-dirty shortcuts. Or as Nietzsche noted, "I skip steps and no step will ever forgive you for skipping it." What follows is an elaboration of each step followed by an application of holistics to managerial decision making.

STEPPING BACK

The art of seeing things whole is harder than it sounds because it is always somewhat mysterious. Like the proverbial tip of the iceberg, every event or opportunity involves more than meets the eye. Thus, the prospect of a new market may be enticing but the totality of that market may be greater or different than initially appears. The methodology of technology assessment may be particularly helpful here.

What is the first, second, third, fourth, and fifth order of impact of the technology being introduced? The durability of each order of impact as well as the probability of spinning off other technologies are all part of the ever-widening process of approximating the whole and of achieving a grasp of the macroreach of the market prior to entering it.

It is probably unfair to lord it over those in the past who minimized the whole and thus underestimated its extent. But what such short-sightedness underscores is the absence of holistics, which compulsively is always more inclusive. Holistics takes off and goes beyond where others have stopped. The assumption of premature mastery, of having plumbed the depths, is usually the infallible sign that we have sold our intelligence and organizations short.

The articulation and analysis of unacknowledged assumptions is the special focus of holistics. Similarly, sizing up the competition is often partial and self-indulgent. Seldom if ever is there an assessment of the talent of our competitors. Planners sometimes do not even know anything about their counterparts in competing companies—where they went to school, what their track record is, what risk management tolerances they employ, and the like. Then, too, often there is little or no discussion of who else is thinking the way they are. Most often that is limited to who else is not planning or doing things the way they are.

Patiently, then, as stepping back and back further proceeds, the whole begins to emerge or much more than what a partial or constrained range of inquiry generally yields. More and more of the iceberg is exposed, the opportunity becomes increasingly three-dimensional. It becomes the table of contents of a total story. It is no longer an idea but a full-fledged scenario. It appears to have all the realism and clarity of animated ideas and opportunities. But it is not finished. It is poised for possible revision.

STEPPING ASIDE

If the first step is thesis, the second step is antithesis. So many plays and films produced somehow seem to have successfully avoided any encounter with sobering reality. So many ventures and new businesses are based on heady expectations but have no sense of gravity. So many careers are fast tracked to oblivion, and so on.

One must step aside so as to see where and when the road may unpredictably veer dangerously off the main path. In short, there is a need to be failure oriented, to hearken to naysayers or the yes-but types—in short, to encourage the loyal and even disloyal opposition. But again, it must be holistic in scope.

It cannot be on a scale smaller than the projected venture itself. That would be deceptive. And even when safeguards and adjustments have been made, monitoring has to join planning as an equal and permanent partner. The venture must never be allowed to become uncritically self-perpetuating or self-directing, especially if it appears to promise success. Thesis has to match antithesis totally in substance, toughness, and scale. We have to worry as much as we dream.

STEPPING AHEAD

But isn't the third step of anticipation—stepping ahead—superfluous or out of order? No, because forecasting is the ultimate check and balance. It comes from another place and time. It has not yet been centrally tapped. It is not part of the original critical apparatus. It is a new player. And it will make or break all that has preceded so far. And its voice is special because it fuses analysis and intuition.

The future is a mixture of the known, the unknown, and the unknowable. We already know a great deal about the future through the extrapolation of demographics and known resources. The unknown is not unknowable. It is available as trends, long-term cycles, various predictors of systems behaviors, and so on. All of these can be tapped and factored into the building up of the original totality. They contribute to the antithesis. But the future is also finally unknowable—that is the way in fact the future remains the future. Nevertheless it is foreseeable, it can be imagined. Utopian, dystopian, and science-fiction writers have been doing it for centuries with remarkably accurate results.

The final step then is to step ahead of the known and the unknown to sense the direction of the unknowable—to try to provide the thesis and antithesis with a future in the form of an intuitive synthesis. This final act, however, is not discontinuous with the two impulses that have shaped this realistic and imaginative whole in the first place. The future compels further, albeit more speculative consideration of totality as well as its future threats. Above all, it adds a dimension currently missing: the future of the future.

So many organizations and managers assume a friendly future. It will agreeably accommodate their planning and thinking. It will always affirm and never question the direction of the totality they have assembled and even the perils. But until and unless one seeks that final reach, not matter how tenuously, the art of holistics is not complete, and the gift of wholeness, contingency, and speculation that it confers upon organizations, planners, and forecasters may be less than generous, enlarging, and bracing. Indeed, that sin of omission may be the ultimate peril.

The value of holistics thus lies in its straddling of opposites—vision and reality, utopia and dystopia. Its correctives are enormous. It brings assumptions to the level of conscious examination. It fixes a quizzical and tough eye on cherished definitions and sacred cows. It requires that the art of conceptualization flirt with intuition and compels vision to be savvy. Above all, at a minimum holistics should make uncertainty more manageable and success more achievable and both permanently incomplete.

REFLECTION AND TRANSITION

Whatever external challenges current managers face, nothing compares to those that directly have affected their basic managerial roles and tasks. They now have to supervise more employees, plug holes caused by downsizing, compensate for workers who often do not have the required work skills, and so on. In addition, there has been a steady erosion of their authority and control. In many plants, teams have taken over. They virtually do everything that mangers previously did. The net result is that in some instances managers have become almost superfluous.

Managers are also finding their knowledge base eroding. New and rapid emerging redefinitions of and demands on their jobs confront them daily: reengineering, balanced score card, employee mission statements and universities, collaborative work covenants, learning organizations, and the like. In short, how does one bring forth a new manager, phoenix-fashion, out of the ashes of multiple crises and dislocations?

The focus would have to be on transition and reflection and above all reflection about transition. One of the hoped-for double outcomes would be the gradual acceptance of reflection as a habitual practice and of transition as a new norm of reality. The rites of a passage to accomplish both goals require identifying three archetypal metaphors to engage both reflection and transition.

One is the figure of Janus, the other of branch-points, the third the learning journey. Janus addresses time; branch-points space; the learning journey process and linkage.

Appropriately the figure of Janus, whose name is the pivotal month of January, sets up the Janerian duality of past and future, retrospect and prospect, genesis and terminus. The past provides benchmarking, the future capacity for anticipating.

The other metaphor is equally powerful. Its classic expression perhaps appears in the lines of Robert Frost: "Two roads diverged in the woods, and I—I took the one less traveled by. And that has made all the difference." The archetype of choice is not only comprehensive, but also recurrent. A choice is not made once and for all time. The road not taken is offered again and again.

Then, too, choice is not limited to externals like lifestyle, career, or calling. It also includes our preferred ways of perceiving, conceptualizing, structuring thought, problem solving, decision making, and so on. In short, it is a complex and alternative identity as rich and different perhaps as the one chosen.

When the metaphors of Janus and branch-points are joined, they support in reinforcing manner a third archetype—that of the learning journey. How do we come to know what we know? How do we develop the assumptions that drive unknowingly so many of our decisions and judgments? What is our relationship to the past and the future? What choices did we make, when, and why? And what are the choices before us?

It is not always easy to reconstruct our learning journey because often earlier ideas have been left behind. They are also not perceived as a lamentable loss. They usually occurred at a formative period when we were still unfinished and not fully educated or acclimated into a career or work-think. Thus, whatever and wherever we were at any given time was always in the process of being revised, retrained, upgraded, and transformed into something so far superior that the old self and its old ways were not worth keeping alive and current.

In any case, what was displaced was regarded for the most part as inferior or inadequate. It served its purpose up to that point but was then cast aside and generally was not available to us any more. It is not unlike the basic difference between science and literature. Science does not have to be cumulative; culture does.

As new perspectives are gained, others are discarded. The learning journey involves an endless and inevitable series of trade-offs. In times of intense change, development may be accelerated and occur with greater discontinuity, just as organizational structures are sometimes altered drastically or reengineered. When that occurs often or deeply the effect may be unsettling.

Managers may be totally unsure of what they are supposed to be and do, just as companies may be confused as to their direction. When things become bewildering, it is perhaps necessary to step back, and above all to look back. That in turn requires adopting the dual directions of Janus, retrospect and prospect, reflection and anticipation. In the process, it may be helpful for managers to reflect back on and benchmark change—professional and organizational—at every stage of their development. In essence, managers inevitably reflect upon their learning journey, which is their individual version of transition. In other words, the learning journey brings together and subsumes the double perspective of Janus, retrospect and prospect; and the ritual drama of making choices. And does it in an extensive reflective review of learning branch-points and transitions. It is to the review of the journey that managers need to turn to find both their new and the affirmation of their traditional roles.

THE LEARNING JOURNEY

When managers recall their past education, training, and experience what frequently emerges is how much the role of the manager itself has dramatically altered over the years and how sometimes they are not happy with the results. For example, many managers were initially given the textbook definition of the five roles of the manager: planning, organizing, staffing, leading, and controlling.

What many found over time is that leading and controlling were altered dramatically. They were called upon to motivate more than lead or to lead by motivating. Control increasingly was eroded by employee empowerment. The dominance of teams meant that singular control of hiring and firing now had to be shared, especially if HR was outsourced. Follow-up became an increasingly bigger part of planning, especially following up the implementation of training. Above all, because of the increasing emphasis on productivity, performance appraisal became performance improvement. And it was the manager's responsibility now as facilitator or coach to bring about that transformation and in the process align employee with business stretch goals.

If one were to compare the job description of managers when they started out with current versions, it might appear as if they were talking about two different positions altogether. But that is precisely the value of retrospective reflection. Indeed, three benefits listed here are conferred by the learning journey of transition.

Yields of the Learning Journey

1. Documentation

    Recording over time the evolutionary history of the job of manager and learning choices. Changes did not just happen. They involved branch-points—roads taken and not taken. In the process, new understandings and perspectives are acquired.

2. Unlearning.

    On a very direct and personal level, managers recognize the degree to which a learning organization in order to be effective also has to become an unlearning organization.

3. Celebrations of Survival and Change

    Valuing resiliency, persistence, and agility that is affirmative; the manger emerges as a survivor of many wars. He also learns to lead and be an advocate of innovative change. He helps to initiate and sustain debate about changing managerial roles. He entertains job and even career change, including going abroad where traditional managers may be more highly valued. Finally, he projects alternative organizational futures that may serve to recover and pursue anew lost opportunities and earlier roads not taken.

The common denominator of the three benefits listed here is to bring the learning review to the threshold of the future. It is at this point where the question of what lies ahead for managers generates a manager's unfinished agenda. The process of retroactively evaluating past solutions or interventions against the realities they were supposed to address may uncover or recover alternative innovations suggested earlier by managers but that like the road not taken, never saw the light of day. The process of future facing thus recaptures lost opportunities in the past. It is like leapfrogging—while we are getting ahead let us also catch up.

Standing at the Janerian threshold where the past and the future converge also provides managers with the illusion of a blank slate. They may wish to speculate not only what mangers are likely to be, but also what they ideally should be. For a change, they might like to design their own jobs rather than having it always done for or to them. In the process, they probably also would have to identify what they need to learn to get from the present to the future. And so appropriately the final yield of the learning inventory may be the training agenda of the future.

In summary, then, the learning journey that focuses on the permanence of transition offers much. The journey brings a probing and self-conscious intelligence to bear on the trajectory of education and training; raises to the level of conscious review, perhaps for the first time, assumptions that drive decisions; and compels an insightful interplay between the past, present, and the future. In many ways, it can serve to structure midlife career change and to provide the rites of passage to renew and restore balance in the future. It can create out of managed turbulence a more informed, innovative, and proactive professional—a manager of transition, ad infinitum.

THE MULTIPLE MANAGER: UNLOCKING EMPLOYEE PERFORMANCE AND INNOVATION

> The kind of people we are looking for in our management ranks is someone who can be persuasive and who can also make people cooperate with them. Management is not dictatorship.

A company will get nowhere if all the thinking is left to management. Everybody in the company must contribute their minds.

—Morita (1986)

A significant way of measuring change or its absence is examining the way managers manage. The options for managing employees and for employees managing themselves have increased significantly. Not surprisingly, so have the ways of communicating managing. In fact, the two often are linked.

There are at least three major directionally driven managerial models operative: the vertical, the horizontal, and the circular. Each is paired with an appropriate communication partner.

There is the traditional directive style of telling workers what to do and how to do it. This is basically a top-down singular style of perfection because there is implicitly only one way to do it. The supervisor, like the proverbial version of father knows best, always has the right answer. Often such paternalism works well, and the path prescribed frequently is in fact the best one to follow. But that method requires nearly total vertical obedience to the chain of command on the one hand and faith in the paternal wisdom and goodness of a boss on the other hand.

Hardly ever is the question asked why this is being done or whether this is the best or only way. Managers generally know why and share it with other managers—that is the official and inside talk between managers—but not with employees. Occasionally, the why may be used as a trump card to eliminate disobedience or mild mutiny. Finally, the dominant communications mode is prescriptive. Following the military models, orders are given.

Another method is coaching or facilitating. The directive has been replaced by a question- and answer-inquiry system. In some case it also may incorporate the Japanese ritual of asking the question "Why" at least five times when a problem arises in order to get at root cause. Applied horizontally and companywide, it is particularly effective when the company also commits itself to being a questioning and communicating culture.

At the heart of this method is dialogue. The degree to which conversation is employed and what areas it covers varies with the security or insecurity of the manager. Supervisors, who are determined to retain control and still be directive, will be reluctant to share all or too much lest it undermine their superior position. Titles and egos are intertwined. Still, even a 50-50 mixture of the directive and coaching styles is usually more productive of creating efficiency, sustaining morale, and building communication bridges than the totally directive approach.

The third mode is circular. It is the most ambitious and complex. It has a number of subsets and is potentially the most robust and most demanding of both managers and employees. The key variable is the degree to which managers are indispensable, dispensable, and finally invisible or nearly absorbed as co-leaders. The progress through these three stages has as its ultimate goal the manager's responsibility to create and communicate an employee-centered culture.

It might be helpful at this point to summarize in matrix form the three basic styles and then to identify the subsets of the third managerial one for further exploration.

Managerial Style	Direction	Communication Modes		Outcomes
1. Directive	Vertical	Prescriptive	Predictive	Singular
2. Coaching	Horizontal	Suggestive		Multiple
3. Team Leader	Circular	Dialogue		Collective

The next matrix identifies the three progressive subsets of management development, except now this will increasingly involve employee participation to the point where they become co-managers.

Leader	Roles	Communication Modes	Outcomes
1. Manager as Directive and Guided Solutions Team Leader/Coach	Dialogue	Exchange Limited	Creativity
2. Manager as Consultant	Suggestive	Guided	Change
3. Manager-Employee	Circular	Exchange Innovation	Shared Leadership

The first version is a transitional hybrid. The managerial role softens, becomes less overbearing and confrontative, and employs a more oblique approach. The manager still holds forth a great deal, moralizes, and sermonizes sometimes but he also listens. His favorite summary question is no longer, "Anyone not know what he has to do?" but rather "Have we heard from everyone at this point?"

The solutions generated still bear the mark of the manager and his preferential way of doing things. But employee input broadens the range of the discussion and helps to make more visible and important the relationship between divisions and between employees and senior management. The latter sometimes discomfits the manager. The tune that goes through his mind is, "How are you going to keep them down on the farm after they've seen Paris?" But he makes sure little or none of that creeps into any written communications. He is sometimes delighted although surprised by some of the more creative thinking that takes place.

The second mode requires the manager to inhabit the periphery of the team. He functions as a resource. His style is thus largely consultative. He generally participates only when asked questions, although he often may try to regain his former indispensability. Generally, he is involved in two activities: the need for factual and technical information, and negotiating conflicts between members of the team.

Serving as a broker in conflict resolution is often a new role for managers. In the directive function, disputes are just ordered to stop and that's that. But here the manager has to employ a craft he may not have used before, and that he in fact may also have to master. Managers who develop the difficult style of negotiation and see both the individual and team benefits it yields, may in the process discover a managerial dimension that more than compensates for whatever loss of authority they experienced.

In any case, depending less on the insistent style of the manager and the pliability and creativity of the team, the solutions generated will be a mixture of the two inputs. It will be somewhat directive, singular, familiar, and even managerially predictable. But if the team is also empowered, and develops a sense of its collective intelligence, the solutions may be more imaginative and robust. The team indeed may begin to sense its difference and even its power to identify alternatives. That happy prospect may be viewed with suspicion and even alarm if the manager believes he is threatened.

In the third or last version, employees share the driver's seat. They basically run and lead the team but they are constrained from taking over totally. After all, managers do not have a monopoly on being the boss. Workers can be just as directive, prescriptive, and arbitrary. Lest that throwback occur, the manager may insist that team leadership at best is temporary and rotational. Who leads varies with the competence required. When the challenge changes, the employee leader changes. As a result, competence is ensured. And the flexibility and security of that rotation by one of their own brings out the best and most creative, out-of-the-box solutions to problems.

At this point the manager in addition to serving as a consultant in terms of data and conflict resolution, becomes a productive member of the team. As such he may take his turn as team leader if he possesses the particular competence required. If he yearns for the good old days when he was boss, he will not be a happy camper.

But if he sees his role as helping to sustain and be an integral part of a shared management environment that contributes significantly to increased productivity, profitability, and performance, and that brings innovative approaches to problem solving, he may find that it more than compensates for what he may have given up. And in his less stressful and more fulfilled moments, he also may even acknowledge that managers do not have a monopoly on management and are not the only and even sometimes not the most important players in the game of thinking, learning, and leading.

The last outcome brings the learning review smack up against the future and the need to anticipate it. It is at this point where what lies ahead generates the unfinished agenda. The evaluation of past solutions or interventions against the realities they were supposed to address may recover and underscore innovative notions or creative problem-solving techniques suggested by managers along the way but that for various reasons never took hold or were tried out. There is thus about this process of future facing the dimension of leapfrogging—let us catch up while leaping ahead. Standing at the Janerian threshold where the past and future converge, managers may wish to indulge in the illusion of a blank slate. They may wish to enjoy the luxury of speculating on what a manager and an organization ideally should be in the future, and where both have fallen short in the past. Finally, because these regrets also may be more global than what surfaced in the series of outcomes noted earlier, they may even be more provocative. That is appropriately futuristic.

In summary, then, the value of the learning inventory lies in the urgent intelligence that is brought to bear, in raising to the level of conscious review assumptions that drive decisions, and compelling an insightful interplay between the past, the present, and the future. In many ways, it is a structured and revealing midlife crisis designed to create or restore balance for the future. It generates renewal and recommitment as a more informed and proactive professional. Undertaken companywide, it can give organizations new vitality, direction, and purpose.

At the end of Mark Twain's *Huckleberry Finn*, our young hero after reviewing his many escapades is not content just to hang around but "to light out for the territory ahead." For Huck, that was the lure of the West. It was also the promise of the future. For America it was both. This country has always had a love affair with what lies ahead. Now there is also the need to find ways of reconfiguring the branch-points for its managers of the future.

REFERENCES

Morita, Akio; with Reingold, Edwin, and Mitsuko Shimomura. 1986. *Made in Japan*. New York E.P. Dutton.

12

LEADER PRACTICES AND PROFILES: SERVANT LEADERSHIP AND EXECUTIVE IMPACT

Senior managers who have served under powerful leaders maintain that for better or worse the company is not the same. How can that be? Can CEOs still be that powerful? Can style become company culture? And if so, have we generally overlooked the tell-tale signs that warn us in advance of substantial, incremental, and even discontinuous organizational change?

In the process, we may be ignoring or devaluating behavior over vision, the thinking process rather than solely the results. In short, what should we look for in the proverbial first 100 days after a leader assumes command that is predictive of what is to come? In addition, should we assume that those differences are precisely how leaders consciously and intuitively choose to put their distinctive stamp on their organizations? There are at least five tell-tale subtle signs to note.

1. Thinking

   How does the CEO think? Is she deliberate or fast, slow or quick, big picture or snapshot, present or future oriented? Does she get impatient with those who think differently? How does she show her pleasure or displeasure? Does the selection of her senior team serve to mirror or contrast to her thinking style?

We are often so preoccupied with external results that we have little interest in the thought processes that were involved in making the original decision. As a result, we pay a great deal of attention to implementation rather than conceptualization. A company should not hire a CEO who is an intellectual lightweight. The capacity for powerful conceptualization is only a step away from powerful leadership.

2. Starting Points

How and where does the CEO typically start things off? What are his recurrent first words or questions? Does he characteristically offer or ask for background or history? How important is the past to him? Or does he prefer to plunge right in, in medias res (in the middle of things), and then move ahead quickly? Does he ever accept interruptions when he is holding forth or pause and seek reflective feedback at critical points?

Many leaders lead by the example of illustrative stories or life-changing experiences. Everything is suspended while a dramatic tale is told that clinches and sums up the argument and pulls together all the pieces and ties up loose ends. The process also may be surprising when other matters or areas are suddenly brought into play as the CEO expands the parameters of the discussion. Finally, he may frequently reframe so that as the return to the original track takes place it may be both more inclusive and consensual. In other words, is how and where he starts with certain subjects expansive or restricted, inviting or excluding?

3. Ending Points

Are his conclusions arrived at cumulatively or sequentially? Does he incorporate opposing positions or are they deleted in his summation? Is he always hot to trot and poised for action? Is he always calling for what's next? Do his conclusions tick off a detailed checklist or are they a rapid and sweeping flourish? Does he take the time to relate all the parts and preserve all? Does he value the whole as a spawning context? And then does he concern himself with follow-up—how are we going to make this happen?—or parcel out and delegate the final communication and implementation of a decision to others?

4. Priorities and Preferences

What does she like and dislike doing? What gets her juices flowing and his heart pumping? What does she seem to just endure? Does she like to fight? Will she sit for hours going over and over again the details and be totally absorbed to the exclusion of everything and everyone else? Is she happy, moody, or angry most of the time? What makes her energy level rise or fall? Is she steady or mercurial? Does she like crossword puzzles?

5. Ego

How important is it for him to be numero uno and be acknowledged as such by all? How does he react to praise? Does he swell or appear uncomfortable? Is he easily bruised or hurt? Is it more important for him to succeed or for the company to succeed? What is his driving mission in life? What legacy if any does he seek to leave? Does he consider himself so indispensable that without him the company will fall apart or do so when he leaves? Does he thank others?

One could go on but I think the point has been made. We need to recognize the power of leadership style to influence the imitative behaviors of senior staff and to shape company culture. Therefore, we need to choose wisely. We need to supplement the interview process for CEOs by raising more internal and indirect questions of leadership dynamics and style once we have determined what we want and what will make the organization flourish. We also have to factor in what kind of CEO style may be needed at a particular point in the evolution of the organization.

The key then is hiring or working with a CEO who has considerable conceptual power (grasp of the situation), values background (knows the score and the competition), starts and ends in a unified way (dots the *I*s and crosses the *T*s), loves to solve problems, especially in a creative way (models innovation and out-of-the-box thinking), and blends his identity with that of the company (vision and mission are one and the same). Anticipating executive style may lead to a more affective assessment of executive impact. Above all, the company may need its own version of 100 days to do its homework before hiring and assessing its choice in a CEO's first 100 days.

> A righteous man asked the rabbi to explain the differences be-
> tween Heaven and Hell. The rabbi noted that both places had
> enormous mansions. Both had large dining rooms in which
> there was spread an abundance of delicious foods. Both sets of
> inhabitants had their arms locked around each other. Those in
> Hell were emaciated. Those in Heaven were satisfied and full.
> In Hell no one would permit the other fellow to eat. In
> Heaven they ate together.
>
> —A Hasidic Tale

Leaders are defined and measured in various ways: results, leadership qualities, decisiveness, innovation, and the like. Robert Greenleaf put service at the top of the list because he claims that is the way to achieve all of the above and more: "One test of any kind of leadership is: Do leaders enjoy a mutual relationship with followers?" (p. 119). He goes on to argue that the critical task of effective leaders is managing serving relationships. Servant leaders are charged with finding commonality, coherence, and consensuality as the means of holding relationships between leaders and followers together. The common ground between leaders and followers consists of power, focus, initiatives, and decisiveness. The dynamic is how the four are sorted out between the two.

Greenleaf claims that there are basically three models of relationships between leaders and followers. The first is the unidirectional or unilateral model; the second the negotiated or shared model; the third the mutual model. A visual version and discussion of each follows.

1. Unidirectional or Unilateral Model

    This model flows in only one direction, from leader to follower as it passes through the four areas.

LEADER   Power   Focus   Initiatives   Decisiveness   FOLLOWERS

Here the chain of command and implementation goes only one way. Nothing is shared. Power derives from the leader. It is a singular not a multiple line passing through and connecting all four areas. Followers learn what is expected of them by announcements and pronouncements, not through discussion. Advice or concurrence is not sought or given. This is a perfect model for a results-driven organization, although to achieve those gains working environments may be punitive. If the CEO is an outstanding Attila the Hun and if the market for the products or services is favorable, the organization will post significant gains and pay a handsome return on investment.

2. Negotiated or Shared Model

	Power	
LEADER	Focus	FOLLOWERS
	Initiative	
	Decisiveness	

The accommodation between leaders and followers is brought about by cooperative and adversarial negotiation. In the first instance, leaders and followers develop more cooperative relationships because of the common need to achieve certain gains and because the special style and vision of the leader eliminates the mentality of them and us. On the outside, business may be at war but inside the organization business is peace. If unions are involved, hard negotiations may have produced this shared model. But it tends to be precarious and contested and regularly open to sudden interventions by shop stewards.

Unlike the first singular model, which enforces uniformity in all four areas, the shared model may be uneven. The extent or degree of the sharing varies with each of the four areas and the degree of leadership commitment to partnership. Although the leadership may be directed more toward liberalizing than controlling relationships, how much also depends on where the company is in its history and evolution. If the goal is innovation, a top-down approach is usually ineffective. Creativity cannot be coerced. The shared model might be more successful in encouraging all employees to be essentially the company's R&D.

3. The Mutual Model

			Leaders/Followers
			Followers/Leaders
Power	Focus	Initiatives	Decisiveness

The mutual model is totally collaborative. Leaders and followers develop a reciprocal relationship; they may even exchange roles. This goes beyond cooperation to their becoming co-creative in all four areas. Greenleaf claims that such an organization can produce results, motivate innovation, and embody a vision of service. Indeed, the relationship between leaders and followers is essentially one of mutual service to each other, the net result being the creation of Greenleaf's supreme organizational vision, the servant institution.

But such an institution and such a model of mutuality cannot be assumed or merely proclaimed. It has to be built. Above all, the model has to be learned and communicated. In other words, the servant leader has two tasks: building and learning the craft of commonality, and developing the communication of consensuality.

BUILDING AND LEARNING MUTUALITY

Greenleaf employs four building blocks to establish a relationship of mutuality between leader and followers: develop people, sustain equal exchange between them, seek, create consensus, and reduce uncertainty.

1. "Develop Everyone You Touch"

The servant leader serves learning. But the learning is not just quantitative or incremental but qualitative and holistic. Greenleaf asks of a goal, "Does it have a healing or civilizing influence? Does it nurture the servant motive in people, favor their growth as persons, and help them distinguish those who serve from those who destroy?" (pp. 114–115). Thus, the learning must face both inward and outward. It has to have as one of its outcomes building a service culture within the organization. That is the only way to develop a customer service company.

Greenleaf pauses to comment on employees who do not always fit in and are outspoken. He calls them "seekers." Frequently critical, sometimes even off-the-wall types, they routinely question the status quo and the orthodoxy of the organization's way of doing things. They need to be protected and even cherished. An institution that is not big and flexible enough to accept mavericks is a fragile or rigid institution and not a learning organization. Then too often the special value of the seekers is embryonic. They may be emerging leaders in their own right. They also may embody a different future direction for the company. In any case, they dramatize the second building block: the interchangeability of leaders and followers.

2. Sustain Equality of Exchange

Greenleaf never supported pyramidal hierarchies. They were edifice complexes supporting excessive ego and separatism, the one being the version of other. Today we might call them Towers of Enron. Such structures create too much distance between leaders and followers, especially for Greenleaf who seeks greater equality and commonality between them.

Greenleaf's argument starts from an assumption that the limits of executive power stem from the limits of executive knowledge. Leaders at the top do not know everything, about everything, all the time. They thus have to recognize that whatever edge they enjoy is temporary: "even the ablest leaders will do well to be aware that there are times and places in which they should follow. And one who seems deficient in one or more of these qualities, may on some occasion rise to save the day" (p. 114).

Thus, the relationship of mutuality extends to the exchange of roles. Leaders will become followers and followers will become leaders when the combination of the need and the expertise are joined to require them to be equals. In fact, it might even be claimed that the assumption of that role by followers is the ultimate form of their professional and learning development. But such elevation to leadership by followers often needs the sanction of the CEO: "The titular leader gives continuity and coherence to an endeavor in which many may lead" (p. 120).

The reciprocity of leaders and followers is not conditional on who has more and who has less. In other words, there is no giver and no taker. Both are "the more able and the less able serving each other." It cannot be otherwise because each needs what the other has for completion. The more able have to offer the perspective and knowledge that their moreness has to give, just as the less able have to define the need and contribution of having less. To do otherwise is to pass off a half as a whole. Genuine wholeness is born of reciprocal partnership and its ultimate achievement is always shared.

One cannot grant wholeness to oneself. It comes from a process of plus and minus, the more able and the less able, the mutuality of leaders and followers. They are co-creators; rightly so, for as Greenleaf puts it, "There is something subtle communicated to one who is being served and led if, implicit in the compact between servant leader and led, is the understanding that the search for wholeness is something they share" (p. 8).

3. Create Consensus

The building block of seeking commonality is one that leaders and followers undertake together. The leader is a "consensus finder," a consensus creator, and a consensus articulator (p. 138). "One leads by the concepts that will enlarge the number who find common ground. The leaders thus strive to bring the people together, and hold them together, as an effective force" (pp. 138–139). Effectiveness is an affirmation of commonality; it is the hoops that hold the barrel together. There is no need to lecture any group about the value of consensuality when they experience directly its collective power. As Greenleaf notes: "There is nothing that builds organizational strength quite like a high order of consensus regarding goals and strategies" (p. 105). But it is not that easy or automatic. There are obstacles to consensuality just as there are to mutuality.

4. Reduce Uncertainty

The biggest obstacle is the desire for certainty in excess of what the world can legitimately provide. The world is stingy as far as assurances are concerned. Similarly, problems exist for which there do not appear to be any solutions and create the impression that collectively our problems are in excess of our capacity to solve them. Greenleaf recommends that we stop calling them problems but rather challenges for they may be with us a long time, and we may never be able to solve them. As challenges we can continue to work together to manage if not to solve them (p. 105). This is not mere semantics because as a consensus seeker, Greenleaf is aware of what can prevent or compromise mutuality. In fact, "defusing the anxiety of people who want more certainty than exists in the situation" (p. 125) is precisely the sign of a consensual leader.

The servant leader has to reduce uncertainty because until anxiety is calmed, common ground will not emerge. When the numbers sharing that common ground increase to a critical mass, a consensual culture is created in which the servant motive can thrive and co-creation between leaders and followers can take place.

But Greenleaf believes that uncertainty can be reduced and consensual cultures can thrive only when the right kind of communication is sustained between leaders and followers. And so his final admonition is to value the communication of commonality.

According to Greenleaf, the three communication modes, which are not unlike the three organizational structures noted earlier, are the coercive, manipulative, and persuasive. Each has its own base of power and its own way of modeling relationships.

1. Coercive

   Greenleaf's analysis of coercive power on the one hand obviously follows the highly directive structure of the first model of unilateral relationships, but on the other hand deals with subtler forms of coercion masking itself under noble ideals. For example, Greenleaf cites the credentialing power of universities that in the name of high standards force students into being certified in only certain ways. The net result is that although few regard universities or similar bodies that prescribe or dictate credentials as coercive because they appear noble in their regard for safeguarding social institutions, the only reason that they can play that self-appointed protective role is that they have the power to do so.

2. Manipulative

   Manipulative power and communication in contrast do not use sanctions or threats or pressures but rather plausible explanations that in fact do not really explain anything. Greenleaf claims that many leaders come to decisions and then seek to find plausible explanations for what was basically intuitive. But when the decision is in excess of the rational explanation, followers feel manipulated, even duped. In addition, because of the availability of superior informational sources at the top, employees are cowed into concluding that they do not know enough to judge and therefore have to go along with the executive decision. But those who are savvier or have watched this manipulative game being played many times begin to be suspicious and ask: "OK, what is the hidden agenda this time?"

In short, such manipulation pays a high price for its shortcuts by damaging long-term relationships. Or as Greenleaf puts it "manipulation hangs as a cloud over the relationship between leader and led, and is the subject of much pejorative comment" (p. 85). In short, manipulation involves passing off a half as a whole, not telling the truth, the whole truth, and nothing but the truth. When that occurs as it does regularly in the world of the second model of relationships, adversarial forces are activated and begin to press for a less manipulative, more direct communication and relationship.

3. Persuasive

Clearly, Greenleaf favors persuasion because it is based on and at the heart of mutuality. Greenleaf begins by claiming that persuasion is initially and finally an internal process. "One is persuaded, I believe, upon the arrival at a feeling of rightness about a belief or action through one's own intuitive sense" (p. 85). Leaders thus do not have a monopoly on intuition. Indeed, it is critical that they recognize that all their followers are also intuitive because then both leader and follower can understand and even agree on what conscious logic can and cannot offer. When that logic falls short, intuition may have to be the deciding factor.

But in a consensual culture it does not end there. Further efforts must be made over time to fill in the gaps. The decision may have been made but the need to complete the partial rationale in other words is still ongoing. Only that way can the leader keep the faith and bring that communication home and full. Thus, "Both leader and follower respect the autonomy and integrity of the other and each allows and encourages the other to find his or her intuitive confirmation of the rightness of the belief or action" (p. 85). In addition to having an immediate confirmatory effect, it also stores up trust for the future: "If this relationship prevails, when a quick action is required, one supported by the skimpiest of rationalization, it will be accepted with the assurance that at some future time there will be the opportunity for intuitive mutuality to be reestablished" (pp. 85–86).

Greenleaf describes how the mutuality of persuasion is employed finally by followers: "A leader who practices persuasion wherever possible sets a model that in time will encourage followers to deal with the leader by persuasion. Power is generated in this relationship because it admits of mutual criticism, spirited arguments can occur, and it does not depend on artful stratagems" (p. 86).

In summary, then, a relationship of mutuality offers much. It structures relationships between leaders and followers along lines of equality and reciprocity. Leaders can lean on followers. They also know that their role is clear: to develop everyone they touch to the point where the relationship of mutuality becomes more intuitive, spirited, and collaborative. The reciprocal relationship is managed through the notion of first among equals, especially modeled at the top, so that all are convinced that at any given time the best people are at the helm for however long that works.

Once again leaders do not have to work so hard at being indispensable on the one hand or 360 degrees on the other. But in two major respects, leaders have to be assertive. First, they have to be tireless consensus finders and persuaders, each being a path to the other. The ultimate achievement of servant leadership is thus the creation and maintenance of a consensual and persuasive culture. Second, the vision of a company is entrusted to and kept alive by the reciprocity of leaders and followers. Or to paraphrase Greenleaf's favorite Tao proverb: When leaders lead well, the people think they did it themselves.

13

LEADERSHIP INSTRUCTION: PROFESSOR CEO

Most orientations for new hires are dreadful. They are variously boring, intimidating, and uninformative cheerleading sessions. Margaret Wheatley (1992) recalls being told initially at one such session that there were at least fourteen ways she could be fired; and then the orientation leader quipped that he could think of at least a dozen more. Is it any wonder that often new employees wonder why they took this job in the first place? And lament all the questions they should have asked at the interview in the first place? Perhaps prospective employees should attend an orientation session before accepting the position.

There are perhaps many obvious and drastic ways of fixing counterproductive orientations. But recently I had the ear of a CEO who put a high value on acculturating new hires, believed he knew a great deal about managing the business (certainly as much as his former professors), and had a big ego. So I slyly suggested that perhaps the best way to reengineer the orientation format was for the CEO to convene a series of breakfast seminars for new employees, play the role of company professor, and introduce them to the company and its culture. He swelled with the idea and then dumped it into my lap to produce an outline of his remarks. Once again, no good initiative will go unpunished.

Because I am generally failure oriented and because I know both the vanity of top executives as well as the uneasiness of new employees, I began with warnings about what not to do: "Don't preach (it is not a form of learning); don't be nostalgic (many of the new employees could be your kids); don't brag (your failures might be more interesting); don't be generic or eternal (stress the specifics of change; all that has happened may be dwarfed by what is to come); and above all, don't try to be funny (unless you are the butt of the joke; then the wit goes deeper and lasts longer)."

The CO reluctantly grunted and then said, "Enough negativity. I am taking over now. I want to talk about—sorry, share—what I believe are the company's central values, and what I therefore think will determine their success and ours. OK?" There are certain questions that do not require an answer. In any case, here is the agenda of Professor CEO.

1. Professional Development

   "As a company, we value professional growth. Who decides that? You do. How much and what do you read? Do you attend professional meetings? Here is a copy of the books and articles I read this past year and the meetings I attended. It is not intended to intimidate. Rather, I am as subject to the pressure for professional development as you are. The dates of my bibliography do not coincide with when I got my MBA. Perhaps, we can read and discuss a book together at a later meeting."

2. Decision Alternatives

   "This is no lockstep organization. Different and even divergent thinking is encouraged. Particularly welcome are decision alternatives. Why are they important? Here are some handouts that describe some real situations. Analyze them and develop decision options and alternatives. What would be the criteria of selection?"

3. Decision Trinity

   "Decision making at every level of the company is not linear sequential but circular. Every decision to do something has to be accompanied by the decision to communicate and implement that something. Problems with any one part affect the whole. If there are too many weak links in the chain of communication or implementation, the original decision may be seriously flawed or compromised. In short, consider every solution a potential problem. Never shortcut the trinity."

4. Negotiation

"Nothing is set in stone. Flux is the norm, Thus, everything has to be negotiated: building consensus, valuing diversity, stirring innovation. That means unilateral bossism is dead. The traditional unilateral warning to workers—'Your job is to make me look good'—has to be changed to the mutuality of 'Our job is to make each other look good.' The declaration of independence has to be altered to the declaration of interdependence."

5. Anticipatory and Participatory Management

"What drives productivity and profitability today may not be in the driver's seat tomorrow. Participatory management thus has to be linked to anticipatory management. The future is to be your constant companion. The reason so many of the books on my reading list are science fiction is that they already live in the future and do so in specific concrete terms. They are not some self-indulgent stargazers, but engineers and social planners who wire the future in place. And that is what you should constantly be doing as well. Seeing in every decision or direction its future forms. Wondering where this company is going to be twenty years from now. Will it be immortal? What about your future and that of your job? If we do not live in the future now we may not have one later."

Who could argue with the points in this list? Besides, it was obviously going to be presented with passion and conviction and that together with the depth of the ideas would carry the day. Although other and even different foci could be added or substituted, the reminder not to succumb to the temptation to be a windbag was accompanied with the recommendation not to employ only monologue but encourage dialogue.

Is this any way to reconstruct an orientation session and to run a company? The answer is yes, twice. To those who believe this may not the best use of a CEO's time, there is nothing more important than delivering the company's future into the talented hands of its new employees. They will ensure that the company has one. Besides, few sources of satisfaction matched the smile and gratification this CEO received when he reviewed the evaluations of his breakfast orientation seminars. He remarked, "Perhaps I missed my calling. Perhaps I should have been a professor. Well, maybe it is not too late. Although what did they mean when they claimed that some of the seminars sounded like sermons?"

REFERENCES

Bohm, E. *On Dialogue*. Ojai, Calif.: The Ojai Institute, 1989.

Buchen, I. "Disturbing the Future." *Foresight* 12, no. 2 (Winter 2000).

Handy, C. *Beyond Certainty*. Cambridge, Mass.: Harvard Business Press, 1996.

Isaacs, W. "Dialogue: The Power of Collective Thinking." *Organizational Dynamics, AMA Journal* (Fall 1993).

Wheatley, M. *Leadership and the New Science*. San Francisco: Berrett-Koehler, 1992.

II

EMERGING DEVELOPMENTS AND TRENDS

14

GLOBALITY: REVISITED, REVIEWED, AND PERHAPS REJECTED

Although economics drives organizations toward globalization, only a few in the game have shown such gains. Bain Consulting of New York examined the 1996–2000 financials of 7,500 publicly traded companies in seven countries with revenues in excess of $500 million. Only 1 in 6 showed a growth in foreign sales and operating profits compared to its domestic operations.

Why? Three reasons: insularity, ignorance, and inexperience.

1. Insularity and Comfort Levels

   Domestic success and savvy do not automatically carry over to and are a good fit with global investment enterprises. Indeed, such experience can be a liability rather than an asset for many reasons. Major corporations are scaled large and are thus less comfortable with small to medium-size versions that are exactly the initial preferred sizes of overseas start-ups.

   American companies are accustomed to being lone rangers and operating without partners. But almost all successful overseas offshoots require some degree of joint venture, which is often discomfiting. Additionally, American senior staff are generally unfamiliar or comfortable with dependency on a joint partner, which often can lead to excessive swings from too much to too little reliance.

If the organization has survived a merger with a foreign company and its different culture, it may be cynical or optimistic or both about such foreign alliances. In either case, there will be considerable uneasiness and even misgivings; more dreadful war stories than happy fusions abound.

Many CEOs have knee-jerked to the "global imperative." They have expanded hurriedly without examining carefully all the costs involved (the financial investment and the human capital) or estimating carefully value creation. The net result, sadly, is either income loss or operating at a financial level far below that of the company's domestic operations. That in turn creates the embarrassment of the home base having to absorb the difference and to subsidize questionable overseas investments.

Most American CEOs were not trained in overseas business. Similarly, their organizations and personnel may reflect the same impoverished knowledge base and lack a global mind-set. Without such companywide focus and staff, the CEO will be unable to marshal the necessary talent to succeed abroad. Finally, whatever the complexities of domestic multiple operations, most senior- and middle-level managers are not adept at maintaining the critical macro-micro double focus: preserving and nurturing domestic markets and at the same time attending to the difference of overseas operations.

In summary, then, the lack of global education on the one hand coupled with the absence of a global paradigm at all executive and managerial levels on the other hand may be a supreme obstacle to overseas success. And that provides a natural segue to the next issue.

2. Ignorance or Sins of Omission

Historically, global experience often was the byproduct of imperialism and the maintenance of empires. But as those faded, often violently and often with a bad after-taste and long-lasting resentments, those original holding countries lost their extensive historical training ground and network for producing global managers and expertise. Formal education had to take up the slack and its record is generally mixed.

Most American MBA programs require only one token course devoted to international business. A rapid examination of the textbooks used shows that the bulk of discussion and case studies are from the 1980s and 1990s and deal primarily with multinational companies who basically replicated their operations totally or partially overseas rather than creating joint new ventures. In short, most current managers are being shaped by a past rather than a current or future model and are acting on dated information. Most professors of such global courses are either Americans with little or no direct overseas experience or natives of other countries with limited knowledge of the structure and operations of American corporations. Most American students are also understandably unaware of or fail to factor in the career dimensions and opportunities of pursuing a globally oriented career. Indeed, they may exclude from their career plans companies that offer such opportunities.

Happily, this vicious cycle appears to be transitional. More foreign-born professors, consultants, and students with American doctorates and corporate experience are being appointed to American universities and being hired by American corporations. The global mind-set may gradually be inculcated to a new generation of MBA students. In the meantime, there are number of alternatives. One is for future American executives and managers to be trained overseas in academic programs, such as INSEAD, which already have built up an impressive international faculty. Equally as important, such programs attract an international student body that is as formative as the program itself and helps to build a global network of contacts that are lifelong.

Another avenue is electronic distance education that enables American working adult learners to enroll in international education programs without having to satisfy restrictive residential requirements. In fact, most such programs often enroll foreign students as well and thus provide a nexus between the two. Chat rooms and instructor facilitation ensure an international dialogue and exchange of different and even divergent cultures.

Probably the most rapid yet highly professional route for current executives, senior vice presidents, and managers is to bypass the universities entirely and enroll in short, intense programs offered by centers or institutes specializing in leadership development programs. Often they do what universities locked into rigid and sequential course structures cannot. For example, two excellent programs, the Center for Creative Leadership (CCL) and the Global Institute for Leadership Development (GILD), build into their instruction initially and subsequently executive coaching sessions to ensure customization of the program. GILD is further distinguished by focusing on preparing global leaders, using an international faculty—including Gorbachev and Bhutto—and on offering differentiated levels of training. The major ones are four: new managers, emerging leaders, senior leaders, and leadership teams. Finally, the learning model and time allocations developed by Warren Bennis and Phil Harkins match and easily justify the $5,000 fee for a six-day period of intense training.

Finally, an intriguing proposal put forward by Trevor J. O'Hara, a London-based consultant and expert on global business, probably should be given serious consideration. O'Hara recommends the creation and appointment of a Chief Globalization Officer (CGO). That would send a clear signal throughout the entire organization of the priority of global business as well as set the standard of its operations. Earlier, GE accomplished a similar companywide priority by appointing Ian Wilson as a resident futurist. Perhaps one of the CGO's first projects would be to secure the budget and time off for attending weeklong programs to bring senior staff and managers up to global speed. Indeed, it is likely that the CGO may be on the faculty.

3. Ignorance and Misgivings

Unhappy overseas ventures may be a necessary initial cost of doing business abroad, especially with uneducated and inexperienced personnel. But that may be viewed as a temporary setback, which will be taken care of in time with more appropriate training and higher levels of commitment. But another kind of misgiving is beginning to emerge at a different and more disturbing order.

Computer programmers in India hired to do at a lower cost what their American counterparts had done, when interviewed exhibited a surprising hostility. In effect, they regarded their appointments as a long overdue form of justice. Salary differentials had created a level playing field by which their equal competence was finally recognized. They exulted that American and British superiority was challenged and found needy. There was an air of retaliation.

Unexpectedly, perhaps, globalization and its companion, free trade have become a political issue. The loss of jobs through outsourcing has already resulted in proposed legislation on both the state and national levels to discourage and even penalize in various ways companies that export American jobs. Perhaps even more serious is the revival of the specter first raised during NAFTA that American workers are paying with their jobs and income for the benefits of free trade. Unions in the United States made overseas outsourcing a 2004 campaign issue. They lined up a list of candidates to support imposing severe limits on the practice.

The net result is that globality is now impaled on the horns of a classic dilemma. On the one hand, CEOs are just being good capitalists doing what they are supposed to do to increase productivity, ensure profitability, and provide return on investment to stockholders. On the other hand, the benefits of lower prices for imported goods and services are of value only if consumers have the jobs and the means to purchase them. The lack of a total picture results in halves being passed off as wholes. Americans are asked in surveys whether they have any objections to their loan applications being processed abroad if it results in lower passed-on administrative costs. But they are not asked whether they have any objections to such savings being accomplished by Americans losing their jobs. Clearly, the debate needs to be reframed along both national and international lines; and just as companies lack the experience and personnel to conduct global business, the United States lacks a comprehensive policy for engaging this double issue.

What is at stake in the United States is the future of the middle class. Already hard pressed, most middle-class families in order to survive and preserve their standard of living have had to become two-income households. Other professionals partially have decided not to have children at all and avoid those heavy expenses. For the first time the birth rate of white-collar worker has fallen below the replacement rate. Indeed, they are now a new demographic category—DINC—double income no children.

To come full circle to where we started with insularity, the political economics of globalism may turn out to be a further obstacle or source of hesitation and timidity. How the conflict between free trade and job (not goods) protectionism will finally sort themselves out is not clear.

The pressure cooker of globality will force the development of new models of internationalism. In the process, the European Union may serve as a future model for an increasingly interconnected and inoperable one world that is economically boundaryless. But if that is to happen soon and intelligently, we need more leaders and managers embarked on a steep global learning curve and above all more chief globalization officers.

In summary, then, globality is emerging as a mixed bag. It nevertheless will go on because it exhibits the classic reinforcement of push-pull. It will be pushed by American corporations to maintain competitive advantage. It will be lured by foreign professionals anxious finally to enjoy a piece of the American pie. But the politics of such economics will engender more heat than light and the enlightenment and knowledge that is needed is in short supply. Given such urgencies, creating the position of GEO (Global Executive Officer) is looking better and better.

15

COMMUNICATION: SELF-DIALOGUE AND TRAINING DECISION MAKERS

In the film *Cast Away*, the character played by Tom Hanks finds a volleyball among the debris washed ashore on a deserted island. It looks like a face. He decides to call it Wilson after the manufacturer's name on the ball and proceeds to have regular conversations with Wilson. Clearly, that arrangement saves his sanity. In fact, when he is on his precarious raft trying to find land or a ship, the ball is swept overboard. Hanks jeopardizes his life swimming after it. But it drifts away, and is gone forever. Wilson is lost, but the castaway is saved.

Clearly, Wilson functioned as a way for Hanks to maintain human contact and conversation. We know it was an active dialogue because Wilson's answers appear in the responses of Hanks. In other words, Hanks not only preserved Wilson's half of the exchange, but also Wilson's evolving character—his difference, disagreements, and dissension—supported the relationship. The exchange was thus enervating. It did not just offer companionship—it offered the relationship of opposition. In fact, William Blake rightly maintained that "Friendship is Opposition." It was an authentic voice because it did not obediently mirror one's own. Through that dialectic, it helped Hanks not only to communicate but also to make crucial decisions.

Can this personalized version of dialogue serve as a narrative metaphor for business and professional exchange? How familiar and beneficial is such dialogue, especially to the process of those charged with communicating and making critical decisions? The linkage with communication is immediately apparent.

Dialogue, internal or external, not only mimics the communication process itself, it also underscores the give and take of making decisions. In fact, one can argue there are minimally two dialogues: the one that shapes the decision, the other that determines the communication of that decision to others. Indeed, to be totally comprehensive, one can include another dialogue, namely, how to implement the decision.

We all know professionals who talk their way through their work. Sometimes it is internal, other times overt. In a number of cases, it also may take place in front of a client or colleague. "Let me see, you want to get this done, fast. Let me try this first; and if that does not work I have a few other aces up my sleeve."

If the customer is smart, he will sit quietly and listen to the problem-solving process make its clever and circuitous way to a solution. The role of the listener is passive. He only has to pose the problem. He may have to answer a few questions along the way to refine and focus the problem, but that's all. He sits back and follows the dialogue, often finding it fascinating as he learns about the way this particular problem solver thinks and solves problems. Although the solution obviously is the bottom line, observing the workings of a mind in a self-relationship process is equally absorbing and revealing.

Self-dialogue does not require another. Many people have conversations with their pets; some with favored inanimate objects or paintings or sculpture that we may also touch. Some talk back to the radio or TV. If viewers are really angry or annoyed they express themselves by clicking it off or switching to another channel, usually accompanied by a few well-chosen exclamations. Others, contemplating but not yet deciding on a course of action, may initiate a dialogue in their heads and call in the warring opposites, one always stressing the downside, the other the upside—two different Wilsons, as it were.

The dialogue of self-relationship becomes a balancing act until enough accumulates to make a decision or to postpone it for another dialogue. Many CEOs and senior managers pay handsomely for this kind of dialogue in the form of executive coaches or trusted advisors. Although it appears there is considerable value to the exchange, it is seldom acknowledged officially as a way of knowing. As a result, it is seldom taught, inculcated, and above all designed as a managerial tool. The structuring of dialectic self-relationships thus may improve problem solving, communication, decision making, and even strategic planning.

Structuring a dialectic self-relationship minimally involves five process steps: scanning, selecting, formulating, trying out, and deciding. Here are the major stages visually displayed:

Stages	Events/Behaviors	Outcomes
1. Scanning	Self-Inventory	External/ Internal Goals Balancing
2. Selecting	Cast of Characters/Voices	360-Degree Thesis/Antithesis Inclusiveness
3. Formulating	Scene and Sequence	Reality Check
4. Trying Out	Evaluation	Revision
5. Deciding	Circular Conclusions	Priority of Alternatives

1. Scanning

   This first step is crucial. It involves an internal and an external inventory. For the dialogue and self-relationship to be effective, there must be self-candor. Thus, it is necessary to identify one's blind spots and the involvement of ego. True self-image, with all its blemishes and warts, must emerge if the dialogue is to stand a chance of being full and challenging. A closed mind or defensive attitude will preclude flow and change. In short, receptivity has to be firmly established. That is balanced externally and objectively by the outcomes that are expected or the decision that has to be made. The bridge between the two worlds of dialogue and action prepares for and sustains the traffic across it.

2. Selecting

   The screening process of preparing the objects of the dialogue, psyche, and objectives now sets up the selection of participants. A cast of characters has to be assembled. The first choice is to always ensure a dialectic—minimally an advocate for one thesis, another for the antithesis. Others are selected to amplify the participants to create a miniature reality. For example, if certain managers and/or their divisions will be affected by the decision and how well it is communicated to them, a communications representative voice must be included.

If the central character has not had the best of experiences dealing with these other voices, he has to build into the process different versions of himself. He has to acquire an understudy who is enough like him for continuity but functions at another angle or frequency to test whether that alters the outcome of both the dialogue and the decision.

3. Formulating

It's time for an initial mock-up. For some it may take a visual form. Revealingly, the main participant may position himself in the middle. The dialogue may then take place all around him. Or he may distance itself from the entire exchange and lurk on the periphery. Whatever his location, the cast of characters is assembled and stages of discussion identified and sequenced.

A preliminary run-though is conducted to determine whether the cast of characters should be changed, added to, or subtracted from and also at what point they should enter the fray. Anyone who plays chess and has to contemplate multiple moves at any time or routinely is involved in strategic planning, that is, estimating first, second, and third orders of impact, understands and feels comfortable with such juggling. Once the number and kind of participants and the sequence are chosen, the dialogue is formally locked in and ready to proceed.

4. Trying Out

Like a play taken out of town for a tryout, all is set in motion in a limited way. Because the entire process is constantly circular, the focus here is evaluative. What has been left out? Is the major participant open enough or do we have to call in his understudy? Are the major participants representative of the whole? Have we left a key player out? Have the outcomes been stated directly and unequivocally? Do the representatives from other divisions properly embody or miniaturize the dynamics? Once revisions have been made according to a reality check, all is ready for the exchange to take place.

5. Deciding (Communicating and Implementing)

Whether or not a visual of the major players and their sequence has been made, it is probably helpful here not just to hear the voices, but to write down their talk in the form of a script. The dynamic of the exchange that way can be reviewed. Such a recorded scenario also compels the major participant to get inside other characters and above all to express points of view other than his or her own. For the process to work its communicative magic, the voices all must be authentic.

The last task, before the curtain drops, is to record the solutions offered and the decisions made. If more than one, they need to be attributed to the different advocates and then prioritized. But they must all be saved for they represent alternative solutions and decisions that still may be called upon or used as arguments to buttress the one selected over all. In addition, before one discards the entire process, like scaffolding after a building is complete, there may need to be one more use and distillation.

The decision or solution must be rendered as three decisions: the decision to do something, the decision as to how it will be communicated, and the decision on how it will be implemented. The dialogue must engage all three dimensions. Moreover, just as the decision-making process involved alternative options, so the same process must now be extended to accommodate the best ways to communicate and implement the decision.

Thus, the dialectic process is circular and bestows its configuration on the decision itself as well as its communication and implementation. A set of internal parts produces an external whole, and does so in real time and real place, and with the potential for growth on the part of all major participants. Each is shaped and extended by all the others.

Dialogue also creates a check-and-balance system. If the decision made poses major problems of communication and/or of implementation, it must go back to the drawing board. The solution may be a problem. The gods of communication and implementation must be satisfied. The decision fails its future tests. The dialogue must go back to square one. A new decision or solution must be found that has to live and function in all the key dimensions of the real world and its cast of characters. Otherwise, it will be stillborn or worse, create problems bigger, tougher, and less repairable than the one that spawned the process in the first place.

It is this last gain that is particularly noteworthy and perhaps un-expected. The entire process seeks to bring about not only more effective decisions and solutions, but also more effective leaders and managers. The new manager, vivified, stretched, and extended by the dialectic of dialogue, will be more inclusive, more balanced, more open, more diverse, and more multiple. In the final analysis the process is a form of professional development that is more ho-listic and dynamic than the traditional tunnel-vision workshops on communication and decision-making skills.

We need to talk our way through to success. Listening and hear-ing voices may lead some to conclude that we are crazy, but crazy like a fox or a Plato.

TRAINING DECISION MAKERS

Most communications training is after the fact. Once decisions have been made, new polices formulated, acquisitions and mergers agreed upon—then communications specialists are called in to wordsmith the announcements. Communications is never involved or invited to play a direct and formative role in any of these processes, only in their final formulations.

But often bad decisions are made, policies are inept, mergers ques-tionable. When that happens, the temptation is to return to the same process that created the problem in the first place, try to be more dili-gent next time, and expect a different outcome. But the problem may be endemic. It may involve the procedure itself or the range of participants or a conflictive interaction of both. Converging process and personnel, it can be argued that communications might be a valued new partner to bridge the two. But for that to happen, companies and trainers have to take the initiative and endow communications with more power as a contributing partner in critical business processes. For example, if chief learning officers (CLOs) trained decision makers as to the muscular and proactive contributions communications can offer there might be fewer lapses and failures. And if a rationale is needed to describe the benefits communications can deliver to decision making, the following discus-sion may serve.

Communications minimally can bring three dimensions to current decision making when invited as partner to the process at the outset. The first is to put the decision arrived at on pause in order to determine its "communicality." The second tests the capacity of various and often conflicting information sources to be sufficiently broad based, reconcilable, and integrated to elicit collective support (Bennett, 1999; Daneke, 1999). The third focuses on decision making as a values process in which a series of smaller values decisions punctuate and stir the final summative decision (Ullman, 2001).

1. Proactive Role of Communications

In this instance, communication functions as a reality check. Managers can be taught the basics of anticipatory or proactive perceptions. How will this decision be perceived and received by a representative array of employees, customers, stakeholders, and shareholders? Is its "communicality" rating high or low? What are some of the ways it can be misunderstood, even distorted? To what extent is the decision a match or mismatch with the culture? Is it a fit with mission and expectations? Is it operationally savvy or is it a square peg being fitted into a round hole? Ultimately, will this decision affirm its makers or give the impression that the emperor has no clothes?

The responses to such questions of communications may be disturbing enough to put the decision on hold. Risk analysis thus becomes perceptions analysis. Communications thus function as an advance guard, an anticipatory manager, and measurer of decision impact. Typically, decision makers are too embedded and absorbed in the process to undertake 360-degree evaluation. They may be myopic and short term. But communications stands between the decision and those affected by it. Its allegiance is to those directly and indirectly impacted and compels awareness of both immediate and long-term consequences. Managers are trained to see both sides of the street. Communications simulate the voices of acceptance, rejection, or ambiguity. That feedback alone is sufficient to affirm or challenge the decision. In the latter instance it warns of failure or miscalculation. And its message then is clear: The decision in its present form and direction needs to be changed. And with that powerful corrective, communications establishes its value as a special and perhaps equal partner in the decision-making process. In short, reconfigured and refocused through training, the decision process becomes a double process: the decision to do something and the decision to communicate that something.

2. Integrative Function of Communications

Communications also have the capacity to be a broker of information input into the decision process. Managers can be given workshops on data sources as alternate communication paths. The goal is always to identify the broadest base possible on the one hand, and the durability and longevity of the life cycle of the data on the other hand. To accomplish and converge that double focus, communications have to champion the integration of information over the long term. That future dimension tests not only the durability of the product or service but of its supporting information.

In the process, managers can appreciate the traditional persuasive power of communications as it seeks to coach various owners of information to share and to integrate sources and outcomes. Those putting forth trends, market segments, and customer-buying profiles tend to be lone rangers riding their own hobby horses and pushing to be positioned as the number one source. Because communications alone embodies audience, it imparts the force of the collective to the decision-making process. It uniquely can serve as the gatekeeper and guardian of integrated data. If as noted earlier communications can serve to give voice to those affected by decisions, here communications have to orchestrate a series of data soloists into a coordinated chorale. This is particularly critical because the common lament is that there is never enough data for decision makers. What communications bring to that perennial gap is at least the optimization of available information.

3. Communications as Values Advocate

The competition of data is compounded by the competition of values. Teams bring forth value-laden recommendations that even cross-functional teams, constituted as they are as a miniature of the whole, cannot harmonize. Assumed or implicit values driving data or recommendations are like the proverbial tip of the iceberg; the full extent is buried underneath. The missing role of arbiter can be legitimately assumed by managers using communications, in at least two points in the process, beginning and end.

Communications becomes an advocate of value trees analysis (Spivey, Munson, and Spoon, 2002). Each team providing decision input has to make explicit the values driving its recommendations and, even more important, what trade-offs and alternatives can be offered to optimize broader corporate goals and mission value. Such vertical alignment can minimize unproductive conflicts. Moreover, alternatives offered can be used to negotiate upward final consensus.

But if the values process has been less than honest or total, communications may be called on to fill the values gaps. In particular, communications can stand at the receiving end and solicit values criteria for decision making. Inevitably ranking or prioritizing will be required. Because communications is not directly involved nor does it favor any one recommendation over another, and because in effect its only allegiance is to optimizing the decision-making process, it can preside with equanimity. It enjoys the high road of the big picture, sometimes matching or even exceeding the range of senior staff, and thus when learned grants all managers executive perspective.

Hopefully at this point companies recognizing the value of communications training not only schedule such training, but also make it doubly inclusive. On the one hand, middle- and especially upper-level managers have to be persuaded to welcome communications into the decision-making process as a critical partner and ally at all levels. Minimally, in that capacity it can serve as an early warning system, practice damage control, help to establish a more integrated base for decision making, and advocate an open values process so that decisions are in fact multiply value-laden in alignment with company goals. On the other hand, communications professionals have to prepare themselves for the challenge of being differently and more comprehensively perceived and used. In particular, they have to learn to envision themselves as possessing unique skills and roles not provided by any other specialization. In other words, for the training to be effective the trainers have to go outside the box and build into the workshops setting up both sets of participants for optimum interactive interfacing.

Communications is the supreme middleman. It presides over the cracks between which data falls. It bridges and aligns the values gaps between competing team recommendations so that the final decision can be inclusive, diverse, transparent, and balanced. Above all, communications experts must directly and knowledgeably enter the management and operations fray. If they are to be brokers and advocates of vision and mission, and to bring to the decision-making and operations process what is currently missing and what is uniquely theirs to provide, they must in fact act and perform like learning leaders. Indeed, communications so redefined may ultimately turn out be the best ally and extension of CEOs and senior staff. Because communication takes place not only at the top but also at every decision point across the board, it miniaturizes and diffuses its connecting power and anticipatory function throughout the entire company at every level of decision making and information gathering. Communications properly relearned, refocused, and championed can diffuse throughout an organization its contribution of optimization, perhaps in itself the supreme mission of trainers.

REFERENCES

Bennett, P. "Governing Environmental Risk." *Progress in Human Geography* 23, no. 2 (1999), 151–159.

Buchen, I. "Employee Mission Statement." *Performance Improvement* 40, no. 6 (July 2001), 40–43.

Daneke, G. *Systemic choices*. Ann Arbor: University of Michigan Press 1999.

Kamikov, N. "Editorial: The CLO's Emergence." *CLO* (September 2002).

Prahalad, C. K. "Managing Discontinuities." *Research-Technology Management* 41, no. 3 (1998), 14–22.

Spivey, W. A., Munson, J. M., and Spoon, D. R. "A Generic Value Tree." *International Journal of Technology Management* 24, nos. 2/3 (2002), 219–235.

Ullman, D. G. "Robust Decision Making." *Journal of Engineering Design* 12, no. 1 (2001), 3–13.

16

EDUCATIONAL, BUSINESS, AND COMPANY CONVERSATIONAL COMMUNITIES

In general in education, the bridges between instruction, administration, and evaluation are occasional, unilateral, or unused. Teachers teach, administrators administer. Each views his or her task as indispensable in its own right as well to the other. But the linkages between the two are often not articulated. They travel in parallel lines that never seem to meet. Even if there is some alignment on the outcomes of evaluation, their perspectives are totally different. The teacher sees a student with a name, a personality, a family, a story, whereas the principal examines columns of performance data. Such separative and myopic foci preclude much. There is little or no coherent environment or culture all share. Although the rallying cry is for a collective effort to increase student performance and accountability, it usually falls on the individual not the group ears of teachers. When the results are disappointing and uneven, the determination to push harder still acts on the assumption that a unifying culture exists. And when it does not work, again, each side blames the other. The search for scapegoats precludes introspection.

The culture of each school is not a given. It is not predetermined or cast in stone. Teams are not born; they are made. The task of principals, often unacknowledged or unacted on, is to shape an interactive, coherent, and collaborative environment. It should be a busy, friendly, caring, and stimulating place to work. It should produce interesting tales, not a litany of complaints later at dinner. It also should be on balance a source of satisfaction, with the good stuff outweighing the bad. Above all, it should not be dreaded as a place to go to every morning.

How is that to be accomplished? The first thing workers frequently answer is, "Get rid of the bosses!" Although lamentable, that underscores, negatively to be sure, the centrality of leaders and their effect on employee attitudes and motivation. Pressed further as to what makes bad bosses bad, the rapid response is, "They don't listen. They are know-it-alls." So it turns out, leaders should not be bosses. Ordering people around and not listening to them is not what leaders should be doing.

Communication and culture always have to be paired. Each is a creative and reinforcing means to the other. A group that does not talk and listen to each other, seriously, frequently, and equally, is disconnected and fragmented. The infallible sign of a coherent culture is that it is held together by communication. The glue is conversation. The principal, in short, is responsible for the conversations that take place or do not in his school.

The first step is to rid himself of all claims to ownership. It is not his but our school; not his teachers and students but the school's. It does not belong to anyone because it is held in common. Top-down possessiveness jeopardizes genuine exchange between equals and partners. The next step is to accept the task of building culture by stirring conversations. But goals for talk are needed. A significant one would be to integrate instruction, administration, and evaluation—to create coherence by talking coherence. Happily, recent efforts of organization building and culture change using strategic conversations can be tapped (van der Heijden, 1996). Introduced and nurtured by the principal, such conversations require no outside or additional materials, workshops, or costs. But to take hold and to bridge all involved, the strategic exchanges have to involve the following three directions.

1. Horizontal
    Distributed leadership (Spillane, et al., 2002) connects instructional practice with teacher and student common learning, on the one hand, and bridges instruction, administration, and evaluation

through a common empowering process, on the other. The key focus question is: How can we be more effective, collectively?

2. Vertical

The vertical direction involves alignment of instructional goals with schoolwide and districtwide objectives so that top down and bottom up are not opposed or contrary to but exist in synch with each other. Differences and even disagreements are not ruled out but are contained within the mission of alignment that precludes mutiny or apathy. The key focus question is: How can we work together to achieve common goals and in the process align the micro and the macro?

3. Circular

Structured mutuality requires a match between how the organization works or does not and how it provides, stirs, and enhances learning (including the self-learning of administrators, teachers, and staff). The critical focus is on environment and how it supports or deflects from achieving shared horizontal and vertical purpose (Elmore, 2002). Such so-called externals are thus made part of the design and action. The key focus question is: How and why is our work as educators organized and structured the way it is, how does it relate to student learning, and is both supportive of collective and common effort and purpose?

To set all this in motion requires a dialectic common to all three agenda areas. As noted, an emerging and significant area of research has been that structured interviewing, strategic questioning, and scenario building nicely summed up and applied by Ratcliffe (2002). It is both qualitative and quantitative, and often incremental. It has been applied to many and different complex problems and yielded impressive scenarios of cities and industries. All applications, however, are governed by the same model as developed by the seminal work of van der Heijden (1996).

THE MODEL

Strategic conversation defines organizational design and flow into three components: (a) All organizations are communities, (b) they are sustained by interactions and exchanges, and (c) the principal mode of interaction is conversation. When the conversations are genuinely strategic, a community of common purpose can emerge.

Strategic conversations are multivalued and functional. They are learning loops, perceptions, concepts, and actions. They are invariably dynamic and as such interactive and always interconnected. They structure the interpersonal relationship of working together.

Focused and purposeful strategic actions growing out of conversations become the basis for developing a coherent action plan. Whether remedial or futuristic or both, the plan is designed to intervene in the evolution of the organization. One of the permanent goals of all such plans is to optimize strategic conversations by having them extend leadership sharing at all levels.

The model is attractive because it is simple, generic, and above all participatory. It avoids the mechanical architecture of organizational charts or the engineering clutter of functionalism. Its scale is familiar and available. Thus, a school is a community where conversations take place. If it is a genuine community, the conversations strategically are sustaining and evolving. If it is an aspiring and goal-focused community, its environment always features intervention and accommodates planning. If it is a future-oriented community, its curricula are always longitudinal and anticipatory. If it is democratically driven, then both teachers and students experience leadership and evaluation sharing.

Although applications of the model in the literature are frequently ambitious and the methodologies elaborate (Ringland, 1998), a simpler, scaled-down version may be extracted that can serve as a basis for introducing and stirring strategic educational dialogue. With some adjustments, such structured exchanges can become part of a principal's tool kit. Although various approaches and entry points are available, one process that enjoys the benefits of extensive practice on the one hand (Silverman, 1997) and is particularly amenable to the role of the principal as Plato on the other hand involves five stages.

1. Meetings

    The principal announces that every meeting of teachers and other staff from now on will include a professional development piece. It will emulate the best of workshop environments in that participatory exchange will be the dominant mode. The focus of such platonic dialogue is reflection. The aim is to encourage a self-conscious awareness of work environments and an understanding of how they support or don't support teaching and learning.

The principal might begin by saying: "I would like to make part of our regular meetings a more reflective series of conversations in which we collectively think and share our views about our work environment and the way it operates and is organized. In fact, I thought we might start with this meeting—in fact, meetings in general—committee meetings, lesson plan meetings, rubric meetings, etc.—and list what is good and not so good about them. This is a genuine no-holds-barred exchange. There are no sacred cows. But all I ask is that the context of effective teaching and student performance guide all exchanges. Let us divide up into three groups of about five each. You know the drill: Select a spokesperson who shall record and present both general observations and any recommendations for change. I think we have enough time to put them all in priority order."

2. Feedback

The principal compiles, prints up, and distributes a composite list of observations and recommendations from the first discussion. In addition to praising the interesting results and noting some exchanges that were less than productive, he also may wish to offer some general remarks about the nature of strategic conversations along the lines of a to-do and not-to-do list (Ratcliffe, 2002): stay focused, keep it simple, remain interactive, pass on ownership, seek consensus, eschew despair and cynicism, and enjoy each other.

Following that, the principal puts together a distributed leadership implementation team to process recommendations for change. He may request that the group not decide by majority rule but by consensus.

3. The Mission

Building on the base of initial feedback about meetings, the principal adds other microareas so as to build confidence and to help internalize the process of self-reflection. They may involve modes of current evaluation, mentoring new teachers, resource allocation, state-mandated testing, parental involvement, and so on.

Once a significant base of success has been achieved, the principal needs to up the ante by introducing the most comprehensive context within which future exchanges will take place. That inevitably involves the mission and vision of the school district.

Even if an official one exists, it can still be reviewed, and supplements can always be added, especially to express the individuality of each school within a district. Indeed, to the standard list of teacher effectiveness, student performance, evaluation accountability, parental involvement, and community relations can be added strategic self-reflection and scrutiny. Above all, the review of mission led by the principal should employ as a guiding overlay the three structural dimensions of the horizontal, the vertical, and the circular noted earlier.

4. The Retreat

Once a critical mass of strategic questioning and recommendations has been centered on the mission and once the mission itself has become an affirmed strategic document, then there is a need to put it all together. That cannot be accomplished at a single meeting but minimally requires a day or better still a two-day retreat, and probably not one but two such retreats spaced at least a few months apart.

The goal of the retreat is to put together the micro and the macro and position the findings of the various distributed teams within the context of the mission, now reviewed and perhaps supplemented. As discussion moves toward action, strategic questioning converts to scenario planning. The outcome of the retreat is the creation of a series of alternative scenarios for how and why the school should organize or reorganize itself, what new questions need to be asked, and what new forms or processes need to be put in place.

5. Reality Check

The scenarios are sequenced into stages according to a timetable. Following the retreat, the recommended changes are not implemented wholesale but phased in experimentally. All understand that this is on a trial basis. Gradually introduced, tried, and evaluated, the distributed leadership teams are now converted to shadowing and monitoring implementation teams. The findings are reported regularly to the principal who is responsible for keeping a cumulative running record. He issues a weekly score card and progress report.

He also may opt to share results on a timely basis with a representative parents group, community leaders, union reps, superintendent, school board members, and the like. But if shared with external groups the principal has to prepare a detailed description of the process from beginning to end. Once sufficient time has been allowed for implementation to do its work of reality checking, then the second retreat is scheduled to adjust and finalize the agreed-upon future school.

Will it work? Positive results abide in the literature of strategic conversations (Ratcliffe, 2002). Besides, in a sense it cannot fail. The only issue is to what extent, how inclusive, how spirited and stirring the dialogue will be. Even a minimal effort will encourage teachers and staff to be increasingly self-conscious about the work they do and the environment in which they do it.

The research conclusively proves that when professionals own their environments and can prioritize their work so that it is aligned with organizational goals, the gains in productivity and morale are significant (Buchen, 2001). Equally as important are the role changes that strategic questioning and scenario planning can bring about.

1. The Principal

He is restored to his comprehensive role of leadership. He does not have to choose between being an instructional leader, professional development advocate, accountability champion, and so on. All can be folded in and subsumed as the principal once more becomes the 360-degree leader of the micro-macro whole. He may or may not wish to evoke the model of the philosopher king but he can certainly and legitimately appear as the advocate for platonic dialogue.

To achieve the integration of administration, instruction, and evaluation is no small feat. Besides, strategic conversations also can carry the same productive focus for individual teacher evaluations.

2. Teachers

Invited to reflect on and scrutinize not only how they teach but also how environments both small and large, intimate and external, affect, shape, and perhaps blunt their well-intentioned efforts, teachers are encouraged to apply learning to structure and structure to learning; and in the process to discover the interfaces that work and those that do not. Encouraged subsequently through distributed leadership to spread those insights over various instructional and evaluative areas across the board as well as up and down, teachers further discover the extent to which horizontal and vertical flows intersect, and what linkages and bridges may be needed to produce the circular formation of common purpose.

3. Students

Whether invited or not to be part of the reflective process, students are the ultimate beneficiaries. Learning becomes more thoughtful and involving. Teachers appear to be all of a piece. Why, what, and how they teach now is matched by environments that are a better reflection of policy, place, and process. Conversations between teachers of the same subject and/or grade level result in a series of more supportive, interventionist, and gradual use of rubric development. The expectations of success become a self-fulfilling prophecy,

4. Mission

Here the benefits include all constituencies. The review, general approval, and creation of supplements provide a center of affirmation for the entire educational community. It steadies the focus, keeps developments on track, and above all speaks the common voice of shared purpose. In fact, it would not be an exaggeration to claim that the most important task of the principal is precisely this search for commonality. His infallible guide is Plato who models the power of strategic conversations to generate shared purpose and coherent cultures.

The business version of structuring strategic conversations centers on work design and performance. An interesting and flexible new methodology is emerging, simply called "Conversation Scenarios" (van der Heijden, 1996), which involves structuring the flow and focus of organizational communications. Although it has many applications, it may be of special interest to human resources professionals in general and useful for performance evaluation in particular.

Conversation scenarios essentially consists of three components: a highly developed and rigorous process of comprehensive interviews on a particular issue or problem between involved parties, often cross-divisional; the recasting of the interview findings into a series of focused strategic solutions but sustained again by conversations; and finally, the conversion of alternative solutions into a series of planning or forecasting scenarios tested and poised for implementation (Douglas, 1985; Ringland, 1998).

The emphasis throughout on constant conversation is absolute. It totally dominates the three phases: tapping the power of dialogue initially to explore and to define issues (stage one); converting generated solutions into strategic alternatives (stage two); and finally developing implementation plans in the form of scenarios (stage three). To be sure, the process on the surface appears to be just another version of analysis, problem solving, and implementation. But the methodology derives its power and its multiple applications from three differences. First, van der Heijden's investing conversational interviews with defining problem-solving capacity; second, requiring planning to remain conversational through the use of scenarios; and third, granting the organization a participating voice. What Conversation Scenarios thus seeks to avoid is the dominance of mechanical and functional analysis on the one hand, and the structural distancing and removal of organizational involvement on the other.

Unusually, the organization occupies center stage. It is defined as not just a place but a persona. It has an identity. Most important it has a voice. It has something to say and to contribute to the various stages of conversations. In fact, if the process did not include the conversational input of the organization, the final result might minimally be flawed or optimally not enriched.

Significantly, the methodology appears to be partial to futures application. It thus has been used for projecting the future of the tourism industry, identifying long-term real estate trends, and even predicting the future of the city of Dublin, Ireland (Ratcliffe, 2002). Employing both qualitative and quantitative sources, it also has been employed by senior managers to help with future task identification, decision focus, mission clarification and congruence, and so on (Converse and Schuman, 1974). But whether the applications are macro or micro, the fundamental model is as presented by its seminal developer, van der Heijden (1996), who describes himself as a humanistic sociologist. The model essentially rests on his three major definitions, or in some cases redefinitions or challenges that, although they have been explored in a previous chapter can be briefly restated: (a) An organization is a community. Its conversations in fact constitute the community (Lambert, 2002). (b) Strategic conversations are multifaceted. A highly reflective and self-examining culture will involve constant revision, review, and correction. New contexts may be sought, assumptions challenged. Above all, how work is organized is a recurrent and constant issue (Spillane, Halverson, and Diamond, 2002). (c) Scenarios are strategic conversations cast into planning modes. Above all, the conversations are designed to intervene and alter the evolution of the organization (Elmore, 2002).

Although its value as a model and methodology has been its multiple and comprehensive adaptability to many sectors and organizations of various size, no application to improving work flow and design appears in the literature. Its immediate value for performance technologists is that it promises and even compels role change. It requires managers to become active listeners and questioners. It requires them to be not just information disseminators, but information generators.

Stirring and sustaining work conversations become a critical requirement of a manager's job description. What makes such exchanges strategic is that they are goal driven. It thus requires conversational exchanges between individual and company goals, between employee and company mission statements (Buchen, 2001). The entire process of work problem definition and solution is collaborative; it evolves and is guided by inquiry and collective exchange. Only then can problem solving really begin; and even then it is recast in the form of planning scenarios.

Managers can use the data of conversation to also assess work environments. By listening strategically, they can determine the degree to which their own unit is a communicating or a separatist community; whether information flow and exchange are clear or muffled; and whether work flow is correspondingly focused or dissipated. Such overlays can be put upon other divisions and aggregated upward. The net result would be a series of interfaces between work and worker, between work design and work productivity that sum up and approximate the companywide whole.

Then, too, learning by listening can provide a valuable diagnostic set of thesis questions. What is the correlation between work environments that lack coherence and conversation as a community and their capacity to achieve stretch goals? More tightly focused, how does the communications and conversational relationships between supervisors and employees impact performance improvement?

Happily, two very different organizations provided the occasion for posing both questions. Although productivity had improved through the standard means of incentives and training, both companies were at a standstill. Contemplating the limits of productivity on the one hand with the increasing demands of competition to go further on the other, senior management was receptive to new approaches to performance improvement. But although the aforementioned questions resonated and brought them closer to the issues they sought to address, they asked that they be more specific. The response was to employ strategic conversations directed toward defining three interfaces:

1. The Work Interface
   Developing a more reflective and self-conscious understanding of each employee's job and performance expectations.
2. The Design Interface
   Perceiving the relationships between work environment and job performance and quality.
3. The Interpersonal and Organizational Interface
   Identifying the nature of the collaborative community within which work is accomplished or not.

The use of interfaces as the foci of strategic conversations carried the day. The first step was the design and implementation of workshops for supervisors. The sequence and the content of the three interfacing conversations were explored and then applied with managers taking turns at role playing of employees.

THE WORK INTERFACE

What was stressed and what the managers had difficulty accepting was that the initial conversation between managers and employees was not to be evaluative. The conversation was to be primarily exploratory. Moreover, it was not to be dominated by the supervisor. The focus, in fact, was on the employee's view and description of his or her job description and the job parts. To be sure the manager was quick to preface the assignment by stating that although no one knows a job as well as the one who does it, it is critical to keep in mind company goals. Jobs do not exist in the abstract in and for themselves but contribute to overall organizational objectives. The manager thus is able not only to certify the employee's expertise, but also to redirect it toward strategic ends.

Because the aim of strategic conversations is to get at root causes on the one hand, and to discourage the routine mechanical response of reciting job descriptions on the other hand, the manager requests that the conversation be reflective. To encourage a more self-conscious attitude toward job definition, the manager suggests that the employee verbalize and talk out loud the kind of thinking that occurs while doing the various parts of the job, confessing that after a while we often do not consciously think about what we are doing, which often sadly results in mechanical rather than thoughtful performance. The manager's prompts go through three stages.

The manager first gives examples based on his or her own work. For example, he or she may describe what kind of thinking and rethinking is involved when he or she has to put together a production schedule or order parts from competing vendors and stay within budget. The manager may even refer to personnel who in the process of handling customer complaints frequently talk out loud while they problem solve. Another tack the manager may suggest is describing the job to someone who is new to the division.

To stir further such internal strategic conversations, the manager then may start the process off by asking some basic questions: What concerns you when you start doing your job? What do you think about? Look out for? Worry about? How much and how often do you look ahead to the next step or where the work goes after it leaves you?

THE DESIGN INTERFACE

The mental responses to the job process lead to the next series of questions: Do you think the way you think about your job is the way other people doing the same job think about it? Let's identify some different types of workers and ambitions and their sense of standards or values. How do you think they might approach the job? What would be the range of attitude and thinking—from the best to the worst?

Finally, the key question: Given all that you have said to date, what would you change in the way the job is done? If you could design or redesign your own job and the work environment, what would you change and for what reasons? How do you think that new way of working would affect your fellow workers in the division and those on your team? If negative, how would you suggest that be managed?

The employee now is asked to develop a more self-critical attitude toward his or her work. The employee minimally refreshes his or her understanding and optimally redefines his or her job. In both cases, the gain in self-consciousness and self-confidence is affirmative. The net result is a more involved, more knowledgeable employee. The worker-job interface is defined. The conversations on the work environment focus invite speculation on the way the work is organized and how it supports or undermines productivity and quality. The multiple perspectives generated by many divisional employees may converge into a consensus of recommended changes. The work design interface is both individually and collectively described.

THE INTERPERSONAL INTERFACE

In the process, the employee also is encouraged to be a worker who explores the collaborative relationships or lack thereof of fellow workers. That includes the redefinition of job satisfaction as give and take. The interpersonal interface now involving many contributing voices is better understood.

As the model of strategic conversations takes hold and is internalized, each unit or division is now perceived not as a separate series of jobs but as an interactive community sustained by thoughtful and self-conscious reflective conversations. That dialogue in turn serves to define in optimal form the three key interfaces of individual, collective, and organizational work design and flow. The individual evaluation process is also now more collaborative. It involves the more contributive and accountable role of the employee matched by a manager more receptive to employee self-definition.

Ideally, a number of the recommended changes of different ways of designing jobs and work environments will increase productivity, improve quality, and stir greater team collaboration.

Although there are various ways to judge the value of a new approach, an unexpected but not unwelcome gain is when the challenge is double: for employees and their managers. They both have to exercise greater self-reflection. They have to suspend judgment in order to listen and learn. A blank slate is assumed. Everything and everyone is at square one. Decision and direction cannot be preset but must be forthcoming, emerging, and evolving, a work in progress. Problem defining and solving must be based on and informed by collective and participatory inquiry and dialogue. Divisional leadership will not be singular but multiple, not unilateral but shared.

In the process, managers may find their own job descriptions redefined and even transformed. They may emerge as community-centered managers now in charge of sustaining strategic conversations, interfaces, and planning. Indeed, that change may not only turn out to be the most important contributory piece of the entire work redesign process, but also redefine the organization happily as a place where employees constantly use talk as the medium of problem solving, strategic planning, and performance improvement. If the walls could talk, what would they say? It may be possible now to know even that as long as organizations are provided with a voice.

When companies are perceived as and become conversational communities, what usually follows is the governance of best practices. Reengineering often involves just such redefinition. Advanced and enhanced by a number of advocates and developments, one of its earliest champions was Charles Handy (1994) who argued that organizations needed to be viewed as essentially a series of political exchanges. To van der Heijden (1999), community is the indispensable base and vehicle for the application of a new methodology of structured interviews, strategic conversations, and scenario planning. For Renesch, the search for best companies inevitably involved discovering communities of best practices; for Champy and Pralahad (1999), best practice always involved being collectively future driven. Senge (1990) presided over the formation of the learning organization as knowledge-based communities. Human resources has become human capital collectives; mission statements affirmed knowledge management cultures.

But obviously these communities did not just happen or come into being by fiat. A mixture of enlightenment and desperation often precedes their emergence. Indeed, both the difference and the impact of community-based cultures become clearer when their range and focus are further spelled out in terms of all the enumerated obstacles that had to be overcome.

HANDY

The benefit of viewing business as a political community is that it places high value on checks and balances and on negotiation as the medium of exchange. But Handy also acknowledges that companies are viewed traditionally as commodities, not communities. They are owned by stockholders. Indeed, in order to hold top personnel responsible and accountable for dividends and profits, ownership essentially has dictated the structure of vertical control. If negotiation exists, it is usually unilateral and downward, not shared and two-directional. In short, ownership and control are not natural allies of community.

VAN DER HEIJDEN

Strategic conversations address mission and planning. But such conversations can happen only in a community committed to dialogue. But many organizations minimize conversation or encourage only standardized rituals of exchange. As a result, most conversations are not strategic, let alone two-way; and most companies do not empower employees to talk, and more important perhaps, supervisors to listen. Strategic conversations can only take place when companies train everyone to talk to each other and when such new conversations occur between equals.

RENESCH

Companies that last and are successful are constantly optimizing. They create an internal culture of best practices to realize the highest levels of productivity, quality, and profitability. But the enemy of optimization is the familiar argument of status quo: "If it ain't broke, don't fix it." Ironically, when inertia is overcome, the new breakthrough may become the new obstacle. That is why best practices have to be created as an on-going community to sustain the commitment to continuous improvement as the new operating norm.

SENGE

The vitality of a company is its capacity to learn constantly. The result is a community of knowledge managers who stir the pot of creativity and innovation. But Senge admitted that learning itself was not a magic bullet. Change did not automatically follow. Often the new learning was essentially incremental not archetypal. Talk changed but thought remained intact.

A common denominator of all the obstacles noted earlier is conversations and communications. That is not surprising since both community and communications share the same root of bringing people and process together. And yet often change agents are so possessed by their visions that they forge ahead without preparing the way for their reception and perception. In other words, a communication stage and strategy may be necessary preconditions.

Often it is assumed both are already in place, adaptable, or automatic; nothing separate or special is required. But a community of communication has to precede, facilitate, and finally undergird the formation of all other communities. Communications not only prepare the way for community, but also are absorbed into it and become its operating system of exchange. In other words, a communications threshold and base are always both anticipatory and anticipatory. To appreciate what communications add to the process of building community requires singling out its following value-added and different contributions. The following figure seeks to capture the four foci of the major advocates of communications:

Community Advocates Communication Contributions

1. Handy   Governance
2. Van der Heijden   Consensus
3. Renesch   Symbiosis
4. Senge   Unlearning

The argument, then, is that communications is a natural ally of community. It undergirds it. Talk is glue. It holds all together. In addition, tapped as the first wave or advanced guard, communications can help prepare the way for other and later communities to form and to take hold. Identifying and engaging obstacles and redirecting perspectives that are counterproductive or inimical to different kinds of communities is essentially a communications problem and opportunity. Taking each community noted earlier in turn, here are some communications strategies that engage the basic obstacles to their implementation.

1. The Political: Communication Antidotes to Ownership

    To achieve structural coherence requires a major shift of focus from organization to governance. Handy argues that the issue of how work is organized and gets done needs to be supplemented and ultimately replaced by how relationships are negotiated and determined by both supervisors and employees. Each checks and balances the other. Empowerment gives both vote and voice. Governance in fact has brought unions inside the gate and facilitated a more cooperative set of adversarial relationships through distributed leadership. Only when conversations flow and only when they are diffused throughout can community happen.

2. Dialogue: Consensus Conversations

    The value that van der Heijden places upon structured interviews, strategic conversations, and scenario planning is in turn contingent on two reinforcing communications conditions: inclusion and consensus. Both involve departing from past traditions and communications hierarchies.

    Traditionally, planning is the prerogative of experts and executives because they alone have the power—360-degree scope and the knowledge. Planning thus is essentially an exclusive rather than inclusive process. Communications between planners and implementers of the plan generally did not exist. But two things have happened.

First, the timetable for the rapid deployment of the plan was jeopardized. The emperor appeared in public without any clothes on. Quickly, the plan had to be returned to the drawing board. In this instance, strategic conversations did their corrective work but alas, after rather than before the fact.

Second, exclusion and majority vote increasingly appeared as versions of each other. The expediency of the rule of 51 percent is offset by the obscuration of minority views, which may turn out to be pivotal. Consensus is a communications process that resists bullying and the herd instinct. It pays special attention to the voices of, "Yes, but." Just as children do not have to be taught how to take but how to share, so strategic conversations are neither strategic nor conversational without being consensual. And that form of negotiated agreement between the haves and the have-nots requires a community of conversation before a community of planning can occur.

3. Symbiosis: Creating Best Practices Collaboratively

The medieval guild system ensured best practice. The four stages devoted to mastering it guaranteed fidelity; the governmental seal of approval ensured quality. And it worked. Indeed, it worked so well that it set the standard. But when change occurred, and when machines replaced hand crafting, best practice was constantly in a state of flux and evolving. Competition not royal monopoly ruled. Innovation not imitation was required. Even the productivity of new technology was not enough. Worker contribution became increasingly the key; and with that communications comes into the arena.

Best practice requires best process. They coexist symbiotically. Worker involvement is the key not only to standardizing the practice but also to continuously improving it. When supervisors and employees dialogue and when job evaluation becomes job improvement, recommendations for increasing productivity regularly emerge. In fact, what routinely has been called best practice might more accurately be designated best conversations; just as what have been designated communities of best practices might be renamed communities of communications.

4. Unlearning: The Learning of Unlearning

The link between learning and memory is tenacious. If the two are not engaged together, new learning may at best be an add-on that remains unintegrated or worst at odds with the past knowledge base. In either instance it is discomfiting. Professionals may be internally operating at ideological cross-purposes; externally the new and the old are not united holistically.

Before Senge's vision can happen, learning organizations first must become unlearning communities. The first conversation is always epistemological: What do we know and how do we know what we know? And finally, what don't we know? Assumptions analysis unearths organizational and individual hidden histories. Raising a priori assumptions to a conscious level leads to the second set of questions, which assesses the external situation: Are the current challenges different and discontinuous enough to require new learning and organizing concepts? Does my tool kit consist exclusively of round pegs when the future is a series of square holes? Finally, what do I have to unlearn and what subsequent replacements do I require to better engage problem solving, decision making, and new missioning and visioning. Only by preceding and building into new learning a review of previously acquired knowledge and how it determines thought and action can a genuine learning environment emerge and direct inquiry and application.

In summary, then, the case for community and best practices turns out to be the same case for communications. Building dialogue internal and interpersonal into performance facilitates making the improvement of work an integral part of the work itself. Being endlessly unsatisfied may turn out to provide the optimum job satisfaction.

REFERENCES

Buchen, I. "Employee Mission Statements." *Performance Improvement* 40, no. 6 (2001), 40–42.

Converse, J., and Schuman, H. *Conversations at Random.* New York: John Wiley, 1974.

Douglas, J. *Creative Interviewing*. Beverly Hills, Calif.: Sage, 1985.

Handy, Charles, 1994, *The Empty Raincoat: Making Sense of the Future*, Hutchinson.

Elmore, E. "Hard Questions about Practice." *Educational Leadership* 59, no. 8 (2002), 22–25.

Lambert, L. "A Framework for Shared Leadership." *Educational Leadership* 59, no. 8 (2002), 37–40.

Ratcliffe, J. "Scenario Planning: Strategic Interviews and Conversations." *Foresight* 4, no. 1 (2002), 31–40.

Ringland, G. *Scenario Planning*. London: Wiley, 1998.

Senge, P. M. (1990) *The Fifth Discipline. The Art and Practice of the Learning Organization*, London: Random House.

Silverman, D. *Qualitative Research*. London: Sage, 1997.

Spillane, J., Halverson, R., and Diamond, J. "Distributed Leadership." *Educational Researcher* 30, no. 3, (2002), 25–28.

van der Heijden, K. *Scenarios, The Art of Strategic Conversation*. London: Wiley, 1996.

17

EXECUTIVE COACHES AND TRUSTED ADVISORS: LEVERAGED INFLUENCE, LEADERSHIP PARANOIA, AND MBA GUIDANCE

Currently there are approximately 30,000 consultants in the United States generating about $50 billion annually. Of these, 10,000 are executive coaches, up from 2,000 in 1996. The number is increasing daily as a result of online training courses and entrepreneurs spreading the gospel at a fee of about $3,000 per person. Finally, there is the even more select and smaller group of trusted advisors retained by a select number of CEOs, heads of state, public personalities, elected officials, and so on. The estimate of this group ranges from 500 to 1,000 but their impact far exceeds their numbers. In fact, it may be greater perhaps than all the consultants and executive coaches combined.

Who are these powers behind the scene and the throne? How did they come to exercise such incredible leverage? What do they have to offer that is so special, unique, and valued? What compels leaders to solicit their services? How are they used? What do they have to offer that is not available from anyone else? Who are the members of this behind-the-scenes society of wise counselors who help leaders run the world with perhaps greater intelligence, wisdom, and caring than they would otherwise? How do these executive coaches and trusted advisors keep so many leaders on the straight and narrow and help to forestall the kind of arrogant and often criminal activity that has characterized recent corporate meltdowns?

Answering these questions and telling the special stories of executive coaches and trusted advisors, especially the latter, is difficult because they are the tales of many who, like me, have taken vows of silence.

I have served as an executive coach and trusted advisor for more than twenty years. The last ten have been exclusively as a trusted advisor to a limited number of executive leaders. No one ever knew what I did or for whom. It had to remain hidden. I was like a secret agent. Although that is not all I did, I treasured that role and believe it offered as much fulfillment to me as it may have provided value to those I counseled.

But the role evolved over time. The challenges were never the same. The CEOs were always different. And of course I myself did not remain unaltered. Indeed, constant and often unexpected personal and professional growth emerged as the first requirement of advisor. The notion of being experienced and even venerated was never enough. Indeed, one had to mirror the changes executives were compelled to make, including the difficulties of making them, if one was to understand even the language of the challenge, let alone help them cross the bridge—in some cases even build the bridge.

But what was absolutely clear is that the job, unlike any other, is temporary, invisible, and finally dispensable. No matter how critical the counseling may be at any time, the advisor must never lose sight of the fact that at best he or she is a sidebar, a wise whisper in the ear, a warning in the dark. He or she never can step forth out of the shadows into the light or speak in his or her own voice. The advisor never can be the big cheese or the main event. At best he or she is like the scaffolding erected on a building, necessary to help build it but once the edifice is complete, gone. Without such self-effacing denial, the advisor is finished before he or she starts. Given the excessive egos of some executives, advisors frequently are tempted to urge similar self-restraint.

Another lesson that advisors frequently seek to impart, although it is often resisted, is fusing personal and professional change. Often it is not enough for the advisor just to offer a model of integration; he or she may have to spell out in explicit detail exactly the way it needs to be done.

Many of my employers have questioned why personal and psychological change had to accompany a change in vision or direction of the company. Wasn't it enough that it had clear organizational benefits and gains? But for leaders that is never enough.

Behavior is the executive version of vision. Language is the lingua franca of direction and initiative. Attitude shapes problem solving. Curiosity makes decision making interesting. Standards drive the craft of implementation. In other words, what sets leaders apart from those who are not is that they have to live totally the life of their leadership.

They have to integrate who they are and what they do. They have to change themselves as they change the company. They can no more be the same afterward than the structures they have altered. They have to abandon the traditional separation that they can be one way at home and another at work. Rather they have to become one, and all of a piece. Unexpectedly, both sides benefit and grow, symbiotically, and often both suffer equally.

Some executives believe they already have reached the apex. They often do not read any more. Many in fact think they are such hot stuff that they pontificate. If they are surrounded by obedient and yes-man types, their principal collective function at times is to be called together to serve as an appreciative audience or hallelujah chorus. Such CEOs always expect others to change, often, and without question. But curiously they often exclude themselves from the process. Their top position gives them the illusion of finality.

As a devil's advocate I remind them that top executives and leaders may or may not have been born but they were always made—and constantly remade and on occasion even unmade. To claim perfection sets them apart in an unenviable way when one of their key functions is to demonstrate for emulation the highest standards—specifically three.

1. Integrity

   Integrity means no duplicity. They always have to be whole and of a piece. They have to not only generate solutions, but also become and embody those solutions. The substance of each has to mirror each other and appear coincidental. It and they had been born at the same time.

2. Communication

   They have to remember that they must always remain the supreme communicators. With authority, patience, and conviction they have to describe, explain, and justify a new direction so that it appears persuasive, compelling, and ultimately inevitable. They have to use whatever obstacles they personally have encountered to making the change, to help others overcome resistance and reluctance. And above all, they have to use straight talk.

3. Futurity

They always have to picture and project the time after. They have to summon the future and position it in front of all so that whatever differences may have existed in the past or even the present, there now is a common future, shared and achievable by all. It is not enough to rally the troops and to give them their marching orders. The future has to become their leader. They also have to feel that it is all within their grasp. Outstanding leaders create leaders. That is their ultimate legacy.

Pretty heady stuff? A lot to lay on leaders? But as a trusted advisor, that is a norm. Otherwise it would to be touchy-feely stuff—happy, happy sessions high on flattery and cheerleading. And that was not what I and they were about.

The art of leadership counseling may find its ultimate value in becoming integral to leadership itself. Indeed, its final benefit may be to raise the bar of executive performance by recommending that the model of friendly opposition, upheld and embodied by their trusted advisors, be internalized.

Coaching executive paranoia is routine. Besides, as Saul Bellow's Herzog observes, "Just because I am paranoiac does not mean they are not really persecuting me." The favorite strategy of coaches is converting obstinate behaviors into flexible attitudes. Sometimes the results are significant and surprising.

What follows is a leadership continuum that ranges from the manageable to the impossible and that stakes out the challenges executive coaches regularly face.

NEUTRAL NORMS VS. WORST-CASE EXAGGERATIONS

Difficult? Impossible
Taxing? Exhausting
Occasional? Daily

Turned around by a persuasive advisor, the result is counterbalancing mastery.

Discouraging? Challenging
Overwhelming? Energizing
Impasses? Breakthroughs

To these situations, the following guidelines and insights drawn from coaching can be added: Leaders generally believe they are indispensable, refuse to acknowledge the limits of their job, can't admit that the job often consumes body and soul, turn to martyrdom as a frequent refuge, and expend superhuman efforts, which generally fall short.

In the past, coaching perhaps like traditional therapy counseled acceptance. Leaders were encouraged to live with the demands of their jobs, and if possible reduce some of the excesses through delegation. They were also urged to see and appreciate the upside—the achievements— the rush, respect, even admiration of those they lead. But for some perverse reasons, such consolation often did not work or last very long.

Why? It is such a sane approach. It blends knowledge of both the nature of the job with that of the client. But recurrent fears persist: not being equal to the challenges, being surrounded by untrustworthy and even backstabbing associates, facing an incredible array of external forces and factors, making success problematical if not impossible, and so on. The net result is frequent and urgent callbacks of coaches. The CEOs then spend their time venting and displaying their stigmata. Finally exhausted, the inevitable question surfaces: "What is wrong with me?"

INTRODUCTION OF PARANOIA

Typically, reassurance is offered but as noted fails. A new direction is to call the spade a shovel and to acknowledge paranoia as a norm: "The job is crazy and so are you. It is a mirror match. No divorce is possible. You have a tiger by the tail. Neither one of you will let go. It will never change its stripes. The only thing you can do is not hide or bury your paranoia because it goes with the job and with who you are. Instead, we have to bring it to the surface and start with accepting paranoia as a permanent tension, for you and your job. Then we have to find ways of making that paranoia work for you—making it protective, purposeful and proactive instead of destructive, guilt-ridden, and draining." I paused and waited. Then, I leaned over and in a softer less assertive voice asked, "What do you think?"

The initial response was a deep breath. It was not a disapproving silence but thoughtful, as if wrestling with a new complexity. Gradually, the leader came back to himself: "Well. I certainly did not expect that. I thought we would have a let-it-all-hang-out session followed by a pep talk and off I would go. But you stopped me in my tracks. Clearly, I am not comfortable about thinking about myself or my job in terms of paranoia. Then, too, if I am really going off the deep end, maybe I should go to a real shrink—no offense intended. But the problem with those guys is that they don't know about business and being a leader as you do. OK. What's the next step? Let's give paranoia a try."

Desperately buying time because I was not sure what the next step would be, I gave him an assignment: "For our next session I want you to think about and make a list of tasks that are daunting, people out to get you, and those on the sidelines cheering you on to failure. That is the first step of making your paranoia work for you. From that point on we will go further."

That experience turned out to be as much of a turning point for my coaching career as it may have been for the leadership of many of my clients. As the methodology of paranoia took hold, major shifts occurred. The value of changing focus from resisting to embracing the limitations of the job, from believing that there is nothing wrong with you to recognizing the insightful nature of paranoia, was confirmed subsequently in sessions with a number of other leaders. And so my curious and perhaps dubious contribution to the voluminous literature of leadership has to do with coaching the development of protective, purposeful, and proactive paranoia for leaders.

What follows is the record of a series of strategic conversations about typical executive paranoia expressed mostly in the form of questions. Often the questions exhibited a surprising capacity to be self-solving and informative.

THREE VERSIONS OF PARANOIA

Although coaching is generally problem and solution oriented, ideally both are provided by the mentee, not the mentor. But here things were different and even new. The client was puzzled. He or she was looking for guidance. The focus was doubly unfamiliar: not just paranoia but rather problem-finding and problem-solving paranoia. Structuring and stirring the muddy waters of paranoia creatively, three recurrent situations surfaced: threats, quandaries, and discontinuities.

Threats—Protective Paranoia

The coach began with paranoia basics. He asked his client to put together a list of threats. Typically, they included who is out to get him, who wants his job, who is undermining his and/or his company's plans, what factions are forming or already exist, what is the rumor mill or grapevine saying about his leadership, what is his general standing with the rank and file, with stockholders, with board members; and on and on? Alongside the traditional to-do list, paranoia thus creates a to-worry-about list, ultimately as if not more important than the first one (Rosen, 1999).

Heeding paranoia and making it serve protective ends, the CEO finds he has to assign a higher priority to information gathering and to follow the sage advice of the Godfather: "Keep your enemies close." A second major set of questions examines his assumptions about his key interpersonal relationships. Who will tell the emperor that he has no clothes? What has been his relationship with his senior staff? Has he surrounded himself with yes-men? Does he require constant approval with little or no dissent? Does he shoot the messenger? In short, has he inspired and developed "followship" (Sergiovanni, 1984)? Has he created a team that will protect the quarterback from being blitzed? Indirectly and ever so gently, the coach uses the occasion of threats to reexamine not only information networks, but also executive interpersonal relations.

The advantage of operating from a base of paranoia is that threats can be accepted as a norm and not a personal leadership failing. That once put in place executive problem solving can be engaged. Thus, what the CEO needs to do is gradually wire in place an early warning or heads-up system. The internal intelligence-gathering function should match that of the external monitoring of the market and the competition. Indeed, the first may feed into the second. Learning about internal capacity or the lack of it may directly affect market performance. Thus, surprisingly, worrying about threats may save not only his job, but also his company.

QUANDARIES—PURPOSEFUL PARANOIA

If one of the ultimate benefits of valuing paranoia is normalizing threats, another is relieving the CEO of the burden of always having to be Solomon. Expectations of being all knowing, all powerful, all successful can lead to a false sense of indispensability. Paranoia does not make the CEO less needed but it does argue that he or she may not be able to solve everything or be the only problem solver. The coach suggests the compilation of another list: What at work dries you crazy? What frustrates or compromises what you believe should be done?

At this point the coach shifts gears. This dimension of paranoia requires a more reflective, thoughtful, and shared exchange. These are not direct threats with teeth bared as much as powerful enigmas that can cause sleepless nights and undermine companies at their core. And so the coach and the CEO together sustain an open-ended seminar on identifying and unraveling Gordian knots (Champy, 2000).

Although many inevitably will surface, especially those nourished by ambiguity, the most difficult perhaps is how to bring about and persuade people to change. Even Senge (2002) recently confessed that his cherished learning organization in retrospect failed to alter fundamental attitudes and belief systems. Revisions in evolutionary theory by Gould (2001) and others using fossilized evidence suggest that species hang on tenaciously to who and what they are before allowing any change in the form of species-splitting to occur. In other words, another generation may have to appear before there is real transformation. But that philosophical perspective may fail to silence the restlessness of paranoia or stop the determination of presidents to act presidential.

The CEO may be led to show a new interest in what the research may have to say on stirring change. Wisely, the coach focuses on the egoless modes of organizational structures and mechanisms. So that change is welcomed not required, invited not coerced, the coach introduces the approach of changing the outside as a way of changing the inside and of shifting leadership from the vertical to the horizontal. In particular, he cites the notion of distributed leadership in which every employee's job description is rewritten to include a leadership component (Elmore, 2002). Or Robert Greenleaf's (1984) notion of rotational leadership of teams, based on the Roman legion's notion that leaders at best are primus inter pares (first among equals). Or contemplating a less mechanical chart of organizational boxes and follow instead the more integrative and ecological design of Mitsubishi Electric, which fused divisions and functions into a more interactive seamless whole, based on the interconnected design of the rain forest (Kiuchi, 1994). In short, shifting the focus from changing people to changing environments that change people.

Often what determines whether CEOs are closed or open to reengineering is their perception of whether it increases or diminishes the importance of their leadership. But nothing feeds the paranoia of failure as discontinuity (Buchen, 2001).

DISCONTINUITIES—PROACTIVE PARANOIA

The high price paid for holding onto the past is that the future may abandon the organization. Instead, the coach and the CEO collaboratively try to engage the future, now. What surfaces are three villains: unacknowledged assumptions, singular not multiple forecasts and plans, and the dissipation of coherence (Hammer and Champy, 1994). Although all three are critical, the last brings everything full circle to square one where it all began.

The major issue has to become, "What kind of leadership is required when discontinuity becomes a norm?" The CEO pulls back and is deep in thought but unlike earlier discussions the issue of leadership was his comfort zone. Almost inevitably, his first overriding commitment is to fuse organizational mission and organizational leadership. In effect he made them one. He came to believe that he was not only in charge of the mission, but also its supreme advocate. At best he embodied it.

The fusion compelled him constantly to search for common and shared purpose. The past may offer some cherished older beliefs that still might have binding power. But vision will have to stretch for new sources of coherence in the future. He finally concluded that the principal task of the CEO is to bind both past and future together and to search for commonality.

The final paranoia was the harmony of time discords and of space continuums, of serving as prophet of science fiction. And curiously, that taxing duality also made wearing two hats much easier, more balanced, and almost respectable.

Coaches for MBA students may seem an expensive and questionable proposal. But one of the most intense pressures put upon all academics by adult learners and their employers is application of course content. That is neither new nor unjustified. And most instructors, institutions, and textbooks have acquitted themselves honorably and sometimes even creatively over the years: case studies are a norm, scenarios and simulations are assigned, collaborative team projects are often required, student chat rooms that feature workforce diversity are offered, and so on. But even such multiplicity does not seem to satisfy the current hunger of application that has become stronger and more insistent, even strident.

What appears to be upping the ante? Of the many new pressures, an emerging one is minimal guidance. It is not unusual to have eight supervisors in as many months. And with outsourcing, sometimes none at all as benign abandonment has become the norm. Then, too, even when available, mentors are stretched so thin supervising more workers than ever before that they have little or no time for individual coaching or counseling.

In short, course instruction is being asked to bear increasingly a double burden and being asked to mediate between a two-way flow: general application of course content not only to the workplace, but also to the new and individualized operating realities of their employed students. Generic coverage can go only so far. It is just about able to manage the first task. Not so the differentiated one. That requires a different and more creative solution.

The model suggested is supplemental, individualized, and optional. In addition to the instructor of record who has basic responsibility for delivering the course content, adult learners also should be offered academic coaches as an option for each course. Such coaches would not be required to hold the kind of terminal degrees that the course instructor must have. Rather, they are preeminent practitioners. They can be professional consultants and trainers, executive coaches, retired executives working for SCORE, alumni of the university, and so on.

Profiles of each coach would need to be compiled and listed. Interested students would review and select the one that best matches their situation. They would pay a modest fee or honorarium. The exchanges would be maintained by e-mail and phone. All e-mail and written exchanges are copied to the instructor of record who may occasionally join in the discussion.

The range of each coach needs to be both restricted and expansive. Although it does not include therapy, it can provide career guidance if requested. Coaches might be regularly requested to address the politics of the workplace. In some cases, it may have to be diversity specialized. It may have to focus on the special needs of women and minorities in the workplace. In such instances, clearly it would be helpful to select a coach who has encountered and surmounted such obstacles. Above all, the recurrent focus of coach and student is to apply the general approach and materials of the course to the specifics of the student's job and work environment. Finally, the hoped-for benefits of this kind of supportive and advocacy relationship will lead the student to consider adding coaching to his supervisory kit as he develops and advances in his own career. Who knows? He may even be involved in payback by serving later as an alumni course coach to a student.

REFERENCES

Bennis, W. *On Becoming a Leader.* Reading, Mass.: Addison-Wesley, 1989.
Block, P. *Stewardship.* San Francisco: Berret-Koehler, 1993.
Buchen, I. "Disturbing the Future." *Foresight* 4, no. 1 (2001a), 36–42.
Buchen, I. "Employee Mission Statement." *PI* 40, no. 6 (2001b), 40–42.
Champy, J. *Reengineering Management.* New York: Harper, 1995.

Champy, James. *The Arc of Ambition: Defining the Leadership Journey*. Philadelphia: Perseus Press, 2000.

Elmore, Richard (2002). *Bridging the Gap Between Standards and Achievement*. Washington, DC: The Albert Shanker Institute.

Greenleaf, R. *Servant Leadership*. Mahwah, NJ: Paulist Press, 1984.

Gould, J. "Fossil Evolution." *Nature* 44, no. 3 (1999), 390–397.

Hamel, G., and Prahalad, C. J. *Competing for the Future*. Cambridge: Harvard University Press, 1994.

Hammer, M. and J. Champy (1994). *Reengineering the Corporation. A Manifesto for Business Revolution*. New York, HarperCollins.

Handy, C. *Beyond Certainty*. Boston: Harvard Business School Press, 1995.

Ratcliffe, J. "Scenario Planning: Strategic Interviews and Conversations." *Foresight* 4, no. 1 (2002), 19–30.

Renesch, J. *Leadership in a New Era*. San Francisco: Berrett-Koehler, 1992.

Rosen, R. *The Healthy Company*. New York: Putnam, 1993.

Senge, P. (2002). "Creating Quality Communities." http://www.sol-ne .org/res/kr/qualcom.html

Senge, P. *The Learning Organization*. New York: Doubleday, 1990.

Sergiovanni, P. *Moral Leadership*. San Francisco: Sage, 1984.

Van der Heijden, K. *Scenarios, The Art of Strategic Conversations*. London: Wiley, 1996.

18

DIAGNOSTICALLY DRIVEN TRAINING: PROFILING, FOCUS, ADAPTABILITY, AND MI

The current process of selecting training topics focuses essentially on what the company believes it and its employees need to succeed together. Relatively little attention is paid to the cognitive psychology of employees, their intrapersonal and interpersonal receptivity, or the range, actual and potential, of their intelligence to grasp and implement the training. The current emphasis on e-learning technology and cost savings deals mostly with the externals of training. It generally leaves untouched assessing and defining the capacity of those trained to contribute to their training.

In other words, training may be guilty of the old myopia of focusing on the business rather than on the customer. Instead, it needs to balance what it is offering with how it is being perceived and received. That also, happily, would accommodate a shift from the evaluation of the training and its implementation to the transformation of the employee trained. Such a focus would include another implementation evaluation too often also ignored or unassessed: the degree to which the training is internalized—the extent to which not only the work changes productively, but also the employee is altered habitually. In short, training needs to be preceded, shaped, and driven by employee data. It needs to be targeted.

Happily, some diagnostic tools are available, at least three. One is traditional, another recently updated, and the third innovative. Training has to catch up and be driven minimally by the diagnostics of how we sell and serve (marketing); how we relate (human resources dynamics); and how we think (cognitive psychology). The first, although tried and proven, generally has been untapped or not applied to training design. The second, Myers-Briggs, recently has been updated and focused on team building. The third, Multiple Intelligences, although around for more than twenty years, has only recently captured the attention of instructional designers in business. In other words, the state of the art of creating learning management systems (LMS) can be advanced by also creating the state of the art of learning management diagnostics (LMD).

Training could benefit immediately, significantly, and obviously from the external and extensive knowledge of customer and market behaviors. Every training program should employ the overlay of customer knowledge and service. Whatever the specific training subject, the customer would be a recurrent, almost obsessive generic focus. Regardless of job title, job description, or customer proximity, every employee would have in front of him or her a dynamic profile of customers using the company's product or service. The principal form that dynamic profile would take is that of simulation especially enhanced by role-playing and storytelling. Indeed, the combination of the three generally has been found to be the most effective mode of communication and training. They even have proved to be invaluable in testing new products and services in terms of customer appeal and purchase. All training would thus feature the demographics and sociology of marketing to the extent that every employee in every training program would be customer driven.

Another key diagnostic that has been used by human resources for quite some time is a series of psychological assessment tools. These include the well-known Myers-Briggs, Strong Personal Inventory, Thomas-Kilman Conflict Mode Instrument, and the like. They are generally employed externally as part of an initial recruitment screening of applicants as well as occasionally internally for purposes of determining or testing for promotion or leadership positions. But strangely, they generally have not been applied to training, until recently.

CCP (formerly Consulting Psychologist Press), a major provider of the basic assessment tools, has developed the MBTI (Myers Briggs Type

Indicator) Team Building Program. The concept is to administer MBTI to each team member and thereby to generate the preferences and profiles of the entire team. (That also must include the team leader who often seeks to solidify his or her role as the team manipulator by not taking the test.) So armed and informed, communication and teamwork can be improved, and the negotiation and resolution of conflicts and differences can be made more manageable. Once again the gain is twofold and synergetic: Both the work process and the worker enjoy greater productivity by being more closely aligned with task and team dynamics. The adage of working smarter rather than harder finds perhaps its major advocate in such diagnostically driven training.

The third tool is seldom used and generally has not been applied to training design. It is Multiple Intelligences (MI) developed by Howard Gardner of Harvard and presented initially in his book *Frames of Mind* (1983). Gardner basically argued that intelligence is neither confined to nor measurable by only one intelligence (the literacy of reading and writing). Rather, there are many intelligences. He originally designated seven, then added an eighth in 1993. Although originally and subsequently mostly taken up by educators and school textbook publishers, MI has the potential by itself, and especially allied with the other two, to offer the most powerful and impactful training diagnostic available today to business. Its ambitious reach was announced recently by Gardner in a twenty-year retrospective reflected in the subtitle to this chapter.

Gardner claims there are eight intelligences: linguistic, bodily, spatial, musical, mathematical, intrapersonal, interpersonal, and naturalist. Equally as important, MI is trackable and traceable as the basic learning pathways of the brain. In fact, when cognitive researchers complete their total mapping of the brain, the results and applications may rival that of cracking the genetic code. But the critical point for the discussion here is the fusion of physiology (brain) and psychology (cognition). Linking human thinking and learning, Gardner claims that MI characterizes not just individual or social behaviors but those of the human species itself. In other words, MI goes way beyond learning styles or preferences and even natural or developed gifts or talents. It also transcends historical differentiation. It is what all humans possess by virtue of being human. Indeed, that starting point enables

Gardner to present the general operating laws of MI that may also be those of training as well.

The range of MI varies with each individual. The extent and depth of that range is determined by genetics, environment, and use. The range of MI is not fixed or predetermined. It can be expanded by education, exposure, and direction. Goals and environment can guide, stimulate, and even determine the configuration of intelligences chosen or favored. But control is never total because MI autonomously operates with a mischievous will and direction of its own.

For goals to be optimal, they should always combine the small and the big, the immediate and the long term. MI is brought more fully into play, mobilized, and energized by task completion and task extension, accomplishment, and incompletion. MI is also stirred when the focus is on "uncovering" rather than "covering" materials or topics. Basic ideas and concepts—square-one thinking or first-cause thinking—stimulate the synergistic interplay between MI and problem solving. It is particularly responsive to the multiple challenges of constructing scenarios, simulations, case studies, portfolios, and the like—in short, to artificial and futuristic realities. Finally, the ultimate value of MI may be to serve in Gardner's terms as "the optimal taxonomy of human capacities" (2003).

To many, the aforementioned may appear too academic and removed from the urgencies of training to have any practical value. But perhaps MI can become less distant but still remain challenging if it is perceived not only as a new way of revisiting human potential, but also a series of multiple smarts. What Gardner is really saying is that as a species we always exceed at any given time the definition of who we are, what we know, and what we can learn. There is thus a need to tap and direct each of the eight intelligences so that they are rendered and extended in terms of immediate growth and long-term expectation.

What may be further helpful is to translate and animate multiple intelligences into action applications. Thus, each MI respectively could be rendered as follows: word-smart, body movement adept, spatially agile, musically facile, math-sequenced, personally and interpersonally savvy, and environmentally sensitive. In addition, clustering preserves and enriches the dynamics of the process. Operationally, one intelligence may dominate but it often taps or engages others in a support capacity to address a task or solve a problem. The process thus features primary, secondary, and even tertiary intelligences all activated by the nature and complexity of the task on the one hand, and the interactivity of smarts of the problem solver on the other. Indeed, the more formidable or unfamiliar the challenge, the more resourceful and varied the team of intelligences marshaled. To be sure, an important and recurrent goal of training is to enlarge and differentiate the range of tools in the toolbox. But the key first step of diagnostics still has to be taken.

Every employee needs to be assessed as to his or her MI range and potential. To tie together improvement potential of both work and worker, the assessment also should be linked and ultimately made part of the job description. Such data would then be used not only to shape the design of training, but also to benchmark growth and realization of potential. Training design also should factor in Gardner's key guidelines for optimum stimulation and synergy noted earlier. In other words, training design would always incorporate immediate and long-term goals, be intellectually rigorous and focus on governing ideas and first causes, be practical and visionary, and offer the multiple challenges of simulation and scenario.

Such a revised and enlarged scope of training would yield outcomes that are both work and worker specific. What is done better would always be fused with what in fact drives such improvement: the application not only of more intelligence, but also of more intelligences. Suddenly productivity would no longer be limited to a singular or narrow definition of the work task or process and workers themselves would no longer be confined to what they have been or used. By tying together productivity and human potential, trainers may be able to tap a whole new vein of learning. Becoming smarter may become not only longitudinal, but also holistic. In short, MI may be able to offer more of the future at the service of the present than ever before.

If there is a supreme art of management and leadership it may be that of problem solving. But learning and training leaders rightly are so preoccupied of late with operational economies and measurement metrics that they may not be able to see (let alone foresee) the vision of the proverbial forest for the mission-driven trees. It is an understandable myopia because success beckons. Steering a middle course between tight budgets and training-driven productivity, learning managers must produce cost-effective gains.

But two related nagging problems are beginning to surface. Are there limits to future productivity? And are there limits to future learning? And if so, are they correlated?

The value of evoking and projecting the law of diminishing returns is its capacity to stop professionals momentarily in their tracks. It compels a proactive calculation of diminishing gains, which if unheeded may stall and place training back in the situation from which it was recently rescued. In short, it may be time to sharpen the saw, except now it may have to be the softer and more speculative cutting edge of theory.

The title is a good place to start because it is taken from a paper, entitled "Multiple Intelligences after Twenty Years," given by Howard Gardner to the American Educational Research Association on April 21, 2003. That double-paired focus on retrospect and prospect also might be just the sort of balancing act institutions need to undertake now on behalf of the future.

There are eight intelligences identified by Gardner that in turn had to survive eight criteria. Looking back to his seminal work *Frames of Mind* (1983) and reviewing his identification of these eight Multiple Intelligences, Gardner comes to a number of general conclusions that can be applied to or alter the future focus of education and training.

All human beings possess multiple intelligences. The profile and range of intelligence dimensions varies with each individual. Multiple intelligences are the intellectual staples of the species. They are not synonymous with learning styles or talents. The former are externally mercurial and appear and disappear with social preferences and fashions. The latter are precious and distinctive gifts of special individuals but are not the common stock of the species.

Multiple intelligences describe all the basic and archetypal pathways the mind uses to learn. What determines which ones are used are a complex of three factors: genetics, experience, and societal priorities. Multiple intelligences rest on brain and genetic research. It is thus a process of describing and utilizing the basic learning pathways of the species. The brain is still being mapped. When completed it will be the equivalent of cracking the genetic code. The ultimate value of MI may be the mainstay of a new science and art of mobilizing and measuring human potential.

To many this may appear to be pretty heady stuff and too far out and off to be of any practical value. But a counterargument that takes the form of reviewing and reevaluating current education and training may keep the subject central, stirring, and beneficial. Here are minimally five critical checklist questions educators and training leaders and managers should ask as they review their current program array.

To what extent if any do the offerings assume and tap multiple intelligences? Are training goals and parameters typically narrow and short term and thus prematurely constricting and limit stretching? To what extent does training address only how and not why, seek end results only, not source drivers? How extensive, if at all, does training encourage multiple, alternative, and even divergent ways of exploring, communicating, and solving problems? Finally, what does the totality of offerings say about the basic institutional assumptions of human potential and productivity? Limited or unlimited, circumscribed or yet to be tapped?

If enough or all of the answers to these questions point to the need for adding MI to the mix, how should it be done? The obvious approach is to employ Gardner's eight versions of MI as an overlay, note where it is lacking, and remedy the various sins of omission. But such add-ons perhaps should be put on hold until more basic spade work is done—until, in short, a list of learning processes is compiled that parallels and invites the learning pathways of MI. Such essential and recurrent processes common to all education and training would include communications, problem solving, interpersonal and intrapersonal relationships, decision making, innovation, and so on. Let us use problem solving as an illustrative example.

As with all the basic learning processes now under the aegis of MI, the starting point with problem solving is to characterize the process as essentially multiple in nature. That assumption, however, goes way beyond the externally oriented notion of the various tools in a toolbox or arrows in a quiver.

MI initially engages not learning outcomes but pathways, not applications but first principles. It assumes the potential and power of all eight intelligences not only to engage, but to multiply problem definition. The goal then is to strengthen the problem solver by enriching the problem—to have it speak to the problem solver in at least eight different languages—to make the problem increasingly multifaceted and more demanding.

Thus, in many ways the initial gain of MI is to multiply access. Each intelligence becomes a learning pathway not only to the facade, but also to the core of the problem. On the one hand, the extent of the impact of the problem is assessed and problem definition now spells out all that it can and may affect. On the other hand, MI approaches the problem as a functioning brain and probes its particular learning pathways in order to define what makes it a problem in the first place. Then combining both external manifestations with internal dynamics, MI finally defines what state the problem has to acquire or how it has to be perceived for it to be no longer a problem.

The goal of problem solving then as with all basic learning processes is mutual enrichment. They tap the optimal taxonomy of human learning capacities. But that involves a double attribution. The first is the recognition that the value of MI is to extend learning range and depth. To be sure, the cluster of MI selected and embraced by each individual is determined according to Gardner by genetics, experience, and societal preference.

But because problem solving itself and especially when driven by MI can both alter experience and be future driven, the potential for expanding the learning cluster is always available and can be tapped. In short, under the aegis of MI, the solution always involves stretching—it must always expand the range and depth of the problem solver. He should not be the same afterward. His growth gain should have not only expanded the range of his productivity, but also stirred the depth of his MI potential. To work optimally, the process now has to be doubling—a win-win.

The first dimension of the problem-solving dynamic is thus primarily internal; but the second is external. MI has to be applied to the problem itself. The problem is now defined or redefined in terms of the eight intelligences. What determines its final version is what cluster sticks to it. That is the equivalent of the problem's genetics, experience, and social preference. It is its core as a problem and the extent of its impacts.

In other words, the problem-solving process has been transformed from a top-down highly directive and unilaterally controlling process to a collaborative, mutually driven negotiating process. It is no longer a subject contemplating an object, but two subjects contemplating each other. Moreover, each is now amplified—more substantial and challenging, more demanding of the other.

In many ways, the attribution of MI to the problem itself and the recognition that what finally adheres to it not only constitutes the learning identity of the problem, but also establishes the threshold for its solution. The ideal is not the cry of "Eureka" by the problem solver but the quiet capacity of the problem to solve itself. In fact, when and what the problem finally selects as its own operational multiple intelligence functions not only as its definition, but also as its core and applications solution. The problem becomes self-solving. Its solution has about it an unarguable logic, clarity, and inevitability.

MI is thus a two-edged sword. It cuts both ways. On the one hand, it opens up the full range of learning pathways and the potential of being more than we are by virtue of learning more than we knew. It also enables learners to attribute to all the learning processes the same expansive array of intelligences. Such mutual attribution in fact changes the basic relationship between learner and what is learned. To borrow from Gardner, it aligns intrapersonal and interpersonal relationships and makes them not alternatives but versions of each other.

MI brings to training the science and art of realizing not only human, but also process potential. It totally engages who we are, what we do, how we think, and how we problem solve. In the process, it also pushes the future forward—to all that we can be and all that we can do. But such gains always are mutual and reciprocal. They inevitably involve the species and its historical and evolutionary partners. It is no longer nature versus nurture but nature via nurture; and in the process it may grant training a new lease on life and perhaps a new future.

Finally, it clearly would be lamentable at this point in history to grant to machines greater potential for intelligence development than to human beings. What would make that also ironic is that bypassing or not tapping the optimal capacity of the human species, the future potential of machine intelligence would itself be impoverished.

What Gardner is essentially claiming is that composing a current obituary on the limits of learning and productivity is minimally premature and futuristically compromising. Indeed, training through MI has been given not only a new lease on current life, but also a new future on stirring productivity and potential.

Adaptability increasingly has become the key measure of performance. Recently a team of math experts found that students across the country regardless of their good scores on standardized tests do not really understand the basic concepts of math (*Ed Week*, 2003, p. 34). Another survey concluded that top scores on high school graduation exit exams are not reliable predictors of college performance (*Ed Week*, 2003, p. 14).

Nothing of such scale and invasiveness ever occurs in surveys of overall business training. Some industries will review the offerings of its members and even rate them by budget allocations and number of workshops. That is usually as far as it goes. To be sure, the introduction of learning management systems has brought new precision and accountability to the entire enterprise. Most notably, not just the training but its implementation has been pursued with vigor. But has it really?

In both educational surveys cited here, the failures were not of knowledge but understanding. In turn understanding is defined as mastery of a wider range of applications than taught. In other words, the students were unable to move beyond the original problem sets provided as part of initial instruction. They were stuck in programmed success.

Are the same limits operable in business training? Standard evaluations survey workshop clarity and relevance of presentation on the one hand, and implementation at the work site afterward on the other hand. But the applications may be prescriptive. The range of implementation similarly may be those of the workshop.

Employees may emerge knowledge rich but understanding poor. Their operational range may rest on a larger information base but it is tied to a stake of limited and known applications. In short, they are compelled to be only prescriptively inventive. But knowledge and creativity need to be synergistically paired. Indeed, the ultimate application of understanding is innovation.

But perhaps the absence of such ambitious gains may not be perceived as a problem. After all, training always is targeted. It has limited goals. That limits the range of applications. If that range needs to be extended or redirected, another workshop can be created or the initial one extended or retooled. After all, is not that the way all education really operates—as progressively incremental? Then, too, the goal of understanding may be excessively egalitarian. Not everyone can be, has to be, or should be inventive. Perhaps, that needs to be reserved for the talented. Doling out some knowledge is sufficient for most.

But the problem of innovation and its sources is not predictable. It emerges unexpectedly and from unlikely divisions or individuals. Besides, a number of arguments might be quickly advanced against forsaking the quest for understanding and settling instead for such mechanical and short-term incremental gains.

First, it costs more to mount more workshops rather than one thorough one. Second, the workplace is demanding more, not less adaptability. Third, productivity gains are driven not by training but by workers reengineering their jobs. Fourth, higher, not lesser expectations motivate. Finally, it is doable. Refocusing may be easier than imagined.

Reconfiguration requires changing the question from "How smart am I?" to "How am I smart?" Or better still, combine and routinely go back and forth between the two by tapping brain research.

Advances in mapping the learning pathways of the brain have reached the point where the art may become the science of learning. In addition, cognitive psychologists are also beginning to link brain dynamics to the human genome and developing no matter how tentatively the genetic drivers of intelligence.

The net result is that we know more now about the way we think and the way we therefore learn than ever before. Human potential has thus become a less abstract and more precise and realizable target. Brain research may be providing educators and trainers with just the sort of leverage needed to address the intense realities of the workplace on the one hand, and to offer optimum understanding and adaptability on the other. Moreover, brain research may overcome reluctance by serving as an overlay rather than an overhaul. That way the baby is not thrown out with the bath water; and professionals have a way of testing before changing.

The goal of the overlay is to pair understanding and adaptability. It is not enough to know. Because it is more difficult and important to understand than to know, we tend to favor knowledge over understanding. That preference is shored up by the way we test on the one hand and the way we measure application on the other.

But the brain values total competence and confidence. The brain welcomes being stretched rather than just being confirmed. The brain wants to experience and affirm its power and to be endlessly enriched. The brain in short is always hungry. Feeding and stirring the brain always requires upping the ante. And it seeks all this from the start.

The overlay provided in the figure here is for completeness. Although each level of each of the three basic operating principles is correlated, only the last triad is the focus here.

1. Progressive Mastery:
   Information
   Knowledge
   Understanding.
2. Adaptability Range:
   Explicitly identified (known problem sets)
   Broadened base (stretched)
   Crossovers (innovative and discoverable)
3. Entry Portals (Instructional Frames) and Exit Portals (Applications):
   Singular (rote and ritual)
   Varied but discrete (diversity and learning styles)
   Multiple and interoperable (intelligence and the range of applications)

The discussion in this section will center on the portals. I hope that will also serve in the process to shed light and serve as a further commentary on understanding and crossover.

The selection of portals rests on the assumption that the way training begins determines whether or not understanding and optimum adaptability occurs. Entry thus drives outcome. Beginnings determine ends. Each portal has to be properly framed to be optimized.

The framework selected has to permit and accommodate the criteria of access and range. It therefore must be multiple not singular in nature. It also must raise the bar and extend the range of applicability. It should always resist closure or finality but remain open ended and unfinished. Finally, although given here in full, the portals form a menu for selection. Not all need be used for any given workshop.

The basic problem Gardner raises is that of singularity: one teacher, one trainer, one textbook, one curriculum for many different students. His familiar argument is that learning styles vary considerably and no teacher can be 360 degrees especially with an unfavorable teacher-student ratio. His solution is to provide multiple learning approaches or his famous eight Multiple Intelligences. That provides a congenial series of learning styles from which students can select their preferred way into a mandated curriculum.

The dynamic offered by Gardner rests on a number of instructional assumptions. The instructor realizes the limits of his or her range and shifts the focus from the server to the menu. The student is not passive but has to be cooperatively engaged in trying out and finally selecting his or her preferred learning style, from which innovation will come or not. The goal of individualizing instruction is to serve as an antidote to stereotypical learning and thinking. Above all, the dynamic establishes the goals of training as real understanding and optimum adaptability.

The use of multiple portals or entry points sets up and enhances the varied avenues to reach those goals. At least seven portals are available: narrational, historical, foundational, psychological, quantitative, esthetic, and futuristic.

To demonstrate how each of the portals can be incorporated or built into training, a workshop focused on employee evaluation will be used as illustrative. Each portal will be followed by two paired descriptors: entry mode and intelligence choice.

1. Narrational
   - Simulation Verbal and Linguistic Intelligence
     The value of story, especially at the outset, is that it establishes the complexity of reality. It simulates real life, issues, and people. It persuasively builds credibility. It may be verbal or visual or better still both. If it is also humorous, that is a plus but not an essential.

     "One company I worked for ran an office betting pool. One had to do with the longest period between evaluations. The winner was twenty-eight years. The other was on the oddest place for an evaluation to take place. The winner was standing in line together at the airport. What does that tells us about evaluation?"
2. Historical
   - Reflection Evaluative Intelligence
     History invites reflection. Evaluation is not perceived as a one-shot or static or nondevelopmental process. Above all, a historical perspective suggests that what is being discussed is purposeful and consciously designed to fulfill certain goals.

     "In the nineteenth century evaluation was generally hurried and crude.

     "Workers were hands and owners were heads. Dickens portrayed the school exit as being the same as the entrance of the factory. Although there were many changes and refinements in the twentieth century, evaluation remained the incontestable realm of the boss. But as unions took hold and productivity became an increasingly important factor, metrics and continuous improvement emerged. Assessment was driven to a large extent by Deming's statistical process controls, which transformed evaluation into measurable performance improvement. What changes have you observed over the years? What are some other changes that may occur in the future?"

3. Foundational
   - Speculation Assumptions Intelligence
     The value of the foundational or philosophical framework is to stir speculation. History addresses how, philosophy why. It invites an attention to first causes or square one thinking.

     "Evaluation seems built into us. We always want to know how we are doing. Even God in Genesis steps back after one of his daily creations to determine that it was good. Imagine if he didn't like it? After all, he regretted creating us. So whatever we are we are also and always evaluating creatures. Describe some ways other than work in which we are always testing and measuring things and people to see if they pass muster."

4. Psychological
   - Intrapersonal and Interpersonal Self-Analysis Emotional Intelligence
     The psychological dimension introduces the ambiguity of evaluation—the degree to which we are pulled toward and away from it at the same time. It compels us to look inwardly at our feelings and points outwardly at our relationships. It presents evaluation as a complex psychological dynamic that reaches into our deepest emotions and fears and extends to how we relate to others. Above all, it defines psychology as a form of knowing.

     "We started out and set the stage by presenting and explaining why an evaluation could be postponed for so long or why it could occur in the unlikely place of a line at the airport. But now let us try to push that further. I need four volunteers. Two will pair off and play the role of a supervisor and employee in an evaluation situation. They do not have to improvise. I have written the script. You just read your part. The other two will play the same roles but they will express out loud the thoughts and feelings going through the minds of each after each exchange. If anyone in the class believes you are holding back or deflecting, he is free to fill in what should be expressed."

5. Quantitative
   • Sizing, Scaling, and Estimating Math Intelligence

   Everything is measurable. It helps however to make it manageable—to get a grip on it. Numbers always help. So does taking an abstract idea and making it visible—like picturing justice as blindfolded and holding a scale. Evaluation is no exception.

   "What percentage of the total budget is earmarked for employee salaries? For benefits? For training like this workshop? OK, while we are at it let us also try to quantify something qualitative. How much time do you spend typically each year in evaluation sessions and formal training? Take home CD-ROM workshops? Personal training on your own: reading work-related books and articles, listening to tapes? Finally, estimate how much time a supervisor typically spends on evaluation. Because undoubtedly the final totals may range, let us ask for three volunteers to put their numbers on the board up front."

6. Aesthetic
   • Shape and Design Spatial Intelligence

   All things are shaped to serve a double master: form and function. In addition, things are not just put in place. They have to fit. Square pegs in square holes. They have to line up with what goes before and what comes after. Engineers generally understand this—that is why placemats exist to make drawings—and human engineers have to understand it more. Above all, access and equity have to partner. One design does not fit all. "One law for the lion and the ox is tyranny." Worse, it is also inefficient.

   "We already noted the historical changes in evaluation. Let us look at evaluation as a design problem. First off, should the system be totally uniform? Should it be adjusted for different departments? If so, how and why? Let's explore differentiated design."

7. Futuristic
   • Anticipatory and Change-Driven Visioning and "What If" Intelligence

   This is not planning—that is a separate and different process, although visioning ideally should precede and inform it. The futuristic is poised for change. It compulsively entertains different, better, faster, and cheaper ways of doing the same old thing the same way. The future and productivity mutually support each other as natural partners. In fact, the purpose of emphasizing the future is to perceive it as an ally not an enemy.

   "To what extent is the present evaluation system current and up with the times? Is it cutting edge? If not, what changes do you envision being made? Let's take another futuristic tack. To what extent is the present performance improvement system time-bound? It leaves out the future—your future and the future of your job. Let's take a few minutes to write a future job description—of what our job would look like two to three years down the pike. And then itemize what training you would need to get there."

SUMMARY

The following matrix provides a summary of all seven portals, their preferred modes of thought, the kinds of intelligence featured, and the growth gains.

Portal Mode Intelligence Gains

1. Narrational Simulation Verbal/Linguistic Memorization
2. Historical Reflection Evaluative Perspective
3. Foundational Speculation Assumptions First Causes
4. Psychological Self-Analysis Emotional Work Dynamics
5. Quantitative Scaling Math Problem Measurement
6. Esthetic Design Spatial Form & Function Fit
7. Futuristic Anticipation "What If" Visioning

Will understanding and optimum adaptability eventually and always follow? Not always and certainly not immediately. But training with multiple portals is an investment and seeding process. It operates on the premise of all brain research: the expanded definition and range of human potential, and the infallible relationship between understanding and optimum adaptability.

Besides, even if all seven portals were selected, such beginnings would take very little time as noted earlier. They might even make workshops less routine and predictable. Most important, attendees would be engaged in a muscular way from the start. Besides, it is after all an overlay not an overhaul. And that may turn out to be enough to surprise employees into being creative.

Although corporate smarts are highly valued, the general impact of MI on the business sector in general and human resources has been minimal. A few consultants have suggested applications to training and leadership (Kravis, 2001). Even a quick review of HR assessment tools reveals that only the old warhorses of Myers-Briggs and personality inventories like those of Strong are still around and generally are all that is used. No major training programs or learning management system show any signs of tapping into MI, let alone reconfiguring the extensive menu of offerings accordingly.

Speculation as to why MI generally has been ignored by business yields three possible answers. The first two are characteristically short-sighted, even snobbish; the third substantive. First, MI's origins are academic. Gardner was advancing theory not application, research not conclusive findings. His primary audience was other psychologists. Then, too, although the criteria developed for determining both the range and operations of each intelligence appeared to be so rigorous and comprehensive and its results definitive, the absolute nature of the original seven shortly was shaken by the emergence of an eighth and now by the contemplation of a ninth and even a tenth. The effect in some circles was akin to adding additional commandments to the original ten. The issue of what the final number would be suggested to many that the research was still an ongoing academic inquiry.

Second, because MI began to partner primarily or only with education, distancing by business occurred. Indeed, that linkage confirmed its lineage: This was basically an academic taxonomy designed for teachers and schools. And as the number of books and articles proliferated, and as the curricula and staff development adaptations began to surface, MI appeared to have found its place and advocates. Given the typical devaluation of education by business, many corporate practitioners concluded that guilt by association once more was operative.

Third, MI seems to be at variance historically with the dominant thought patterns. After all, it originally was presented and subsequently proliferated in book form; and literacy is still in fact the principal form of thought and expression. Glasser (2002) and others challenged whether multiple intelligences were merely a more ambitious version of learning styles or the traditional exceptionality of talent or gifts possessed by a relatively few lucky individuals. Finally, MI appeared to be unmanageable. There are too many, the range was bewildering, the way they internally interact still a mystery, etc. In short, perhaps it would be better to ignore MI completely or adopt a wait-and-see attitude because if it were to be taken seriously and implemented, it might require a total transformation of a number of business operations.

But in the twenty-plus years since its first appearance, at least three major related developments have made it more difficult for professionals committed to performance improvement to play ostrich. First, brain research has made major gains (Dennison, 1994; Carter, 1998; Greenwald, 1999; Jung-Beeman and Bowden, 2000). New professions have emerged: cognitive psychologists, genetic physiologists, cognitive programmers, and the like. The mapping of the learning pathways of the brain is offering breakthroughs in many areas as extensive as those following the cracking of the genetic code. Indeed, the links between the two are shaping a future research agenda of convergence. More relevant to this discussion, brain research not only has identified and confirmed the specific pathways for each of the eight intelligences, but also registered the electrical synergy of their interaction. In fact, Gardner's own initial research began with examining brain-damaged patients and relating specific impairments to intelligence deprivation. In short, the science of brain studies has served to anchor and to impart empirical credibility to MI's academic origins.

Second, Gardner himself has become less tentative and more aggressive and explicit about what MI is and has to offer (Gardner, 1999). Largely emboldened by the successful educational applications of MI, he has argued that these various intelligences are not culturally or psychologically driven learning styles or preferences determined or shaped by history or fashion. Nor are they the precious monopoly of a small number of talented individuals or idiot savants who may be fortunate to be blessed or cursed with certain intelligences in abundance. Rather, they are congenitally the basic equipment of the human species. In fact, when Gardner was invited recently to give a speech on the occasion of twenty years since his book was first published, the subtitle of his address defined MI as "the optional taxonomy of human learning capacities" (2003). In short, MI is being presented as the new science of human potential. It has given new meaning and precision to Maslow's supreme goal of self-actualization.

Third, major changes in business training and performance improvement have taken place. The competitive quest to do more with less, to work smarter not harder, to raise levels of productivity, quality, customer satisfaction and profitability, and so on have changed training root and branch. Nonduplicative and cost-sensitive e-learning has come to the fore. The need for greater management and leadership of learning coupled with cost-effectiveness led to the creation of corporate universities, learning management systems, and even new executives, CLO or CIO (Chief Learning/ Information Officer).

The net result is the recognition that attracting and retaining human capital requires constant upgrading. Training has in effect become a company's competitive edge. But because of the relentless pressure of the global economy not only to remain productive but also to exceed previous levels on the one hand coupled with downsizing as perhaps the key American way of achieving such gains on the other hand, two disturbing future issues are emerging. Are there limits to productivity? Are there limits to learning? And are the two openly and/or secretly linked? In other words, asked again and again to repeat and even exceed the stretch goals of last year and perhaps in the process beginning to encounter the law of diminishing returns of productivity or its outer limits, CLOs, LMSs, and performance improvement professionals may be more receptive to what MI has to offer. Fortunately, business does not have to reinvent the wheel. The general and specific benefits MI can provide already have been spelled out in twenty years of applications to education.

Limiting the focus to what business would value, two educational patterns emerge. The first is disturbingly obvious: students graduating from MI schools and curriculum gradually will apply to organizations for jobs.

Disparity will be immediately apparent, comparable perhaps to students of e-learning coming to paper-and-pencil organizations. In fact, almost all organizations are generally not aware of the extent to which they are structured fundamentally to function as singular rather than multiple intelligence organizations. In other words, these prospective new employees, many the best and the brightest, may compel a total review of basic organizational assumptions about intelligence. The sign of a genuine challenge is that it affects both root and branch. Organizations may be forced to assess prospective candidates by Gardner's version of the key question: not "How smart are you?" but "How are you smart?"

The second yield is more focused and may have a major impact on recruitment and selection, promotion, team productivity, and ultimately training. Happily, the range of that change already has been identified by educators. Following is a summary of the common operating conclusions of different educators with varied curricula and at diverse school levels on the value and application of MI to learning (for teachers read trainers, for students, employees).

MI teachers assume, develop expectations, and act on the belief that students are intellectually competent in multifaceted ways. Students respond accordingly. The range of student responses and combinations of intelligences are unlimited, elude final classification, and designate long-term potential. The school's mission is rewritten to support and promote intellectual diversity. Instructors become acute observers of student learning behaviors, take their teaching cues from such observations, and link the immediate snapshot with the big picture, the short term with the open ended.

Student learning is routinely multimodal. Teachers encourage and direct students to use their strong intelligences to work on and improve their weaker or less used ones. Students develop autonomous skills and habits through independent project learning. Self-reliance rules. Students develop collaborative and team skills and habits through multiage and differentiated groupings and through multidisciplinary and integrated studies. Interdependence rules. Finally, assessment takes as many multiple forms as there are intelligences, the favorites being rubric self-assessment, portfolios, simulations, and scenarios.

Although not all these impressive outcomes of education may carry over totally to business or performance, their principal value is compelling a review of what minimally would be required if MI were to be applied to business structures, operations, and human capital. Specifically, five reengineering principles can be distilled as guidelines for business from the above:

1. Inclusive

    Application to all employees at all levels at every stage of their development.

2. Benchmark

    Initial identification is to be noted, factored, and followed by constant and seamless data tracking of potential.

3. Alignment

    Individual employees and the company are joined at the hip; the process must be undertaken jointly and tested and monitored regularly by the degree of its reciprocity.

4. Pervasive

    MI must permeate everything. Although ubiquitously invasive, initial foci on productivity and innovation, for example, may reflect company priorities.

5. Interoperable

    MI also must define all work descriptions and interpersonal relationships to the point where in aggregated form they collectively become and sum up the company's mission.

Translating these guidelines into a plan requires a five-step process: identification, interpersonal dynamics, focus, reflection, and mission. The first stage is identifying the MI range of every employee. Happily, a number of assessment tools are available, all online (Accelerated Learning, BGRID, and Midas). The more difficult task is replicating that process organizationally, which many companies have never undertaken. It requires defining what intelligences the organization values and predominantly uses. That is enriched by identifying the organization's preferred forms for communicating the range and diversity of its intelligences.

Sooner or later such organizational self-assessment has to engage company vision and mission. If a task force of senior staff, middle-level managers, and representative employees were appointed to analyze and to tease out the essential intelligences assumed or implicit in those statements, and the input of human resources on the problem-solving and creative factors that actually have shaped hiring decisions and promotions were added, the final profile would identify the company's archetypal smarts and competitive edge. Whatever the results, the process of getting there would be enervating.

The next stage is contextually dynamic. The intelligences identified cannot remain as stills. They have to be animated in real time, terms, and work contexts. They have to appear as interactive and communicating behaviors operating in the environment and culture of the company. In other words, they have to be intrapersonal and interpersonal. Inevitably, this again involves a double assessment: how employees work together intelligently and whether smart work flow and design as well as team performance are facilitated or impeded by company structures. The goal is to achieve optimum interoperability of smart interpersonal relationships and fluid environments.

The third stage follows Gardner's definition of the tasks of the eight intelligences in the first place. They all are involved in problem solving, creating innovation, and fulfilling goals (Gardner, 1983, 1999). Of the three, the last is the mobilizer. To work effectively, MI needs goals and direction. MI is not self-activating or -directing. It is driven by work or play. It reaches optimum levels when the two are fused. In education they are the learning goals of the school and the social goals of the community. In business they are the performance goals of productivity, quality, profitability, and customer service on the one hand and the collective power of company vision and mission statements on the other. In other words, goals animate and direct MI, not the other way around. The companion task of the company then is integration: to determine the extent to which by informed hiring and training, employees have the smarts to achieve smart goals.

The fourth stage may be the most difficult because it is the most individualistic, speculative, and fluid. It requires reflection and self-observation. Essentially, each employee has to generate a series of mini-narratives or films that describe the interactive dynamics of their individual intelligences. The initial step only identified the intelligence inventory and range. Now that needs to be rendered interactively: why different intelligences organize themselves internally for problem solving and creativity. For example, one standard cluster typically may show one intelligence dominating and others in a supportive role. In some other instances, a number are all equally and simultaneously active and contributing. But again, such self-assessment is not free-wheeling but targeted by and against specific and recurrent work goals, activities, and patterns. What also needs to be emphasized is that this like the first one of identification is also a benchmarking process. It establishes the growth point for each employee's future potential and thus sets the stage for a series of later growth steps.

The final stage of applications is where MI displays the full range of its potential applications. Minimally, what appears are critical applications to training, personnel, performance, and mission. In addition, the entire training menu and its delivery systems can be reviewed toward the end of being reshaped as an MI training program. In fact, the principal responsibility for implementing the five-stage MI process probably belongs to CLOs and directors of performance improvement and LMSs.

All personnel processes and procedures need to incorporate MI screening and assessment as conditions and criteria for initial hiring and subsequent promotion. But such a commitment to a new fusion of human capital and human potential in turn requires executive willingness to revisit and reformulate company vision and mission. In many ways and in the final analysis, the company unexpectedly is asked to play a larger and more proactive role through MI than through current modes of operation and measurement. MI also may grant organizations caught in ever-increasing spirals of having to outdo themselves with new ways of doing so. Above all, it would provide business with the opportunity to display a vision and mission of embracing human potential rather than its dispensability.

What follows is a visual summary of the five-step MI process:

MI Application Stages
Process Focus Yields/Gains
1. Identification
    By individual: How are you smart? Employee MI Profile
    By company: What do we value as smart? Company MI Profile
2. Interpersonal Assessment
    By individual: How are smarts interoperable? Team smarts
    By company: How does structure facilitate relationships? Fluid Design

3. Goals Focus: Customer
   By individual: Customer knowledge base? Customer Targets
   By company: Knowledge gathering. Customer is data
4. Reflection
   A. By individual: How do smarts internally interact? Synergy Range
      By company: What kind of interaction do we need? Preferential Patterns
   B. By individual: How do team smarts interact? Team Optimums
      By company: Structure to facilitate teamwork? Collaborative Culture
5. HR Applications
   A. To Training. By individual: Problem solving and innovation MI taxonomy
      By company: Big picture and long term. Diagnostically Driven Training
   B. Personnel. By individual: Recruitment and selection. MI Screening
      By company: Promotion by smarts. MI Reward System
   C. Mission. Of individual: Customer and innovation focused. Employee Managers
      Of company: MI organization. Future driven

Clearly, MI is not a panacea or magic bullet. It can't solve systemic failures or executive lapses. It is also not a template of one size fits all. Companies like MI itself will display multiple MI versions and visions. Above all, it is not a quick fix. It requires trainers, HR and performance improvement professionals, and company leaders to pause, to step back, and to contemplate total reengineering.

Happily, it can be done in stages. It also can accommodate company priorities. Only certain divisions or operations can be initially targeted. But as training and human resource professionals link forces through MI, what in effect will gradually occur over time is that companies will be given a future lease on organizational life, and employees on their unfinished human potential. That double gain or integration is what in fact MI has to offer: the fusion of company and individual smarts.

REFERENCES

Armstrong, T. *Multiple Intelligences in the Classroom* (2nd ed). Alexandria, Va.: ASCD, 2000.

Jung-Beeman, M. J., and Bowden, E. M. "The Right Hemisphere Maintains Solution-Related Activation for Yet-to-Be Solved Insight Problems." *Memory and Cognition* 28, no. 7, (2000), 1231–1241.

Campbell, L., Campbell, B., and Dickinson, D. *Multiple Intelligences and Student Achievement*. Alexandria, Va.: ASCD, 1999.

Carter, R. *Mapping the Mind*. Berkeley: University of California Press, 1998.

Dennison, P., and Dennison, G. *Brain Gym*. Ventura Calif.: Edu-Kinestics, 1994.

Fogarty, R., and Stoehr, J. *Integrating Curricula with Multiple Intelligences*. Palatine, Ill.: Skylight, 1995.

Gardner, H. *Frames of Mind: The Theory of Multiple Intelligences*. New York: Basic Books, 1983.

Gardner, H. *Intelligence Reframed: Multiple Intelligences for the 21st Century*. New York: Basic Books, 1999.

Gardner, Howard. "Multiple Intelligences after Twenty Years" http://www.pz .harvard.edu/Pls/HG_MI_after_20_years.pdf

Glasser, William. *The Quality School: Managing Students without Coercion*, New York: HarperCollins, 1992.

Kravis, de Roulet. *Multiple Intelligences and Leadership*. New York: Lawrence Erlbaum, 2001.

Lazear, David G. *Multiple Intelligence Approaches to Assessment*. Palatine, Ill.: Skylight, 2001.

Martin, J. *Profiting from Multiple Intelligences in the Workplace*. New York: Gover Publishing, 2002.

Martin, W. C. *Assessing Multiple Intelligences*. International Conference on Educational Assessment. Ponce, PR, March 1995 (ED 385 368).

INNOVATION: STRUCTURING A RESEARCH WORKFORCE, CREATIVE THRESHOLDS, AND RADICAL BREAKTHROUGHS

Motivating change is difficult, perhaps even impossible. One can surround employees with all sorts of incentives, inspiring pictures on the wall, cheerleading sessions with managers, and the like, but it may not take. Why? Because motivation is internal not external.

The two basic techniques of the military—bribery and fear—are never internalized. They constantly require a sergeant standing by with a 2x4 or basket of goodies to be persuasive. The moment he and the stick or the carrot are gone, behavior reverts to whatever it was initially. A horse can be led to water but he may not drink. So what else can be done? Nothing apparently, if the only approach is a direct one. But a totally different tack might work.

An unusual opportunity and challenge surfaced. A relatively small high-tech organization with a strong reputation for innovative products and services was facing stiffer competition, especially from abroad where copyrights and patents were not always respected and where wages were much lower. The only solution was not only to make the company more innovative, but also to involve everybody in the process. Only by improving across-the-board ways of doing things could the advantages enjoyed by competitors be offset.

Although every company seeks that goal, two factors complicated this assignment. First, the organization was not starting from square one. The employees had a healthy respect for leveraging information. They were in fact already knowledge workers. Second, the goal of total involvement of all employees was tied to total improvement. As such it offered the challenge of uniformity (a singular standard approach) working its way through diversity (top to bottom, CEO to mail clerk).

The associates I worked with huddled, brooded, brainstormed, wrote ideas on the board, searched the Internet, consulted books and articles, called a few other seasoned veterans, and so on, but nothing emerged. To be sure, because of the emphasis on ministering to all employees, the focus had to be more basic and essential; not so much creativity as curiosity. The image of over 200 horses standing at the trough and refusing to drink drove us crazy. Then serendipity intervened.

One of our associates just had an article accepted after having been rejected. The reason for the initial turndown was lack of attention to and utilization and documentation of the research in the field. He happily threw the manuscript and its congratulatory cover letter onto the table. Like the proverbial hat thrown into the ring, suddenly we all realized that a new and different model had been put directly in front of us. Why not train all employees to be researchers? Why not alter "needing to know" to "needing to know more"? Could curiosity be engaged and be then prodded ever so gently toward creativity? And what would be researched?

We put together a plan for all employees. There would be no exceptions, even at the top. It involved five stages: introductory training of research design and sources; development of a research agenda of topics by each employee; creation of a research proposal and budget to be sent to an interdisciplinary research committee; review, revisions, and approval of the project and the appointment of a mentor team; and undertaking and completing the research project according to an agreed-upon timetable.

The first step was for every employee to compile a double research agenda. The first one was global and involved the company as a whole and the entire industry worldwide. The second focused on each employee's division. The same key questions of taking stock were to be asked: What do we know, and what don't we know? The employees themselves added another: How do we know all that we don't know? To facilitate the global agenda, we arranged for cross-divisional and top to bottom discussion groups and teams. Employees who had never met, let alone worked with each other, were brought together to interact and to develop a collective research agenda.

A feedback newsletter was created and disseminated. Anonymous input was invited. Initially, the process was the butt of humor. Some were familiar: "Who ever heard of a Nobel prize being given to a committee?" Another contribution offered the Research Angst: "Analysis, analysis; paralysis, paralysis." But perhaps the best came from a mischievous but philosophical wag that summed up the entire effort: "Where there was light there shall be darkness. Where there was clarity there shall be confusion. Where there was order there shall be chaos. And with that as our creed, the research warriors of Company ABC go forth in search of the Holy Grail of Forbidden Knowledge. Your Devoted Servants, The Creatively Discontent."

It took hold immediately. It was reproduced everywhere. Some copies were put over inspirational pictures. We welcomed humor as the first sign of the creative juices beginning to flow. Never minimize mischief.

The research agendas produced were so incredibly impressive that we quickly recommended to the CEO that he dub all items as proprietary and to be held close. That had an immediate salutary effect. The entire effort rapidly was invested with importance. All employees found their curiosity and creativity affirmed, acknowledged, and appreciated. The momentum increased and proposals were generated. Quickly a call was put out for writing and editing assistance. The communications division was pressed into service. The CFO developed a research budget accompanied by guidelines of limits and exclusions.

The training on research design and methodologies sought to demystify the process. Practical, everyday models were developed of survey formats, interview protocols, data analysis, display of findings, and so on. The employees reveled in it; it was like being given a brand new toolbox. Mentors were internally identified by an anonymous survey form—a quick and dirty research project in its own right—supplemented by some retirees who had not gone to Florida or Arizona and were pleased to be again involved. Finally, each approved research project was assigned a supervisor drawn from the ranks of senior staff. Even the CEO carried a load of research projects.

Was it successful? Immensely. Some ten research projects were completed in six months, nearly thirty by the end of the year. Because the proposal process required a detailed plan for implementation and sign-offs in advance from the major principals involved, the time span for changing operations based on research findings was short, easy, and fast. The fear that the research process would peter out and the projects dry up, betrayed a lack of understanding of the research process itself. Just as technology creates technology, research begets research. Indeed, the company gradually developed the reputation in the industry of being a totally R&D company. In fact, one research survey project sought to assess the impact of the process on employees. Among the findings were increasing self-respect, a reputation as a smart company with no equal in the industry, and a very satisfying and even exciting place to work.

Although the specifics of the research projects were under seal, three general patterns can be identified, shared, and briefly discussed. All were unexpectedly diagnostic of company operations, processes, or structures. One critical pattern dealt not so much with matters within as between divisions. What was discovered again and again is that much is lost between the proverbial cracks. One research proposal claimed in fact that if such gaps could be bridged the gains in productivity would be greater than could be produced cumulatively and separately by each division. A related project proposed to study the effects on interdivisional operations after each divisional manager was trained as a broker.

The second favored area of research was customers. One proposed to study the effects (before and after) on employees whose work location or situation forced them to be distant or removed from customers, but who were then brought into direct contact with a representative sample. Another sought to survey and tap the creativity of customers; asking for their suggestions for new products and services. Still another asked for the specifics of customer satisfaction or lack of it. Since many customers are also vendors running their own companies, unexpectedly their answers included how the business should be run differently. In short, the customers became data. It was a rich vein for research to tap.

The third pattern was not just unexpected but transformational. The professional researcher is usually associated with a research lab, a university, or a think tank. The dominant image is that of a detached, dispassionate, and objective searcher of knowledge. That traditional image was explicitly targeted as part of the process of demystifying the research process and the researcher. In particular, what was introduced is the notion of action research pioneered by Carl Lewin.

Lewin argued for three changes. First, he was an advocate for lay researchers. Second, he embraced the study of fluid, ongoing situations in real time and place. They needed to be studied in a state of action outside of a controlled environment if the findings were to be authentic. Finally, Lewin claimed that researchers did not require objectivity or total noninvolvement as an absolute condition. The researcher could be directly involved in the situation and even affected by its outcomes. Who else has more knowledge and motivation, and more to gain? Besides, such bias is a small matter and can easily be corrected for.

Historically, action research had found its largest number of users and supporters among teachers who have produced a substantial body of classroom research on best practices. Lewin's adjustments made all employees breathe easier. The harness of action research was something they could function comfortably within. But it also produced a change in perspective that was generally unexpected.

Research inevitably involves repositioning. The most obvious change is from passive to active. One is no longer merely the object but the subject of study and operations. Another change is one of perspective. No longer does the employee perceive himself as solely part of a process. Now he sees the entire process from beginning to end. He perceives its systemic nature. Moreover, because the research process itself compels framing the subject of inquiry in the widest terms (although the final research topic will narrow that down to what is manageable), the employee suddenly finds himself in the captain's chair of a big oceangoing liner. If the subject is financial, he may feel like a CFO; informational, a CIO; personnel, a VP of HR; decisions systems, a CEO; and so on. In other words, this goes way beyond the involvement of ownership to that of leadership.

The final outcome was the gradual emergence of a new governance structure—that of distributed leadership. Leadership would no longer be the monopoly of the CEO and senior management. It would be written into every job description and exercised by every employee at every level of the company. Research had helped equip them for that role. It had given them a holistic view of the company. It had led them to understand operations from a systems point of view. They also learned that solutions are not always proximate to problems. The emphasis on the future of the industry and the company had made them sensitive to trends and to a larger vision of the next twenty years. Research had helped to create a company of researcher-leaders.

Post Script: In the process, however, a Frankenstein may have been created. Human resources reported a significant increase in requests to expand the undergraduate tuition remission program to now include enrolling in master's and doctoral programs at research universities.

CREATIVE THRESHOLDS

Preparing the way for anything new or difficult is a neglected art. It requires anticipatory reflection and creative thresholds instead of direct and impatient assault. For example, the senior management of a small high-tech firm made an executive decision to promote companywide innovation. That was summarily announced as not only a crash course but also a crusade. Everyone in the organization would be involved. A designated steering group was appointed. Tangible results were to emerge within six months. Breakthroughs would be rewarded with one-time bonuses.

Does all of the aforementioned sound disturbingly familiar? Does any of it cause you to squirm and groan? Or do you find nothing wrong? In any event, by the time six months came around the company had nothing to show for its efforts. As a consequence three of its vice presidents (marketing, human resources, and strategic planning) were dismissed. Then, troubled and confused, the CEO decided to call in a consultant with the idea of performing a quick fix and cleaning up the debris. I was that consultant.

Our first meeting started off with the CEO venting for ten minutes. My reaction was to listen and to wait patiently and then afterward to slow everything down and try to engage him in a general if not almost philosophical discussion of innovation. "Innovation is one of the most difficult objectives to accomplish. It is never easy to introduce. Its definition is slippery. Many argue as to what's really innovative and what isn't. And whether everyone is creative."

Then I moved on to specifics. "How many of your managers in your judgment exhibit innovation? What percentage of the workforce do you estimate are creative? Do you believe employees can be trained to be creative or is such ability basically innate?" We also talked about innovations that occurred in the past in the company, as well as in the industry. "What were they? Who brought them forth?"

My strategy was to suggest that innovation is complex and not in the same league as announcing a salary increase or benefit package. In short, my goal was to encourage a more reflective and deliberative approach. I tried to give the impression that we both had all the time in the world to sort this thing out.

The approach worked. In closing the session, I suggested another one the next day to go over what apparently hadn't worked and why that was the case. The CEO responded: "Let's make it early in the day before things get cluttered and my time is gobbled up." I found the CEO the next morning, not anxious to have another philosophical discussion but instead to get down to cases. His game plan clearly was to come up with a new and this time successful launching process for innovation in the company. I was reluctant to totally abandon the process of dialogue or lose what had been captured the day before. But the CEO was hot to trot, so I tried to weave together all three elements of reflection, evaluation, and action—what I viewed as the essential trinity for preparing the way for all new initiatives.

"OK," I said, "But first let's look at how we launched this initiative in the first place." That immediately puzzled the CEO: "Why should an announcement even be an issue for reflection, evaluation, and action?"

"We could get into an extensive discussion of how you announce decisions in general," I responded. "But I know you are anxious to get to the heart of this particular situation. So let me just ask whether there is anything special about innovation—the way which we talked about it yesterday—that might affect the way the announcement was made?"

The CEO, musing out loud, recalled "Many are uneasy about innovation, many feel they are not creative. And I would even say that many may not know what innovation is, or be fully aware of what it could mean to the future of this company."

"Exactly! Given all these apparently legitimate concerns and hidden questions," I asked, "What, in retrospect, would you have done differently about announcing the initiative?"

"With the benefit of hindsight, I guess I would have discussed it first. I would have used examples. Big ones, and many little ones, as many as I could think of; some of those we talked about yesterday. I might have told them the story of what was done at 3M. You know that article you gave me on their fifteen-minute system. Above all, I would try to strike a balance: While I don't want innovation to appear facile or accidental, I also don't want it to appear distant and impossible, beyond their reach, reserved for only R&D types."

"Good! So now we know that we can't just drop an announcement like a bomb without taking the chance that it will blow up in our face. OK, so that was not the best way to start and you already have to find another way. It is interesting that you mentioned R&D. A little sidebar if I might?"

The CEO nodded and leaned forward. I continued, "Thomas Edison still holds the record for more patents than anyone else to this day. Of course, he may have been an inventing genius but he had others working with him who were not Edisons. So he developed for himself and all his employees idea quotas. But he also knew that some ideas were big and many would be small; so, for example, he gave himself six months to come up with one new major idea, and a number of smaller ones. I mention Edison because he may be telling us something. His emphasis was not on inventions but ideas. Maybe that holds a key for the company and innovation. Maybe the process we want to get going is IG—Idea Generation. And maybe what we have to do is to encourage each employee to work on his ID—his own Idea/Innovation Diary—which is private and which is not available to anyone unless he says it is."

The CEO nodded reflectively. "You're right. The focus is really on ideas. We can't all be Edisons and match his record, but if we can get our people to write down what they think and what they have come up with we will be way ahead of the game. In fact, I never told anyone this but I keep an idea journal by my bedside. OK, let's keep going. This is good stuff."

"OK, let's go on to the next point. The initiative was presented as a crash course and a crusade. Put yourself in your employees' place. How would you have reacted to such a statement?"

The CEO snapped, "I would have resented it. I don't like being stampeded into anything. And I personally don't warm to the cheerleader role. Worst of all, it sets us up for success or failure. We either make it or we fold. Besides, nothing could be further from the truth. We are actually doing quite well and all indications are that we will have solid sales for the next three to five years. So this was a future-oriented activity. But, OK, I see where you are going. What you are saying is that we should have just told it like it really is—as a way of getting a leg up, insuring our future success. Right?"

"Absolutely," I quickly answered. "And maybe even to grow another business or at least another division. When the juices start to flow, you never finally know what people will come up with. Now, pressing on, why a timetable of six months?"

The CEO bristled, "Now, I think that was perfectly defensible. You can't have an open-ended arrangement without limits and without closure. I would let that stand."

"OK," I said and then paused. "But suppose nothing happens within six months? Do you shut everything down or let it just go on? Or suppose then something surfaces by month seven, something else by month eight. What then? How will that six-month deadline look?"

The CEO interrupted: "Maybe arbitrary, even dumb. But there has to be some oversight and control. They have to know that they will be held accountable."

I mildly protested, "But accountable for what? You did not put a dime into this. You are not providing any training. You are not giving people time off. You are not sending them to any conferences. You are not even buying them books and magazines to read. You put this pot of money aside for bonuses but if no one comes up with anything, even that money won't be spent. I understand every executive's need for control and outcomes, but deadlines and innovation are not compatible, unless you are willing to settle for half-baked goods prematurely delivered before their time."

The CEO was quiet. Had I pushed too hard? I stepped back and took another tack, "Instead of control, you may want to go for indirect monitoring. Schedule weekly brown bags or pizza lunches (you pay). Mix divisions, levels, shifts. Have the supervisors just listen; tell them not to talk, just take notes. Carry forward those notes to the next level then to the next and then to senior management. Walk around, drop in on sessions unexpectedly, listen for a change."

The CEO sighed, "Well, it makes sense not to dictate creativity. It's like pushing spaghetti. It just won't behave the way you want it to. Well, I guess you're also questioning my picking an innovation steering group. Did I do anything right?"

I said reassuringly, "You came up with idea of an innovation initiative, and that is right as rain. But I am curious. What was your thinking here? What did you hope to accomplish with this steering committee?"

The CEO sat back and thought: "Well, we picked people from each division. Each had an excellent record and had given some evidence of being creative. The idea was they would model for each of their divisions the behaviors to produce results."

I agreed. "That makes a lot of sense. Modeling is critical. That is what Edison did. But here's my problem. It's either going to be companywide or it is not. It is either going to be collective or not. Innovation often occurs with the least likely people and in the least likely ways. Besides, most selected steering groups are political. Those chosen are always the same ones picked. The winners of trips to Hawaii are always the ones who win again and again. Good for the few winners, lousy for all the rest who may get used to being losers; and there are always more of them than winners. Besides, everyone in the division will rib their representative to death and make him or her regret he or she ever was chosen in the first place. Finally it will be seen as a transparent way again of maintaining control. Make it egalitarian. Inclusive not exclusive. Fish or cut bait."

The CEO protested, "OK, OK, but what's wrong with incentives? It's been used since the beginning of time and it works."

I conceded, "You're right. Generally it works. It certainly has been effective for years in sales especially. But money and innovation have nothing to do with each other. It is a mismatch. Incentives stimulate only the familiar not the different. Besides, such incentive-driven innovations will be generating a lot of look-alikes of what you already have. But you will not get anything different."

The CEO was not ready to toss in the towel. "Well, what should we do? Drop the idea of incentives altogether?"

I again became reflective, "I am not sure. My instinct tells me that it is a question the employees should tackle. See what they come up with.

Make it part of the creative challenge. I have to confess. I am a little old-fashioned. To me the best incentive is the future of the company—the future of my job. Or as one worker put it to the COO: 'Your job is to keep this company around so that I can collect my pension.'"

The CEO leaned forward, "I agree. I am old-fashioned that way, too. And that worker is right. You can't have growth and change unless you are around to try both. But it's the executive's job to look ahead and to decide now what will keep us around later."

He stood up and held out his hand. "Well, I think our exchange has set us on a new course. I now see why care must be taken with certain initiatives—preparing the way as you call it—thinking it through. I would like you to stay with us on this project, through all the stages for as long as it takes."

"Be happy to do so."

"And let's get together soon and hold another seminar. OK, Professor?"

Postscript: I nodded smiling and said to myself, "He was right on both counts. I am a professor and it was a seminar." But after I left and was walking down the hall, I realized that he was a professor as well, and that good seminars are always shared if they are to be seminal.

In any case, in less than three months three major employee-generated proposals for innovation passed the review committee and were on their way to implementation. Many others followed. All were energized by the Idea/Innovation Diary, which often led to small non-dramatic changes that could not be called innovative but just different ways of doing things. Above all, the employees entrusted with the future of their jobs and the company rose to the challenge and became pre-eminent and permanent idea-generators.

In the process, what were the lessons learned? Innovation should never just be announced. Preparation is required. Examples should be given from the company itself, from the industry. Innovation should not appear facile or fortuitous but never beyond reach of the rank and file. Speed is not relevant. Deadlines are the enemy of creativity. If you have to have quotas, stress number of ideas. Urge all to develop an Idea/Innovation Diary. Deadlines and innovation are not good partners. Keep all open ended like the process itself. But stir the pot. Schedule weekly brown bags. Top management should not pick innovation teams. The effort is collective or it is not. Besides, it is not a political popularity contest.

Money and innovation have nothing to do with each other. It is a crass mismatch and will not stimulate difference but incremental familiarity. If you need an incentive system, let it be employee designed. It is likely to be creative in its own right.

The ultimate preconditions for innovation are environmental. The key variables are identified and summarized in the following figure:

Situation	From	To
1. Culture	Directive	Questioning
2. Focus	Same	Different
3. Structure	Closed	Open
4. Systems	Mechanical	Biological
5. Information	Limited	Shared
6. Distribution	Insiders	Network
7. Communication	Vertical	Horizontal
8. Status	Official	Unofficial
9. Incentives	Financial	Environmental
10. Quality	Prescribed	Evolving

RADICAL BREAKTHROUGHS

Desperation sometimes leads to radical creativity. For example, imagine creating a change pill. With one stroke, workers would change; so would teams, so would managers, so would organizations. To many frustrated CEOs and consultants it seems that is what it would take. So much already has been done, written, and researched about changing or reengineering people and organizations; and so much has been tried with often unimpressive or short-term results that we seem to be at the end of our rope. Perhaps, we have reached the point finally to contemplate going off the deep end—pursuing desperation rather than enlightenment—considering excesses rather than rational incentives.

The basic reason change is difficult is that people are stuck in success. The tried, the true, and the tested have generally served them well. The basic problem-solving tool kit has worked most or all the time. The kinds of benevolent and often heady learning dislocations that occurred in college or graduate school have been replaced by steady and sober affirmations of standardized operations and hard-nosed conventional wisdom. In many cases work development has been continuous rather than discontinuous, incremental rather than different.

In short, who are we asking to change? Someone who has been successfully set in her ways, who already is persuaded she has been changing and growing for many years, who has acquired the language and behaviors of change via various workshops and books, and who has learned to pick the fruit of productivity from the lowest branches.

Also, many current efforts to change behaviors and environments are manipulative, punitive, or excessive. Workers are offered rewards or gain-sharing incentives. Employing a more direct frontal attack, employees are told that if they fail to achieve their stretch goals the company will find others who will. Finally, CEOs and managers communicate endlessly: They talk about global competition, industry problems, customer alienation, and the like. But it mostly falls on deaf ears because what all these techniques translate into is a request or demand to do more. But what is needed is not more of the same stuff, but different stuff—innovative stuff.

In a nutshell, what are we seeking to accomplish and how far are we willing to go? If the goals are basically incremental, we will get more of the same; and if that is acceptable then stay with the manipulative, punitive, and excessive.

But if the goal is something more substantial and radical—to change the fundamental assumptions and perspectives of inquiry, thinking, and conceptualization—then we have to engage in a strategy that is more oblique and even mischievous. In the process we have to outflank success. We have to come from the side and from the back and from the top and the bottom. We have to unthink our basic way of thinking. We have to unlearn our basic way of learning. We have to unlive our basic way of living. We have to become in short someone different. The enemy is thus not outside but inside the gates. The strategy being proposed here is threefold.

Instead of asking for change, ask for innovation. It does not make any sense to beat around the bush. Go for the brass ring. Whether you are officially a learning organization, if you become an innovative one you will be an outstanding learning organization, for innovation is the ultimate learning experience.

Recognize that the brain is designed for survival. It becomes creative only when survival is imperiled—in other words, dislocation drives openness.

Outflanking the brain on the one hand and its successful habits is initially slow. The mind has to be weaned gradually; it has to be teased into being surprised by itself. But once a new flow starts, movement can be rapid.

What follows here is a series of dislocations designed to gradually separate the familiar from the different. In increasing intensities, the aim is to move the center off center in order to create the space for the gradual emergence of a new center. This new center may not be really totally new. It may be a previous center in which the experience of creativity occurred and in which learning was still incomplete.

The goal is to bring that past forward into the present, not to compete or replace the present identity but to complement and converse with it. The ultimate synthesis will be a fusion of the old and the new. It introduces a new tension between success and exploration, between the operating reality of the tried and the true and the experimental and the new.

The first strategy involves a gentle disorientation produced by assumptions analysis. That helps to set up an other-than-linear or either-or kind of thinking. The second invites the dislocation of adopting a totally new temporariness, of looking at the world and problems as transitional, always unfinished. The third and last is the most destructive and vigorous because it involves a process of emptying the self and the mind, casting out the obstacles remaining to a new curiosity and experimentation.

DISORIENTATION OF ASSUMPTIONS INVENTORY

The first step of exploring assumptions involves in this case innovation itself. Here are five pairs of statements:

1. Innovation is easy.
   Innovation is hard.
2. Creativity is something you are born with.
   Creativity is something you acquire.
3. Everyone is creative.
   Only a few are creative.
4. Intellect inhibits creativity.
   Intellect supports creativity.

5. Creative types are strange.
   Creative types are normal.

Typically, individuals choose one half of each pair. And usually a divide is set up between analysis and innovation, with each group following a consistent pattern of self-identification. Thus, those who are highly intellectual often construct the following composite: "Innovation is hard except for those who are born with it. These few creative types are often anti-intellectual and eccentric."

The other construction is 180 degrees away: "Innovation is relatively easy especially for those who are used to it, although one learns all the time. Creative people think but not primarily; and they are not so much weird as different, sometimes."

So there we are, each group passing a half off as a whole. In addition a number of permanent and false oppositions are proclaimed: innate versus acquired, intellect versus creativity, normal versus abnormal, easy versus hard. The first conclusion one therefore can come to is that such divisiveness is the sign of being stuck on one side or other of the brain. The process of constantly confirming that precious partiality is the very antithesis of innovation. The proper answer to all five pairs is duality: not one or the other but both. Innovation is both easy and hard, born with and acquired, resistant and accepting of intellect, strange and normal, and available to all but especially to a few. In short, the first stage of change is to establish harmonious discord, dwelling comfortably and without irritation with opposites, and becoming comfortable with ambiguity.

THE INCOMPLETION OF TRANSITION

Creative dislocation needs to be followed by another disorientation: an introduction to precarious states of mercurial thinking and imagining. Enter the five terrible "Ts": the temporary, the tenuous, the transitional, the transient, and the tentative. The aim of any one or all five of these icons is to breed impermanence, to create a willing suspension of disbelief that anything will last or be unique. It is an acceptance of footsteps in the sand, a recognition that what will emerge or be produced will not dominate the landscape forever. The Etruscans painted on wood knowing full well that, unlike their Roman counterparts, it would eventually crumble just the way they also would.

To flourish, innovation requires a sense of experimentation—it cannot be oppressed by permanence and its companion fear of making mistakes. The forms must be made of rubber, not concrete. Nothing must be etched in stone. Edifices first exist as scaffolding. Drafts must become the norm. A tinker toy mentality shall reign supreme. Things should be put together and taken apart again and again, not desperately or with anxiety, but with a sense of play and even mischief.

The new attitude to be gradually developed is that there is no end to anything or any activity. There is no final solution to any problem. Rather, the best is temporary—it is what we currently can create. But nothing is finished. The evolution of the organization is far from over. It may have future incarnations that are not known or anticipated. The current products and services provided may not be what will be offered or created five or ten years from now. The company may become more of an electronic than an actual place. And most important, I am not finished; I am not done with myself yet.

The net result is everything is shaken out and loosened up. Everything becomes subject to flow rather than divisionalized or standardized finality. Rather than only and always being masters of our fate and captains of our ships, we become objects as well as subjects of that flow. Work becomes more interesting. We are carried along. We are not totally known or owned. There is a permanent transience to all things, an unfinished and incomplete series of expectations that workers are invited to compete and finish, no matter how tenuously.

Once this kind of thinking takes hold employees become multidimensional rather than singularly focused on the one way to do things. Curiously, then, transition becomes not only a new norm, but also a new source of difference.

EMPTYING OUT THE VESSEL

The last strategy is made easier by the first two. At this point the world and the employee experiences a sense of multiple impressions. There is déjà vu as previous experiences of creativity and learning are tapped again. There is a dawning and growing respect for complexity and ambiguity—that things are not what they seem, that there are links and connections not previously acknowledged, that the world is more entangled and perhaps more secretly and subtly interconnected than it initially appeared. And finally that every current way of doing or conceiving of things masks many alternatives that were not chosen on the one hand and many others that were not originally thought of. The rush to get on with things is tempered by the recognition of constant change and transience. Above all, there is the sense that there is more to everything, especially me, and there is enough time to do all the things worth doing.

At this last stage, the individual turns on himself all the altered states that he has experienced in order to claim himself anew and to make himself whole and wholly his own. This is the most reflective stage. It involves a double process of emptying oneself and being filled up. The worker must trash his mind and purge it of everything but the problem he is trying to solve. His world must be occupied by that problem. There is no past or future, only the present. Rather than irritably being busy with his problem-solving tool kit, he has to be quiet so that he can hear what the problem has to say to him, including what its solution is or more accurately its solutions. And when that happens, change occurs, innovation appears, and the future is incarnated.

Risky strategies? Perhaps. But the gains are potentially great. Besides, the only way an organization will be able to claim its future is if they grant it fully to their employees first.

20

EMPLOYEE CENTRALITY: WORK COVENANTS AND PROGRESSIVE EMPOWERMENT

Advocates of capitalism often argue that "poorly managed and poorly led companies deserve to disappear." But what about the innocent? Why should the workers pay for the ineptitude of their leaders? Perhaps the standard for wars should be not how many soldiers but how many generals are killed.

Increasingly, employees are questioning those in charge and wondering how smart and anticipatory they really are. The first thing a savvy consultant does when brought in to solve a problem is talk and listen to employees. Invariably, they know not only what is wrong but also how to fix it. But they are never asked.

Increasingly, employees are not blinded by hero worship or codependent on a father who knows best. They value their own intelligence and refuse to accept suffering the consequences of the incompetent and the paternalistic. Too many have endured downsizing and reductions in force associated with mergers and acquisitions to have much confidence in a leadership that gives lip service to participation but essentially practices benevolent authoritarianism.

On the other side of the aisle a similar rebellion is brewing, only in this instance it involves managers. Thinning or flattening out the organization has made overwork a norm. Fewer managers are being asked to accomplish and supervise more, to fill in gaps left by loss, and to rely on less qualified workers to accomplish ambitious "stretch" goals. Moreover, to do all that they have to create, train, and sustain worker teams. Afterward, they have little or nothing to manage. The team does it all. As managers become aware that they are being asked to cut their own throats, they are less than enthusiastic about supporting teams whose increasing effectiveness increases productivity but forecasts their own demise. In short, there is discontent on both sides.

Workers want more say; managers seek to preserve their status. Employees want to become not just shareholders but stakeholders. Managers want their expertise of planning and supervision valued. Workers argue that their experience is critical, managers their education and training. The net result is an impasse in which neither side will yield. Employees will not surrender their recently achieved centrality nor will managers, after all the years of dominance quietly take a back seat. But alas, the rope in this tug of war is the organization that employs both. When the CEOs or senior staff speak on behalf of the organization, all the familiar declarations come from the mount: We are in charge, we set policy and choose direction, we determine who is hired and who is fired—in short, we rule.

Not so any more. Too many major misjudgments, flawed products or services, failed companies, unprofitability have torn or tarnished the mantle of infallibility. Moreover, the dissension on both sides of the aisle is generally ignored and thus nothing or little is done to bridge or converge the two. Current CEOs and their senior staff preside over a divided house, which is immune to traditional monarchical harmony and capacity to resolve.

The net result is a wobbly three-legged stool. The CEOs and senior staff (and Board of Trustees) no longer provide constant support for managers because of the pressure for worker productivity. The managers still have to do all the dirty work, fill in holes brought about by reductions in force, and trade off their traditional control with worker teams. The employees are becoming increasingly distrustful of upper management's judgment and resentful of their obscene salaries, often increased precisely when layoffs occur in some kind of perverse reward system.

In many organizations distrust has become the norm. Replacing CEOs solves credibility temporarily. But it is recognized soon as an external public relations game of duplicity as managers and workers see no internal changes follow in its wake. In short, disunity reigns among the three major components of an organization: upper management, middle management, and rank and file. When surviving global competition is factored in, what follows is a total preoccupation with the bottom line. Then virtually everything and everyone becomes expendable.

The dilemma is clear: How do we put Humpty Dumpty together in a new way? Can a different alliance between the three major constituencies be forged or negotiated? If so, what is the glue? There are some tentative and partial signs that a new understanding and even rapprochement is gradually surfacing. The standard official negotiations between workers and their organization have been extended unofficially between workers and managers. Some CEOs are willing to limit executive power to bring about internal alignment. They are beginning to understand that their central task as leaders is not to glorify their role but to find and proclaim areas of commonality. Increasingly, middle-level mangers are warming to their new and different tasks of being team leaders and coaches of improved performance. Employees are increasingly aware of the need for a less adversarial more cooperative attitude and of their own productivity and creativity offsetting the lower wages of global competition.

In other words, historically we appear to have reached a major branch-point in which all sides are more open to changing their fundamental relationships with each other and of producing a whole that may even be more than a sum of its contending and divisive parts. There is a need then to explore and to define no matter how tentatively the different roles of all the major participants in what I have called collaborative work covenants. Although what is offered here is not prescriptive, it is based on perceptible changes of practice on the one hand and major shifts in the literature of leadership and empowerment on the other. If such covenants are to take hold, however, there cannot be any take-backs in the hard-won battle of employee empowerment. New interfaces born of mutuality and commonality must be found to close current gaps. In the process, private enterprise may find itself moving more in the direction of socialism than capitalism.

How are covenants and collaboratives different from their earlier predecessors, the social contract and union contracts? The most obvious is that the focus is not limited to workers. In fact, the major problem is not eliminating adversarial relationships, which may be sometimes of contributory value, but getting all three parties to the table together to negotiate or renegotiate their roles with respect to each other. That, in turn, requires all to acknowledge that what is at stake is the company itself and its future. Indeed, that is the first and most important area of commonality to be acknowledged. The company may be owned by stockholders but its fate belongs to all those who are there equally at the table. Each one brings his or her special expertise to bear but that expertise is not exclusively held. It is available for input and overlap from all the others as well.

In addition, whatever form the negotiation shapes, it will never be final or emerge as a singular, legalistic, elaborate formulation. Rather, it will be a mosaic, a series of clusters, a compilation of agreements of understanding. It will also be consciously incomplete. Negotiations can go only so far and then they must cease. The endless and often trivial details of union contracts cannot become the substitute for basic operating principles guiding new relationships. Moreover, room must be left for fleshing the skeleton and accommodating the subsequent contributions of all those who have to implement the accord.

Unlike union contracts, which like bibles spell out every chapter and verse and that require often as many to monitor as to implement, a work covenant is intentionally incomplete. It is routinely discontinuous and preserves gaps. It compels constant dialogue and negotiation on every level and between every division and unit.

In addition, it is defined not so much in terms of the individual but the group or team. And there are no jurisdictional limits. Nothing is off bounds. If the team lacks anything, it can be imported. The group may have a core but its periphery and final extent may vary with the focus and the process. It is free to expand and even cross divisional boundaries in pursuit of its quarry. And when that happens successfully, new configurations of operations may emerge, not even anticipated in the original agreements. Structural dexterity follows goal pursuit. Form catches up and supports function.

But no addendum to the contract is required to freeze this new variation. To etch spontaneous change in stone and finalize its shape may preclude a different configuration from emerging at another time and for another purpose. If anything, the work covenant process resembles the metaphor of a river flowing through an organization described and extolled by Margaret Wheatley. Self-learning and self-organizing, the process affects the fundamental structure and culture of the company and brings about changes gradually from within. The organizational chart itself no longer imposes order from without but benchmarks change points. It is the history of a work constantly in progress. Lest all this appear easy or rapid, it does not happen without extensive and intensive reconceptualization of work and work relationships by all the members of the triad. Effective groups attuned to process rather than function are not born. They have to be made, remade, nurtured, coached, challenged. They are newly created. In other words, there is the need for all to master at least five skills of group dynamics.

First, conflict is a norm. Managing opposition is the key to higher levels of understanding and performance. Second, interdependence of teams becomes the model for all. If a worker is dependent or codependent, he must become more independent. But ultimately, he and all others have to become more interdependent, not at the expense of their individuality but in addition to it. They have to become a new composite: collectivized individuals. Third, transition has to be accepted as a dominant and recurrent norm. Paradoxically, it provides the overriding and ambiguous benefit of an organization permanently in flux and committed to the dynamic give and take of collaboration. Fourth, work covenants require constant negotiation and persuasion. The process is endlessly consultative. The agreements reached are always tentative and situational. How they are arrived at is as important as what is finally agreed upon. It is an optimizing skill. Finally, communication must be constant and total. It is the stuff of mutual empowerment and a way of leaving no one behind or outside the circle. Persuasion is the key to bring groups back together into new wholes, healing wounds in the process, and forging a new consensus. Again and again the recurrent summary and debriefing has to include the same litany: "OK. What have we learned? Where have we been? Where are we now? What is our future focus?"

The skills must be supplemented by an understanding and examination of the assumptions, expectations, and agenda of each group. Often that requires reflection, assumptions analysis, and subsequent unlearning. For example, CEOs believe they have a monopoly on leadership. Managers are convinced that workers must be managed. Workers often think they know more than their immediate supervisors or the top brass. But a central covenant value is the self-organizing principle of groups managing themselves.

Overcoming limits to productivity may require that the traditional distinctions between workers and managers be blurred. Workers assume managerial roles and managers worker roles. This is the ultimate cross-training. It is also the key to how and why covenants can accommodate managers. Managerial functions are thus shared and are not the monopoly of one class of employees. But aside from the commonality of training and objectives that now tie both groups together, what is also required is a different definition of leadership.

It's not enough to claim that leadership is shared. Expertise is leadership and it must be acknowledged and given its due at all levels or directives and initiatives will not be hearkened to or respected. Such recognition means that every level leads. Each one not only possesses and practices its unique version of stewardship, but is responsible for harmonizing all the others as well.

Traditionally, shaping the whole was the distinction or cross that top management alone had to bear. Bits and pieces of the cross were parceled out to managers so that they could serve as mini-leaders. But that pecking order pecked at and muzzled or minimized the leadership of each level below CEO. But the work covenant functions not unlike the way a multidisciplinary task force does: The whole belongs to the whole. It grants not only all common purpose and focus, but also collective responsibility for sustaining and if necessary altering it. The covenant thus defines and celebrates commonality.

One of the key problems of effective group collaboration is keeping the big picture in front of everyone and not passing off a half as a whole. Indeed, the primary responsibility of all leaders at all levels is to preserve and optimize the collective individuality of the group so that the full force of its diversity can be brought to bear on all problems and opportunities. Finally, one of the key distinctions of such groups is the creation of the collectivized individual, who epitomizes the behavioral and cultural power of work covenant collaboration.

What might a work collaborative look like? And how would it work? Perhaps a defining way of rendering that is to offer a profile of each of the four members of the trinity after the negotiation. It should be noted that they have not been blurred into each other. Each set of characteristics has been developed to focus on what is now within their altered power and province and how they now contribute to the process of creating new interfaces and a new set of working relationships.

THE ROLE OF TOP MANAGEMENT

Constantly draw, shape, and share the big picture, routinely, periodically. Not summarily announce or promulgate decisions; instead, provide persuasive reasons and documentation for decisions. Align policy with vision and mission and be value driven. Be proactive, anticipatory, future driven. Conceive and present initiatives in clusters of alternatives and tradeoffs. Recognize, reward, and value innovation, small or large. Be intellectually rigorous, savvy, interesting, and occasionally daring. Signal clearly that the era of top-down, heavy-handed, punitive bossism is dead and buried. Give to get: If you want more accountability offer more choice.

Finally, always tell the truth, especially if it is bad news.

MIDDLE-LEVEL MANAGERS

Minimize noes; maximize yeses; optimize maybes. Don't play the blame, shame, or gotcha game; go for root cause. Don't play favorites. Be a straight shooter and talker. Be a worker; get your hands dirty. Do not oppose or suppress opposition; incorporate it. Keep the customer alive and in everyone's face, every time and everywhere. Listen always; especially two-eared listening—hear what is said and what is not. Develop everyone you touch. Recognize that success is always multiple.

WORKERS

Have a say and stake in everything. Don't allow yourself to be treated like children and accept pablum when you have the teeth to chomp steak. Claim that expertise resides with workers. No one knows the job better than the one who does it. Constantly ask, discuss, and explore. Act as if there are no limits to individual and group development and capacity. Acknowledge that all are collectively responsible for what is done, said, and sold. Treat everyone with respect and dignity. Value the diversity of commonality and commonality of diversity: everybody is the same in a different way. Practice what is preached.

TEAMS EXHIBITING THE COLLABORATIVE WORK COVENANT

Create a team that is change ready, able to shift direction and focus as needed. Be intolerant of mediocrity in everything: quality of product, service, communication. Shape the values of the collaborative work covenant to align with the vision of the company and vice versa. Be smart about your industry; position your company to take advantage of emerging trends. Minimize bureaucracy—weeds push out flowers. Be obsessive about customers. Meet them, talk to them. The customer is data. He may not be always right, but that is still the challenge. Move authority always closest to the point of action and expertise. Examine stats. Challenge assumptions. Check alignments vertically, and to the right and left. Give a prize for the best question of the week. Create employee universities in which teams teach. Create happiness, camaraderie, and enthusiasm as a unique expression of the team but never use it to shut out newcomers. Always seek to be interesting. Recognize and embody Blanchard's dictum: "None of us is as smart as all of us."

In many ways, collaborative worker covenants are being built upon previous breakthroughs and hard-won achievements. But these new agreements in many other ways are basically new. They signal a new competing centrality. No longer is the spotlight solely or even largely on CEOs, managers, or employees. Rather, the focus is on the interfacing relationships between them. Commonality is king. The commons of the old village is what is shared and owned by all. All collectively shape a new organizational configuration. Both vertical and horizontal alignments can be retained but only if surrounded and enclosed by a series of multiple concentric circles of common cause and purpose. The circular thus governs the architecture because all the Knights of the Round Table are equal and all are leaders. Jurisdictional boundaries are no longer sacred. Everything must flow and meander like Wheatley's river through the entire enterprise.

Leadership is not the monopoly of the CEO or senior management. Leadership is distributed and written into everyone's job description. Cross-training and work interchangeability are common best practices. Above all, collaborative work covenants hopefully create a new and interesting home for a new kind of worker-manager-leader as a collectivized individual.

To many, perhaps, the prospect of such a covenant appears utopian. But given the realities of the economics of competition on the one hand and the forces of empowerment and commonality on the other, workplace collaboratives and covenants may emerge merely as the embodiment of a transitional present and a transitional future.

How do things change? Three ways: We will it, we negotiate it, and it just happens. Those who claim to be in charge of making and shaping change, whatever their level and fulcrum, would have us believe that the last member of the trinity is also within their province. It has no separate power or even identity except what they give to it. On a national and international level, the counterclaims of history, past, present, and emerging, are not allowed to prevail over forged policy and image. But the truth is otherwise. André Gide correctly noted that "We believe we posses when in reality we are possessed."

We should will and shape with vision and mission. We should seek to be masters of our fate. We also should sometimes achieve those ends by the less dramatic and self-glorifying means of tweaking, revising, recasting—all the ways we serve and honor adjusting to our times, challenges, and circumstances. But we must also develop a healthier respect for and tolerance of the extent to which we are determined from without, no matter what that does to our self-definition and esteem.

History in partnership with emerging trends is the DNA of change. Circumstances drive decisions. If the illusion of control is still important, then we designate transformation as a paradigm shift. We may be affected from without but at least it takes place with the permission of our conscious understanding.

Categories BE, AE

1. Structure Centralized Decentralized Vertical Horizontal
2. Job Description Prescribed Self-Directed
3. Mission Statement Organizational Employee
4. Operations Function Process
5. Employees Workers Assets
6. Leadership Specified Distributed Top Down Available
7. Pay Salary Gains Sharing
8. Human Resources Recruitment Retention
9. Relationships Individual Group (Independence) (Interdependence)
10. Training Homogeneous Heterogeneous
    Singular Cross-Divisional
11. Information Hoarded Shared
12. Performance Blame/Shame Improvement
13. Manager Boss Coach
14. Listening Limited/Selective Feedback/ Feed Forward
15. Decisions Top Down Consensual
16. Innovation R&D Learning Organization
17. Forecasting Planners Lay Forecasting
18. Agreements Contracts Covenants
19. Voice Singular Multiple
20. Roles Given Negotiated

Figure 20.1. Empowerment Matrix

The argument here is cumulative. Over the last two decades what has gradually, increasingly, and tenaciously determined change and the responses to it is enfranchisement—especially of the bottom at the expense of the middle and the top. In scope and intensity it is comparable to the exodus from Egypt and the Declaration of Independence. Neither event resulted in immediate and total freedom. That not only evolved, but also was shaped and negotiated, and enshrined in vision and mission. Thus, willful self-determination still plays a critical role but it is not self-initiating. At worst it is reluctant, at best responsive. But willy-nilly, history holds the trump card.

To appreciate how pervasive and invasive empowerment has been, one needs to review the matrix in figure 20.1, which features in various categories what was in place before empowerment (BE) and after (AE).

No commentary is necessary. The visual display says it all.

MANAGER ADJUSTMENTS:
UPS AND DOWNS

It is probably politically incorrect to endorse obsession. This is especially true now when many urge balance between work and family, between matters of the spirit and the bottom line, between being a kindly coach and a forceful leader. But professionals are working harder and longer hours than ever before. Boards favor organizations that are vision driven, future driven, and leader driven. Driven is not exactly nonobsessive. The proverbial quest for fame and fortune has never been more realizable. More new millionaires and billionaires were created in this last decade than in the entire twentieth century

If such behavior is encouraged and even sanctioned, it seems somewhat hypocritical and yet understandable for organizations to hold aloft the image of the nonexcessive manager. No company wants to acknowledge that under the velvet glove there is an iron fist. Perhaps the wisest course is to find a model that at least somewhat redeems or softens the edge of that drive and yet maintains its ruthlessly singular and intense focus. One recommendation is to apply a phrase often repeated, invoked, and urged: become a student of the business (SOB).

SOB often unambiguously describes a manager who compulsively lives, eats, breathes the business and in the process may have developed uncanny instincts for what is central and futuristic. Students of the business always search for the piercing idea and the one who has it.

What are the characteristics and qualities of a student of the business? What distinguishes that special state from the conventional knowledge worker? There are at least five qualities: instinct, self-learning, convictions, endless inquiry, and problem solving.

1. Instinct

   The SOB has an ear and a smell for what is genuinely new, even groundbreaking. Students of the business develop instincts, hunches, feelings; they have highly developed antennae. But such reliance on intuition is not merely an early warning and opportunity system—although it can significantly function that way—above all, it is a way of knowing. They can ferret out something about to disturb the universe. Like Rick, they do not have to be the one doing it. Their obsession is initially to recognize it, then to give it credence and finally perhaps to lure it into this world. Like collectors of anything—pens, spittoons, stamps, coins—students of the business are always looking for the rare gem, for the Holy Grail.

2. Self-Learning

   Formal education often has little to do with the process. In fact, it can be an obstacle. MBAs may be more imprisoning than liberating. The SOB develops his own favorite way of seeking and acquiring knowledge—his own curriculum. But the respect for insight is total and pivotal. Unexpected "eurekas" can set the SOB off on a life journey. A teacher or colleague may embody a kind of endlessly probing curiosity that is seminal and stirring. A student may ask a question that comes out of nowhere and that does not follow the familiar trajectory and further is inimitable because that student is wired that way. A book or an article may stop the SOB in his tracks and rapidly become a personal bible. Or an opportunity to do some original research may result in being bitten by the bug of discovery. And if that happens again and again and lasts, one is permanently possessed.

3. Convictions

   The problem is that although the aforementioned experiences may happen to many, they come to naught mostly because of many fears—of being perceived as uncompromising, the intimidation of conventional company culture, and the paralysis of taking risks.

Many are more comfortable on the sidelines cheering the obsessives on to oblivion. Indeed, such intense SOBs are often condescendingly advised that if they want to get ahead and be accepted that they ought to toe the mark. That wisdom is pushed again and again at every stage until most buckle and begin to love their captors and slavery. But convictions dictate otherwise and preserve persistence and singular integrity. After a while the genuine SOB realizes that his strength and difference are part and parcel of his very identity—they are who he is. William Blake over two hundred years ago proclaimed: "I must create my own system or be enslaved by another's."

4. Endless Inquiry

Such types also are endless probers. They never stop asking questions. They are reminiscent of Louis B. Mayer's classic statement: "For your information, let me ask you a question." They are relentless. They get the scent and they are off like Sherlock Holmes pursuing the mystery until it gives up the ghost. They are often boring and even pedantic. They start conversations with "Did you know. . . ." They are capable of ruining dinner parties or being brushed off and told to get a life. But nothing stops or slows them down. They shake those comments off and look for another victim. Although they may be tiresome to others, they are never bored with themselves. They cover the waterfront and never miss very much if anything. Pedantry aside, they frequently find shortcuts to the basics or circuitous approaches to the center. A student of the business is searching for the impossible, which he secretly hopes he will never find because it is the search not the end prize that stirs him.

5. Problem Solver

He is an inveterate problem solver, an admirer of those who pull rabbits out of hats, tireless seeker of the state of the art. One could not find a better champion of innovation and creativity. What he finds particularly creative are new theories and metaphors that force reformulation, that require the entire world to be viewed differently. Such insights approach revelation. He operates on the assumption that nothing is known forever, and that knowledge will be overturned regularly and without warning.

Finally, he is a major advocate for the future, which he believes will be incredible and beyond present imagination. Ultimately, all students of the business seek to approach the threshold of time, to know all that can be known up to that point, and then to gaze and search for the new, the dazzling, and what has not yet been thought of. They all read science fiction and compose scenarios.

In summary, then, what does this obsessive managerial model of the student of the business offer other managers and confer on their organizations? At least five benefits. First, it urges other managers to think back to a time and place and person that compelled them to be obsessive—when they underwent an all-nighter not because they were cramming but rather totally possessed—when they did not so much decide to write something but rather it selected them to write it—when they were possessed by an idea or a vision that they could not let go of and that gave them no peace—finally, when they thought of going into business for themselves or actually created such a business—because all obsessives are entrepreneurial owners. Such experiences minimally will establish a basis for identification and kinship and enable managers to contemplate as a real future a mode of operation that is not totally unfamiliar or unattractive.

Second, the model of the student of the business can be used to assess and examine the degree of complacency and comfort of managers. How much is routine, how much is accepted as absolute gospel that will never change, how much inertia is built into the company culture? Is the organization driven to possess a future unique and discontinuous from everyone else in the industry? In short, is the organizational culture itself a student of the business?

Third, it compels probing and dislocating questions to be asked. Have any been raised at meetings, in teams, in formulating policy and planning? Are challenging questions and analysis generally rated highly and viewed favorably? Is the culture a questioning or pacifying culture, risking little, playing it safe, always being predictable?

Fourth, does the organization settle too quickly for answers or solutions? Is everything solved with the same solution system or tool kit? When was the last time that anyone pushed the question or issue harder, beyond conventional wisdom and familiar thresholds? Is the environ-

ment placid or passionate? Are there any resident madmen, idea lu-
natics, obsessive searchers?

Finally, has everyone been reading the same business books? Are they
ever discussed? Put on the agenda for a meeting? They all can't be right,
can they? Where's the synthesis? Who are the company's innovators?
Are they recognized and rewarded? How is creativity and futurity tied
together? How many students of the business does the organization
have?

Imagine a CEO who could boast: "My managers generally are all obsessives. They are all SOBs."

In the good old days managers were called bosses, never missed a day,
barked orders, never heard of psychology, and got things done. And the
workers always knew where they stood. It was either his way or the high-
way. But they too were never absent, did what they were told, had high
standards, respected authority, and exhibited a superb work ethic. Job
satisfaction was a bonus. If they experienced it occasionally, that was
fine. If not, that was OK, too.

But of course many of those bosses were brutes and bullies. In fact,
workers in many companies sometimes would band together and form
"dirty tricks teams" whose sole purpose was to drive bullies crazy or get
them fired. And there actually were consultants who would help them
out. Of course, now things are more civilized. Bosses are now called
managers or supervisors or, best of all, facilitators or coaches. But if
things are so much better, why in a recent Internet survey in Career-
Builder (2001) did more than 50 percent of workers indicate that they
would like to fire their bosses? As a consultant visiting many different
companies in many different sectors, I would push it to 75 percent.
Many could claim that 85 percent of all company problems were the
fault of bad managers.

What is going on? In this enlightened period of worker empowerment, intellectual capital, team management, and people productivity,
why should the old problems of bad bosses persist or resurface? Strange
as it may seem, an old pattern may come not from the past but from the
future.

According to future trends, managers are a disappearing breed. They
are like displaced gentry in late nineteenth-century Russian novels walking around and bemoaning, "I am a superfluous man. I am a superfluous

man." (Even the repetition proves the point.) They find themselves redundant. They have become marginal, peripheral, and in some environments trivialized.

Teams and robotics run a number of factories. The engineers appear to be on a daylong coffee break. Workers properly trained do not require the kind of extensive supervision managers insist upon to justify their jobs. Statistical monitoring of performance is automatic and does not require human bean counters. Maintenance schedules are known and followed. Safety factors are observed. Output per machine or unit is set up on dashboards. Metrics program and measure the process. In fact, the entire schedule of work assignments, stretch goals, and quality standards are often determined by the workers. If a piece of equipment breaks down, there is an employee fast response repair team quickly there, often trained by the vendor of the equipment. And then the head of the team is immediately in touch with the manufacturer by computer to display visually the piece of equipment, the problem, and possible solutions. A great deal, in short, that has been done by managers has been taken over by teams.

What happens when supervisors find they are not needed? They become endlessly intrusive and invasive. They cannot leave workers alone. They invent work. They call numerous meetings. The agenda is recycled, nothing is ever decided, and nothing is accomplished. They request endless reports and then reports of reports. With little or nothing to do, they become busy and bossy all over again, and spawn dirty tricks teams. Worst of all, they are throwbacks. Creations of an unwelcome future, they ironically are more past than future oriented and thus imperil the need to bring about employee change by facing forward rather than backward.

But the same circumstances have compelled role change. Rather than being totally superfluous and overbearing, many bosses and managers rightly have become coaches to facilitate the realization of potential. They have not totally crossed over the line between managers and employees but they have become closer than ever before. That makes sense and in fact has been a very productive partner and even indispensable component of performance appraisal and performance improvement. In short, the new manager is not only evaluating performance, but also coaching change. But for that to happen effectively, the database, range of evaluation, and coaching competencies have to become more robust and extensive.

When an employee sits down now with his manager coach, what are the dynamics? In the past, the coach would have a folder that contained the employee's work documents and history, a self-evaluation for that quarter, and perhaps an elaborate 360-degree feedback report (outsourced and produced separately by a specialist HR company at considerable expense). But the employee also has a folder. It contains his or her self-evaluation form, the report from the last time, and a printout of all his or her activities and achievements from the electronic portfolio that he or she has maintained and constantly updated. The supervisor is also familiar with the basic coaching steps and knows how to coach upward. In short, the first and perhaps the most noteworthy difference is the new equality between the two. The playing field is now really even and level. Exchanges between coach and employee are data-based. Claims and counterclaims require documentation. Each has a fat folder. The first change to note then is coaching is not a casual, quick-fix process but more of a professional and well-prepared negotiation. A key coaching competency, therefore, is doing your homework.

Another critical difference is the addition of collaboration to the traditional adversarial relationship. The latter echoes the past, the former anticipates the future. If he has become a genuine coach, not an all-knowing boss in sheep's clothing, the manager will welcome the relationship of partnership and perhaps be surprised by the equality and value of the give and take. Thus, they both sit on the same side of the desk like equals; contribution is mutual; at its best there may be the surprise of one plus one equaling three.

Far from losing respect, importance, or value, good coaches find new substance and challenge in this partnering role especially if they come to value and incorporate research. They become fascinated by work challenges, problem solving, and innovative solutions. They understand, unlike the old bosses, that they do not have a monopoly on wisdom, and that creativity can emerge from almost everyone and everywhere. They also can become fascinated by the dynamic interplay between various personalities and their attitudes toward work, work relationships, and standards of performance. In fact, it would not be inaccurate to describe a good coach as an outstanding example of a knowledge worker. But as such he needs to recognize that he may have more to learn, that his knowledge base may need to be as constantly expanding, as much so as that of the employees he coaches. In other words, he needs to practice continuous improvement and be exposed to the state of the art. He requires an advanced or graduate course in coaching. Specifically, his new integrative role requires greater awareness of the research in the field and its incorporation into his change kit. The third change then is to become a student not only of the business but also of the best information, research, and practices of the business.

In summary then, what is clear is that coaching is not just an expression of the warm fuzzies but because of the challenges of productivity and downsizing has become a far more thoughtful, anticipatory, and professional managerial role. Specifically, the coach has become a human resources director. His questions are always based on solid data. His task is to negotiate perceptions, and always to tip the dialogue to future aspirations.

The coach also must recognize that the employee enjoys a new role of equality. He is equally armed with data and documentation that at times may be superior in detail and depth to that of his coach. If he also has developed his own professional growth plan, his expectations and exchanges with the coach on career pathing may at times resemble role reversal. In short, the old, paternalistic role will not serve a new relationship based on equality. But the new coaching competencies can raise the dialogue between the two to a much higher and more collaborative level in which it may be impossible to tell who is the manager and who is the employee.

Finally, a distinctive role offered the coach is that of research into best practices. Again functioning as an ideal version of the director of human resources, the coach needs regularly to review the literature of his industry, of career development, and the changing demands of the workplace. Only in this way can the coach bring something unique to the table and to the employee. Perhaps these three competencies will restore some of the substance and insight to often marginal supervisors, and equally important, restore and underscore their significant contributions to worker productivity and future growth.

Overcoming limits is a recurrent obsession, especially those of managerial leadership. But hereby limits is not meant what leaders are unable or fail to do because of ineptitude, indecisiveness, miscalculation. Rather, it is what they should not be doing even though they have the capacity to do it.

Such inhibition may appear to be a strange course of action to recommend. After all, managers are hired precisely because of what they can do and what needs to be done, hopefully a marriage and fit made in heaven. And historically that is the way it has been. But there is too much at stake now and in the future for that course of action to tap the increasing independence and interdependence of the workforce.

The psychologists tell us that if you don't allow and encourage children and young people to do things on their own, even or especially if it seems to take them an excruciatingly long time, that they may grow up to be managers in organizations who routinely do not complete their tasks, fail to dot the *I*s and cross the *T*s, miss deadlines, and can't delegate. In fact, our experts of course have a name for it: Completion Deficiency.

Organizations need to create room not at the top but at the middle and at the bottom. But that can't happen with a management that is too invasive, too intrusive, too relentlessly needed. If the increasing independence of the work force is to be affirmed and advanced, then increasing the space and place for employees to be decision makers, innovative thinkers, and future driven needs to be provided.

To accomplish that the following nonsteps should be taken by managers:

1. Step Back

    Don't always insist on being number one. Be gracious. At best you are first among equals. Good managers recognize good managers among employees. They know who is good and who has the right stuff. Give workers a turn.

2. Step Down

    Don't chair every task force in sight or put your cronies in charge. Create opportunities for trying out abilities. Send workers out to sites like farm teams but give them letters of authorization and lines of credit. Multiply your number of representatives. Write down not the vertical but the horizontal chain of command so that if you are not around and even if you are everyone knows whom to consult or blame.

3. Step Aside

Establish company priorities by management sharing. Create co-leaders. Dramatize new options as essentially leadership opportunities. Identify key themes of the unit. Create the illusion that it is the company in miniature. Aspire to top roles. If technology or e-business is a new direction, act like chief information officers. If innovation is to be a major initiative, behave like R&D. If there is an increasing need to be sensitive to customers, make visible and present a cadre of selected customers to maintain relationships with.

4. Step Away

Every decision is minimally two decisions. One is what to do. The second is how it should happen. The mistake is that the first may be so prescriptive that it steals away the many subsequent decisions of implementation.

Authoritarian managers steal. They do not allow applications and follow up to take place without nervous micromanaging, incessant prodding, busy-body monitoring, and indispensable threats or rewards. Good managers step away to create the opportunities for seeking the closure of implementation. Rather than being sages on the stage they instead become guides on the side.

It may appear that these steps appear to be going against the grain of the basic managerial process of stepping forward or stepping up to the plate. But what is important: hitting a home run or winning the game? And sometimes that happens best by using pinch-hitters.

STEALING EMPLOYEE'S DECISIONS

The singular homogeneity of corporations no longer exists. In its place, there is incredible diversity—of employees, divisions, structures, multinational operations, alliances, partners, acquisitions, and mergers—in short, a whole host of different cultures currently coexists (Adsit, 1997). The quest for corporate unity, therefore, routinely encounters the patchwork quilt of the United States and even more so now that of the global market. And yet the search for such unity is a tenacious and determined job requirement of CEOs and managers.

It is an awesome, recurrent, and relentless task that, alas, more often than not falters and fails. It may have a better chance of success, however, if the following guidelines are heeded.

Commonality and unity are not the same. They also are not equally valued. Although initially unknown and unavailable, commonality is discoverable. The energy of the apex and the middle derives from the base. Inquiry of common purpose should follow reverse delegation. Power belongs to the lowest point of the organization. Managers, not CEOs are positioned for optimum access and definition. The secrets of commonality may be more discoverable and accessible with employee participation and involvement. Such bottom-up contributions should always pursue internal alignment with company objectives. Managerial guidance structures such alignment and priorities congruence.

The focus of managers is therefore clear: to discover what holds their units together as the avenue to what holds the company together. It is critical at the divisional level because that is not only where it has to happen, but also possesses sufficient diversity to test comprehensive applicability. In the process, the manager has to share the leadership of his task with the employees of his unit if the search for commonality is to become both generic and diverse, and thus both applicable and adaptable to all other units. Involving all and undertaken across the board, the discovery of commonality may be consensual.

The temptation is to limit the search to known or identifiable weak or soft spots suffering from a lack of common purpose. But that may be deceptive or distractive—fast and dirty. Better to be comprehensive and archetypal. Miniaturize the search to organizational essentials: mission, future planning, employee demographics, leadership, and training.

1. Mission

Mission is listed first because obviously that is where common purpose is expressed. But how obvious? And how well does it serve as a nexus? Two extremes dominate: Many companies have not revisited their mission statements for years; others seem to do it every week. In addition, the level of the review process itself may be exclusively the province of senior officers and thus not really serve the cause of diverse corrective revision. The CEO and his or her senior staff may shuffle words around or jazz it up with the latest buzzwords but it may still emerge as the same tired, interchangeable, and predictable statement that could apply to many companies. The pressure of commonality compels that another and more basic source of mission be found.

A number of organizations have been experimenting with employee mission statements (EMSs). In its basic form, managers ask employees individually to identify their job parts in the form of a mission statement. They then designate how their performance will be measured. Then because each employee shares that job description with others doing the same job, the next phase involves developing a master EMS of all those job parts and measures common to all doing the same job. "I" at that point changes to "we," an important symbolic inclusion and change. The net result is a collective template and identity, cutting across different divisions, sites, even countries, of occupational identities and goals.

The third phase seeks to assign priorities to each EMS and its parts, but this phase is negotiated not determined unilaterally. What fixes the priorities are the overall business goals of the corporation. Employees with their supervisors select those job activities, goals, and measures that serve best to accomplish those business goals. Thus, employee missions are aligned with the company's mission.

The company mission statement now becomes an aggregated core of common employee mission statements. Every individual and every group of job-specific individuals—indeed, every employee in the company—is welded together to articulate and share a common purpose and focus. The alignment of priorities clinches the process by creating a nexus between top and bottom. The flow of the organization cascades downward and ascends upward. The functions of the organization now can move more easily from the vertical to the horizontal as work and goal commonality emerges.

2. Future Planning

One of the most effective ways of determining whether everyone is on the same page is to identify a common challenge or opportunity, especially in the future. But again that can serve as a rallying point only if all are genuinely invited to face it together. It cannot remain a monopoly of the CEO and the senior staff or strategic planners. In other words, like the EMS process itself, it must be comprehensively participatory. In fact, that EMS can be used as a future probe.

Some managers experimenting with EMS have pushed the envelope further. Designating the compilation of an EMS as the current version and benchmark, employees also have been asked to create an aspirational version. That would incorporate and factor in skills and attributes to be acquired, especially in light of future challenges. The yields from this exercise are equally and impressively multiple. Most obviously, the workforce becomes future directed, even future driven. A comparison of the current with the future version quickly yields the training agenda needed to get from here to there. Finally, if a company wishes to capture the momentum of such a collective effort and to render it with greater precision, employees already are primed and receptive to participate in an environmental scanning process that, buttressed by books, articles, and speakers, can shape and create an in-house, companywide, employee futures collective. Such anticipatory commonality would produce a projection of decision alternatives, which might model perfectly the future core of the company itself.

3. Employee Demographics and Diversity

Currently, at least five, soon to be six, generations coexist in a large organization. The earliest were born in the 1940s, the latest in the 1980s; the range of their retirement runs from 2025 to 2065. Nearly fifty years of history span and determine the five cohorts and display their different and often conflicting value systems. Of late, that has been compounded by companies forming overseas alliances with cultures that are often at variance with some basic American drives. Software programmers from India, for example, employed by American companies do not seem to be as comfortable with the challenge of initiative and opportunity as their American counterparts. Instead, they would prefer decisions to be made and tasks to be assigned by others. In short, how is commonality to be found in the midst of such straining diversity?

Discovering common denominators may involve valuing paradox or ambiguity rather than an either/or attitude. For example, extremes are often posed as false alternatives: Everybody is the same or everybody is different. Typically, people are invited to choose one or the other position. The truth of paradox is that everybody is the same, differently. The commonality of sameness offers a common core for understanding, action, and communication. Difference then is available as individual variations.

4. Co-Leadership

Discovering commonality ultimately rests on leadership sharing. Indeed, to a large extent leadership itself is a source of commonality but only when it is parceled out, even multiplied, and is no longer a monopoly of the top. Many have endorsed distributed leadership as a companywide empowerment strategy.

For Greenleaf, distributed leadership takes two forms. First, it extends servant leadership across all decision points. Everyone thus would serve first and lead second. It also transfers leadership ultimately and selflessly to the organization rather than being a prisoner of executive superstars.

Handy was convinced that distributing leadership among all employees and even writing it into all job descriptions would not only provide but also require everyone to exercise leadership whenever and wherever it presented itself. Handy's clients found that such shared or common leadership enervated the company, generated creativity, and identified future leaders for promotion.

Finally, in a completely different area, that of public education, Elmore sought to address the situation of principals routinely being overwhelmed by the demands of the job as well as the increasing shortage of new educational administrators. His solution was to call for distributing the leadership horizontally to all teachers and professional staff so as to create a more manageable, accountable, and productive structure. In the process, what emerged increasingly as a new source of commonality was the teacher leader comparable to the middle-level manager. But these teacher leaders remained in the classroom. In the process, they uniquely embodied the integration of administration, instruction, and measurement.

5. Training

This final item returns the discussion to where it started. When employees are asked to compose their own mission statement followed by the increasingly inclusive process across the company, and when further future sights are raised and incorporated, what is produced is the commonality of shared purpose. In addition, that happily is not an abstract or imprecise understanding but rooted in the specifics of every job each person does. But perhaps its most powerful expression is the common desire to be more than they currently are. When the expression of personal potential is extended horizontally and transferred vertically from the base to the apex, and when leadership is shared and diversity valued, both commonality and the future become the nexus and mission of the company.

Discovering and nurturing such aspirations programs the company's future. Training and development then is harnessed on behalf of commonality of potential. Specifically, the training must incorporate the commonalties discovered. Thus, the training agenda itself should not be determined unilaterally but collaboratively, not from on high but from rank and file needs and aspirations. Training also should not be limited to incremental updates, but anticipate future developments. Harvesting companywide identification and evaluation of trends should be a training objective just as developing distributed leadership should be supported by training exercises. Above all, a major thrust of training should be stirring innovation. For such creative outcomes to involve everyone, all efforts need to ride the coattails of distributed leadership and benefit from the diversity of different people doing the same things differently.

What is perhaps now clear is that the search for commonality is inevitably reinforcing. It is a circular process. Each of the five areas mentioned earlier increasingly becomes interactively aligned. The orbits of leadership and diversity overlap and together they both support new ideas and future creativity. The net result is an organization structurally more like a network than a pyramid, more interconnected than separative, and more multiple than singular, steered in one common direction, even though thousands are at the helm.

REFERENCES

Adsit, J. D. "Crosscultural Differences." *International Journal of HR Management* 8, no. 4 (1997), 385–401.

Ashford, B. E. "Social Identity Theory." *Academy of Management Review* 14, no. 1 (1989), 20–30.

Buchen, I. H., and Zdrodowski, P. "Coaching Complexities." *PI* 41, no. 9 (2002), 27–29.

Flamholtz, E. G. *Entrepreneurship to Professionally Managed Firm.* San Francisco: Jossey-Bass, 1986.

Harrison, R., and Stokes, H. *Diagnosing Organizational Culture.* San Francisco: Jossey-Bass, 1993.

Hofstede, G. *Cultures and Organizations.* New York: McGraw-Hill, 1997.

Van Muijen, J. J., and Kooperman, P. L. "The Influence of National Cultures on Organizational Culture." *European Work and Organizational Psychologist* 4, no. 4 (1994), 367–380.

22

EMERGING LEADERS: CEO INTERVIEW QUESTIONS, SOLOMONISMS, AND RECONFIGURING THE EXECUTIVE TEAM

It is conventional wisdom to list, examine, and celebrate top leadership traits. That is occasionally followed by a list of tips for surviving the first year. Of course, both are after-the-fact lists. Neither compilation addresses before the fact. So hot and heady is the CEO pursuit that we ignore or minimize the prospect of failure. The interview needs to be perceived as an early warning system.

The sin of omission is similar to all the leadership development programs at centers and universities stressing how to get there but seldom addressing how to stay there. Or perhaps most important, what questions should a prospective candidate ask during the interview as a way of both getting and staying there? In essence, the five questions listed here seek to unearth the various ways a CEO can fail. The comments immediately following suggest how and why it can happen, and how to forestall its happening.

1. Subject: Workload

Question: "Would you be good enough to share with me the typical week of the current holder of the position? Might I see, for example, his calendar, his travel schedule, his after-hour business-related social engagements, the involvement of his significant or insignificant other?"

Comment: Most executive jobs are currently conceived positively or negatively by the behaviors of those who previously held the office. In some cases the schedule was crushing. Days of fourteen hours are normal, longer when business travel and related social engagements are factored in. Even if the candidate is in great physical shape when he starts, he will have little or no time to exercise and stay that way. Do you want to make important decisions, complete critical reports on time, and attend difficult meetings with a few hours sleep? And if the social calendar is heavy, consultation with spouse is essential.

If that is the way it has to be, then at least negotiate a six-month or one-year transitional period of adjustment in which you can gradually become acclimated on the one hand and absorb the overtime and traveling schedule on the other hand. In the process you may discover more civilized ways of running the job before it runs you.

2. Subject: National/Global Business

Question: "National and overseas branches, affiliations, partnerships? Where? What language(s) is involved? Do we have attorneys and translators to handle business? How often must the CEO carry the flag and visit? Typically for how long? To accomplish what? To what extent is the company involved in e-business? Future expansion planned? If so, do we have a CIO?"

Comment: Aside from perhaps too much time away from the main office, determine whether or not the company is equipped to conduct its present business nationwide and abroad. Also if that scope as well as expansion of e-business is set in the strategic plan. If so the job you are interviewing for may be like the proverbial iceberg—much more may be involved than is visible. Again, that may not be enough to be of concern; in fact, it may appeal to you or have drawn you to the position in the first place. But what it clearly signals is that you must pay attention to infrastructure, and you need to ask what and who is already there or being planned for.

3. Subject: Board Members

Question: "Who are the board members? Profiles of each? What other boards do they serve on? All holdovers? Any new slots available or likely? Have they had any specific assignments so far? What have those been? Is there a special liaison with the board from the CEO's office? If so, I would like to meet with that person separately. If not, what is my budget for such a liaison or trusted advisor?"

Comment: Boards hire and fire. Find out what you are up against and what their record and mode of operation have been. Hire a board coach who reports to you only.

4. Subject: Employee Demographics

Question: "Unions? Demographics of employees? Education? Years with company? Competency ratings? Performance appraisal and improvement reports? Empowerment practices and expectations? Expectations of new CEO? Last one? One before that? Disappointments? Distrusts?"

Comment: CEOs now more than ever have to be leaders of workers, because that is where the future of productivity, quality, customer service, and creativity reside. If little or nothing positive has been done, a new CEO will have to purge, build, and reengineer—not the easiest or the most popular of tasks.

5. Subject: Expectations

Question: "What are the various constituencies looking for? Is there any commonality or is it at cross purposes? What is the degree of change expected? According to what timetable? How much time in other words do I have to accomplish the goals of the board? Any room for negotiation here?"

Comment: Excessive expectations of followers can doom a new leader. The famous 100 days for new presidents invariably has resulted in some ill-conceived directives and hasty appointments. Ask for 200 days, better still, 365. Nothing ensures short tenure like the seduction of a CEO to the role of the savior or miracle worker.

POSTSCRIPT

If CEOs are to exhibit whatever special traits of leadership they may possess, they first have to survive and stay the course. But to their detriment the use of the "f" word—failure—has been avoided. Prospective

CEOs are at risk when they do not ask the right questions during the initial interview. They need to be prepped; they need to be suspicious especially if all is made to look and sound too good to be true.

Pallas Athena, the goddess of wisdom and patron of Odysseus, after a grueling session of trying to answer all his endless questions, finally in exhaustion says: "What I admire about you, Odysseus, is your suspiciousness. It is the sign of a civilized leader."

In the midst of all the welcoming greetings, smiling faces, and hearty handshakes during the interview process, prospective leaders may not be fully aware of all those on the sideline consciously or inadvertently deciding to cheer them on to failure. Above all, they have to recognize that asking the right questions also will spell out the emerging demands of the job of leadership.

SOLOMONISMS

Case studies and scenarios essentially offer real-world dilemmas safely cast in generic or disguised narrative terms. They nicely serve to distance the problems being featured and to protect the guilty from obvious detection. And generally it works well. Indeed, for many the preference of that indirect mode becomes the sign of where they secured their graduate degrees or how they problem solve. But it does have its limits. It tends to be depersonalized, dry, and often humorless. It also tends to focus more on organizational or structural matters than those associated personally with leadership. The challenge then is multiple: have the leader occupy the center stage; surround him or her with situations that would challenge Solomon; and offer extrication in a deeper and more palliative form of "Solomonisms."

What are Solomonisms? They are situations that leaders frequently find themselves confronting that require the wisdom of Solomon. The situations vary and can be classified into three main types: head's up, job threatening, and quandaries (the second one always gets the immediate attention of leaders).

Head's up are advanced warnings of dark clouds on the horizon. Job threatening is like life threatening; an ax is being wielded and may be ready to fall. Quandaries are the imponderables of life and leadership,

extremely difficult if not impossible to solve, and requiring the proverbial wisdom of Solomon. What follows are response options of leaders.

1. Head's Up

    Head's up is also called watch out, protect your back, and the
famous advice of the Godfather: "Keep your enemies close." In
many cases, such situational threats require not so much leadership as followship: the strategy of followers protecting their leaders, just as defenders prevent the quarterback from being blitzed.
In other words, leaders have to build, cultivate, and nurture a network of followers who serve as an advance guard, a buffer, and
above all a protective shield. They also are the leader's eyes and
ears. They have to listen to gossip, rumor, and venting. The tidbits
they pick up are like the bits and bytes the FBI collects for further
analysis.

    In other words, how good is your early warning system? How re-
liable are the people who man it? How extensive and deep is the
network? Above all, what guidelines should leaders provide their
followers about how to respond initially to potentially embarrassing situations or accusations? In short, do you practice preventive
medicine? Is your own house in order?

2. Job Threatening

    Never minimize or underestimate threats. Don't bewail the ac-
tivities of nay-sayers by exclaiming indignantly, "Don't they have
better things to do?" Don't make the mistake of scaling down the
issue and its impact and downgrade both to that of a local and
harmless storm. Above all, don't discount the source by claiming,
"Those people always complain. If it is not one thing, it is another.
This week it is me."

    But chronic dissenters are more powerful than occasional ones
because they possess a complaining agenda. They find fault with
everything on almost every occasion. They are the people who always say, "Yes, but." Above all, they never go away. They are perfectionists and thrive on finding fault and flaws. And they love to
argue. In fact, they get stronger if you take them on. They will
wear you down and exhaust you. Afterward, you will appear limp
and the glint of victory in their angry eyes will signal your loss.

Another temptation is for leaders to bewail their lot and call out "Woe is me!" They lament that they cannot get to the important things because instead they are always fighting rearguard actions or putting out fires. They often develop a persecution complex and believe others are out to get them, and sometimes deservedly so.

Paranoiacs always have their defenses ready. In the case of the CEO it is a constantly updated, comprehensive, and extensive list of data-driven and documented activities and accomplishments. The full report is always ready for distribution to members of the Board and senior staff. An executive summary version is for companywide e-mail dissemination. Timing is everything. Fight heat with light.

3. Quandaries

Gordian knots cannot really be untied. They represent the eternal issues of how organizations can be changed, how diversity can be honored without alienating the old majority, how American companies can retain employees and still remain profitable and competitive in a global market, and so on.

The only Solomonism that regularly has worked is balance—striking a middle position of yin and yang, push and pull, two steps forward, one back. But the balance must be genuine and not hide behind paralyzing ambiguity. The CEO must be pained by the stretch involved. His most important response should be genuine empathy rather than false relief. He may have to heal rather than solve or healing may be the only solution an executive can legitimately offer. Being Solomon does not guarantee wisdom. It just signifies its worth and the value of searching for it.

RECONFIGURING THE EXECUTIVE TEAM

The standard arrangement at the top is for CEOs to create, maintain, and hopefully nurture executive teams. They usually consist of the heads of all major divisions. Minimally, they include the CFO and COO and routinely vice presidents of marketing and sales and human resources. Depending on the industry and growth cycle of the company, they also may include a chief legal officer with expertise in acquisitions and mergers. Of late, with the increasing centrality of external and internal data management and tracking systems, a newcomer to the constellation at the top has been a CIO (chief information officer) or CTO (chief technology officer). The increasing emphasis on optimizing human capital through training has led to the creation of learning management systems and the emergence of the CLO (chief learning officer) and his international version, the CEO (chief executive officer). Finally, there is the holistic presumption of intellectual capital and the emergence of the chief innovation officer (CIO) (or at Dow Chemical, CIA).

The addition of so many additional top-level positions so rapidly has led some CEOs to pause and to reexamine not only the new composition of their executive teams, but also their dynamics. In the process, reconfiguration has become a new option. When exercised, that in turn has involved at least three major determinations: who shall be on it; what shall be their relationships with each other; and what shall be their relationship to the CEO.

ENLARGED CAST OF PLAYERS

The first step a CEO must take in reconfiguring his executive team is to recognize that he now will be working with or inheriting not only an enlarged cast of major players, but also a changed script. Not only will more voices be heard; some will be using unfamiliar language and acronyms. The key issue here is the comfort level of the CEO. Many top executives prefer to keep their teams lean, small, and close. They read each others' slightest signs. They function like executive coaches. Such CEOs thus may employ a gradual or peripheral process and initially grant only semi-permanent guest or as-needed status to the new additions during a shakedown cruise. But whatever assimilation strategy is employed, the pressure for more comprehensive and differentiated input will remain if not increase and compel enlarging the executive team.

NEW DYNAMICS

Often such horizontal expansion provides the additional opportunity to review the relationships between members. This is particularly critical when there is a mixture of the old guard and young turks, compounded by age spans and exotic specializations. Indeed, the CEO may detect (and sometimes exploit) an emerging rivalry or competition between the siblings. Although there is perhaps no sure way to forestall or spike such uneasiness, the CEO must take the lead to establish interoperability in all areas as the focus of the executive team. That in turn requires a new and deep appreciation of the kind of integration and symbiosis characteristic of fluid rather than mechanical systems and of circular rather than linear sequential communication processes. In particular, it requires the CEO to initiate and preside over a new orientation training, perhaps best provided at an executive retreat, that introduces the principles of holistics and convergence as the new shapers of vision and mission. That has the further advantage of putting everyone not only on the same new page, but also on one that is future driven.

STRUCTURALLY WORKING TOGETHER

The third reconfiguring factor to be considered is structural. Traditionally, executive teams help to develop broad strategic goals and plans and to be involved in decision making. CEO style plays a major role here. Some use their teams as sounding boards. Others work at negotiating consensus. But perhaps all approaches might benefit from altering the structure of the way the team operates. One suggestion has been advanced by Robert K. Greenleaf. Like the other two options, which seek to accommodate the new pressures of greater comprehensiveness and interoperability, respectively, this structural alteration seeks to address and better manage recurrent transitions.

Typically, transitions have been temporary and awkward. They had to be endured and the storm had to be weathered before calm and stability was restored. But now a transitional period gives way to another transition and that in turn to still another. The net result is that transition has become permanent. To address such morphing change, Greenleaf reached far back into classical times to resurrect the structural arrangement of each unit of the Roman legion.

Leadership was summed up by the concept of primus inter pares— first among equals. There was always a head of the business, but all the others were his equals, not his inferiors. Indeed, it had to be that way because a companion principle was that the head position was not permanent but rotational. When circumstances or transitions changed that required a new expertise, and one of the equals was better qualified to take the lead, he became temporarily numero uno. Such a rotational and egalitarian process would structure the dynamics of the executive team.

Throughout, the CEO remains the head of heads. He alone embodies the range of 360 degrees and of the whole enterprise. He alone must preside over, guide, and prod his team of equals toward their common future global goals. He designates who is the point lead. He is ultimately accountable for survival and success. Moreover, he alone also can shepherd and implement the principle of rotational primus inter pares companywide and thus fuse and embed his vision of optimizing relationships into structure.

Reconfiguring the executive team thus offers current CEOs with an emerging kind of internal leadership. Moreover, what finally surfaces need not exhibit a one-size-fits-all form. Indeed, it should not because diversity not uniformity should rule his experimental reconfiguration. Above all, new arrangements offer executives the unique innovative opportunity to acknowledge and to multiply the management of transition as a new norm of realty. There is enough about such an early response system and structure to blend and to strike a new balance between old and new team members and to make bedfellows of ancient history and science fiction. CEOs may still stand on the shoulders of giants, but they now rotate on a sufficiently diverse axis to accommodate stargazing and to see the whole of all the parts.

III

THE FUTURE OF THE FUTURE

23

E-LEARNING: SECOND GENERATION, E-LEARNING CURVE, AND EDUCATIONAL ENTREPRENEURS

In less than a generation, electronic versions and delivery of education and training have altered virtually all learning institutions and professions dramatically. Distance education, which now spans K–16 and includes both master's and doctoral degree programs, really should be dubbed distanceless education. In the process, training also has bypassed the logistics and expenses of f-2-f residencies, and effortlessly has achieved a global range. Why and how has e-learning taken hold so tenaciously and rapidly?

One of the key problems that e-learning addressed and successfully solved is instructor variability. Avoiding the extremes of creativity and ordinariness, e-learning instructional designers wisely opted for the solid middle road of competence. In the process of channeling to a central performance core, the designers also have built in a range of best instructional practices that typically would exceed that of even the most extraordinary instructor. It is thus not surprising that when such smart and resourceful strategies are joined to cost controls, technology advances, and ROI, e-learning has become the favored training mode.

But what is the next stage? Will the evolution be primarily or exclusively technological? Will dazzling gadgetry dominate and obscure the need for content and instructional design similarly to develop parallel forms of growth? Perhaps it is time to reassess the basic assumptions of e-learning design.

Traditionally, e-learning like all instruction involves three components: content, format, and delivery. With the commitment to cost controls, overarching evaluation was added. That bridged instruction and implementation and in many cases was embedded in course design to ensure follow-up. But although the harmonizing of these components has significantly upgraded training, is it the state of the art? Is it the best that can be offered given the unrelenting pressure for productivity and innovation?

Perhaps the best way to begin that process of review is to acknowledge from the outset a number of fundamental limitations built into the very format of current e-learning, and that if identified and addressed can prepare the way for a second generation of development.

Five limitations of current e-learning training are identifiable. First, course expectations narrowly focus on how not why, on knowledge not understanding. Second, the range of applications provided is predictably reassuring but fails to encourage wider and more creative adaptability. Third, learning capacity is assumed to be fixed or limited but in either case is not engaged as an active cooperative learning partner. Fourth, the range of audience intelligence is untested and hence untapped. Finally, the training focuses solely on measuring institutional and incremental gains not the monitoring and tracking of learner continuous improvement.

To bring e-learning to a new plateau and to overcome the limitations noted earlier requires two changes, one external, the other internal, each reinforcing the other. The external involves employee testing but of a different and expanded kind. The internal requires not only tapping such employee diagnostics, but also refocusing the training to address understanding and optimum adaptability.

EMPLOYEE TESTING

Current e-learning design avoids the limits of a singular instructor by offering a broad-based composite. In effect, the course or more exactly its format becomes the instructor. Even with interactive formats using an electronically sustained teacher-trainer-coach, the kind and levels of interaction are usually prescribed by the course script. Then too, although open-ended prompts may stir a greater range of response, the intelligence capacity of learners has not been factored in. So the first corrective is to help the instructional designers be smarter about their audience's contributions to the learning process—to perceive them not solely as objects but subjects of instruction. And that involves a different kind of employee testing.

Two kinds of metrics are needed to sustain a new level of e-learning: relationship styles and learning styles. The first can best be accomplished by the administration of some version of a personality profile such as Myers-Briggs (especially the new team version), the second by a multiple intelligences test. Although both already have been examined as part of the emergence of diagnostically driven training, the focus here and now is on applications of employee testing to e-learning.

Character profiles define not only interpersonal but also learning relationships within and across quadrants and divisions. They also determine hierarchical preferences for either directive or nondirective management and instruction. Who we are and how we relate is thus how we learn. Multiple Intelligences (MI), which identifies archetypal learning preferences, capacities, and pathways, invest how we learn and how far and deep with almost unlimited individual variations and combinations.

Testing and then fusing relationship and learning styles generates with rare precision the learning range and variety of both individuals and groups. Such learning thresholds and benchmarks become the new and expanded database and targets for training design. Performance expectations are not only raised, but also targeted. The metrics specify the attainable higher performance levels. The goal is more precisely bigger.

In addition, the expanded focus on the psychological and intellectual contributions of participants also can sustain a more individualized and long-term evaluation process. Monitoring and tracking employee continuous growth can provide a significant supplement to course evaluation. But for such metrics to yield the greater gains of productivity and creativity, they have to be optimized. That in turn requires developing new conceptual frameworks and designs.

UNDERSTANDING AND ADAPTABILITY

The change of focus from "How smart are you?" to "How are you smart?" involves a double shift not only from the singular IQ to the multiple MI, but also from what is fixed and known to what is evolving and discoverable. In other words, human learning potential comes back into the equation. Diagnostics joined to the unique and generic ways people are smart grants two growth gifts: employees now know more and training can ask for more.

The knowledge gained is extended and extending. Employees now can better understand their interpersonal dynamics on the one hand and their multiple talents on the other hand. Their self-knowledge is greater and more available. Above all, they are in a state of informed self-actualizing readiness and thus are poised for greater performance expectations.

But the shift in framework also requires a change in learning goals: from knowledge to understanding, and from predictable implementations to optimum adaptability. Diagnostics helps facilitate both. The level and reach of training no longer addresses the lowest but the highest common denominators, individual and group.

The learning and performance expectations of attendees is thus immediately but realistically more expansive. Parameters are stretched and thus can better address stretch goals. It expresses confidence that incremental success is within the range of their ability. Most important, the ultimate learning goal is not just knowledge but understanding.

Additional knowledge is always desirable but it does not always offer or lead to innovation and optimum adaptability. Knowledge and creativity are not inevitably linked; understanding is. In fact, the sign of deep understanding is innovation. The value of the symbiotic relationship between understanding and creativity is that it positions employees for questioning current operations as the optimum way of doing things. So if real change is desired—the how—the goal has to be understanding—the why.

The other limitation of knowledge is application. Training routinely includes a range of illustrative applications. But typically the examples are scripted to be of a piece with the training and institutional goals. They are what the company wants to see happen, now and precisely.

The sample applications are thus invariably prescriptive and limited in range. How restrictive and limiting appears when evaluation is properly done and is generally free of the limited workshop parameters.

What emerges is that the follow-up implementation of the training is limited to the original problem sets. Application is so confined that employees emerge so programmed for prescribed behaviors that success becomes predictable and limited. Not only is innovation jeopardized, so is optimum adaptability. Thus, training is always less and reaches for less than what it can be; just as it shortchanges its participants and their performance potential.

Incremental training yields just that—a prescribed series of baby steps. What usually determines such parameters is the assumption that employees and workshops can only be effective if they are narrowly focused on limited competency acquisition. If and when further progress is needed, another incremental session is scheduled.

But control is still vested exclusively in the trainer and the training; it is not shared. Everything comes from one side, which in turn calls the shots. Even when extensive participation techniques are used such as role-playing and simulations, they are driven by already defined workshop goals.

Knowledge is thus paradoxical. It expands but limits; it opens doors but only to a preselected room. It gives but does not ask for a different and unpredictable giving in return. Turning knowledge over to understanding begets a different process. It welcomes with thanks the incremental knowledge extension but now seeks to go deeper, to go inside the knowledge to see what makes it tick, to speculate on what is behind it all.

To be sure, here too limits will be encountered. Indeed, they may predictably be determined by individual metrics. But the limits will be deeper. In addition, more of what makes each one smart will be engaged and stirred to be smarter; more and less predictable applications may surface. Occasionally innovation will emerge and surprise even the innovator.

When e-learning dynamics involves such two-way sharing, knowledge crosses over and partners with understanding. Linking the known and expanded ways employees relate and are smart to goals of understanding and optimum adaptability can create the threshold for a new generation of e-learning.

It potentially also would have a profound and lasting impact on the way employees engage and relate to each other and to each other's smarts. In fact, that interpersonal process as well as work redesign constitutes in fact the new requirements for horizontal implementation and application. In effect, the development would be carried forward with each employee charged with sustaining multiple and hopefully optimum relationships with both human and work design. Tracking the effectiveness of workshops now can be supplemented by a system of monitoring the continuous improvement of individuals, teams, and divisions.

Finally, the emergence of this now optimized e-learning and new data tracking systems would enjoy vertical alignment. It even might persuade organizations to review and rewrite their mission statement. That would now reflect not only how its employees currently are smarter individually, collectively, and collaboratively, but also a future of second-generation e-learning based on optimum growth, adaptability, and creativity. In this way, the future of the company and the future of its learning become one.

E-LEARNING CURVE

Although learning curve expectations regularly increase, they surprisingly are rapidly accepted, assimilated, and accommodated often with relative ease and finally emerge as new operating norms. In addition, there is evidently a prior hidden hand or winnowing and discriminatory screening at work otherwise matters would be overwhelming, distracted, and superficial. The competition of change factors ensures that only the most deep-seated and essential developments are comprehensively passed on and achieve currency. The survival of the fittest has become the selection of the best practices.

Still, the acceptance range and rate have been remarkable. Thus, human resources is now comfortably human capital; work contacts, work covenants; objectives, stretch goals; training directors, chief learning or learning officers; learning organizations, learning management systems (LMS); and so on. The new language and acronyms carry change into our conversations with such adjusted comfort that updating is automatic and even seamless.

There is another development, less noticed perhaps because it is so obvious, that may exhibit the same potential of being elevated to the Parthenon of new perceptions. It has to do with the increasing multiple external relationships learning and training basics are beginning to manifest. What is curious is that the content remains fundamentally intact. The focus is on the connections. The busy part is in the externals—in the constellation as it were that surrounds the star subject matter. It appears to be thus more a matter of learning extensions than of learning creation. The net result is that it may suggest a more expansive and inclusive version of the learning management systems. Indeed, because such connective compulsion applies across the board to all subject areas (evaluation, leadership, ROI, strategic planning, etc.), it may serve to establish the future agenda for LMSs altogether.

Although the constellation of learning connections extends outwardly in a number of directions, they seem to organize themselves in three basic categories: competency-enhanced increments, progressive holistics, and new wholes. Each of the three finds expression in an alphabet soup of letters that extends the learning.

1. Competency-Enhanced Increments
   Thus, under the first appear e, o/s, a, and d/r.
   • e-learning (delivery)
   • s/o learning (organization and self management)
   • a-learning (assessment feedback)
   • d/r learning (differentiated rubrics)
2. Progressive Holistics
   Under the second are l, i, and c.
   • l-learning (linkages)
   • i-learning (interfaces)
   • c-learning (convergence)
New Wholes
   Under the last is i/a.
   • i/a-learning (imagination and art)

This checklist of e-options serves a double function. First, to consider extending and amplifying current in-house staples of existing training to new dimensions. Second, to adjust the content to support and even optimize the learning enhancements. Most adjustments are likely to be modest. The more pressing focus is selecting which extensions would best organically suit different training goals and modes. However, all should initially be considered, no matter how gradual or sequenced, as a progressive and multiple series of incremental gains.

Hopefully, such additives individually and collectively may have the power to vivify basics with the immediacy of new transfusions, turn catching up into getting ahead, transform mission into vision, and cumulatively suggest a whole that may be greater than the sum of its parts. It would impart to all training the unfinished quality of lifelong learning. But first, a discussion of each of the additives.

COMPETENCY-ENHANCED INCREMENTS

1. Delivery of e

    Increasingly learning is e-learning. All academic subjects are also acquiring the delivery prefix. Thus, English comp is now e-English comp; economics, e-economics. But when e is prefixed to training or academic course, it is really a double e—it offers a double delivery: the obvious delivery of the training itself and not-so-obvious delivery of the Internet resources of that training. The workshop not only has been delivered to the workplace, but also to the home, office, or hotel of the employee or student. Moreover, it also has delivered the employee or student into the cyber space of an enhancing and extending cyber library. Indeed, this nicely sets up and segues into the next dimension.

2. s/o-Learning (self-organizing)

    If the learning has been well designed, it should stir the initiative of the learner to structure his or her self-organizing and self-managing of the training. Specifically, he or she should be encouraged not only to apply the learning to his or her special set of differences and perceptions, but also to make that now altered identity his or her new organizational center of self-expression, action, and performance improvement.

3. a-Learning (assessment)

   Much of the distinction of LMSs and CLOs is the high value placed on measuring training effectiveness. The same focus has to be built into all training so that it becomes compulsively and habitually ruled by a-learning and its constant feedback of assessment. For the connection between doing and reviewing to take hold, reviewing has to become part of doing. In its effect, the extension of a-learning is capable of producing not only measurable change, but also culture-changing.

4. d/r-Learning (differentiated rubrics)

   Critical though it is, it is difficult, sometimes impossible, to design training that universally is adjusted or responsive to all. And yet differentiation remains the goal. If the range of personalities can never be totally or adequately addressed, perhaps the challenge of range should be shifted instead to the job itself and to its variety of performance levels. All differentiation should take the form of performance rubrics—a matrix system of work-disaggregated parts, subject to minimally three familiar performance levels: does not meet, meets, and exceeds. The rubric not only accommodates differentiation, but also promotes self-selected benchmarking. That in turn provides the basis for job performance improvement.

Summary: All four versions of learning mentioned earlier are incremental. Their modest goal is quantitative change. Their strength is to encourage the internalizing of new habits of thinking about work that make the process less mechanical and more reflective, less dependent and more autonomous, less dispersed and more focused, less generalized and more rubric driven. For a more ambitious reach for training, it is necessary to turn to the next level.

PROGRESSIVE HOLISTICS

If the first set of extensions focused on the individual, his job, and the self-management of both, here the emphasis is on the interpersonal and the interstructural. A number of years ago the CEO of Motorola sought to reduce the total number of days between an initial order for a cell phone and its delivery. He discovered that there were more productivity gains to be found and realized between rather than within divisions. Thus, here, crossovers of various kinds characterize the three dimensions of l, i, and c-learning.

1. l-Learning (linkages)

Minimally, two bridges are encouraged: interpersonal and interdivisional. Linking the training to both personnel and structure not only extends its application, but also empowers employees. Securing individual work satisfaction now begets the additional obligation to provide satisfaction to co-workers. Similarly, recognizing the interdependence of functioning parts, employees learn to face outwardly as well as inwardly, and to find ways of being dependent on each other closer together. Doubling thus rules. Employers are asked to be takers and givers, dependent and interdependent. The paradox celebrated is that each half finds its secret sharer in the other half. Linkage learning is probably the most productive and dramatic way of conveying the big picture in both miniature and intimate form.

2. i-Learning (interfaces)

Most linkages are proximate: the fellow employee next to one, the division before and after yours in the process. If linkages rule the near, interfaces rule the far. Here the training travels vertically not horizontally to other less obvious distant areas such as customer service or strategic planning. The interface grows out the perennial question: What does my job and my division have to do with those that are totally different?

Often, that even taps and releases a hidden resentment that such departments and employee are parasitical and do not directly generate income or increase productivity. The value of the interface is that it can be used not only to correct misperceptions, but also to prepare for the commitment to alignment—the ultimate yield of interfacing.

3. c-Learning (convergence)

This is one of the most ambitious and difficult extensions largely because it goes beyond the individual mission of the company mission to the collective vision of the industry. It thus pushes much further the distant but relatively close linkages of internal divisions, to entertain developments and breakthroughs that ostensibly have nothing to do with either job or company viability. It requires investing training with surprise and playing with wild cards. Above all, convergence introduces training to forecasting, to megatrends, and to the geometric and exponential speed of change. The risk of dislocation hopefully will be offset by the gain of creating minimally a notion of the future of the future as well as a future driven workforce.

NEW WHOLES

1. i/a Learning (imagination/innovation and the art of both)
   The signs of a proactive culture and a creative culture are the degrees to which they are versions of each other. Whenever innovation appears, the future is created. But that fusion can be enhanced by introducing or further advocating the tools of the imagination: scenarios, simulations, case studies, and so on. To further stir the stretch of convergence, science fiction may be invoked or sampled as a model.

The selection of more imaginative tools and resources, however, requires that the traditional high value placed on analysis be supplemented with that of the imagination. Imagination is ultimately the most fruitful generator of questions of "What if?" Shaping and re-creating the present stuff of reality may produce the new wholes that unite the future and innovation. Imagination has the power not only to react creatively to the world, but also to recast it imaginatively. It alone also has the integrative power to link the two.

In summary, then, what appears earlier are the multiple offspring of e-learning. Limiting the variations of a theme to eight probably will suffer the same fate as Gardner encountered with his initial list of seven. But no matter the kind and number of additions, what hopefully is clear is that e-learning especially gathered and linked in its systemic LMS version is a rich learning world that is also rigorously self-disciplining. It also signals a training future in which the learner not only receives but also gives. Diagnostically driven training is thus also finally participatory learning.

EDUCATIONAL ENTREPRENEURS

The current trend from singular to multiple training and from f-2-f to electronic delivery has been accompanied and even propelled by the unacknowledged emergence of non-university educational entrepreneurs in all fields and sectors. In numbers and substance, they represent a formidable alternative to institutions of higher education. Here are some cases in point: the Federal Leadership and the Management Institute of the U.S. government in the last decade has trained over 10,000 federal employees nationally and even internationally; some 2,000 charter schools (and growing), which never existed before, have challenged education's monopoly. In addition, between one to two million K–12 children are successfully being home schooled; the World Future Society (WFS) like many professional associations holds annual meetings that are preceded by a mini-university of futures courses generally not available anywhere else; the Glasser Institute of Chatsworth, California, has trained and certified thousands of psychotherapists and K–12 teachers and administrators in reality therapy and choice theory. No credit or degrees are granted, and no university offers the program; the Center for Creative Leadership in Greensboro, South Carolina, trains outstanding leaders from all over the world, enjoys a reputation that rivals that of the Ivy League, and is not licensed or accredited to function as a university; Ford University like some fifty other corporate universities collectively trains millions of employees each year in their state-of-the-art facilities and/or delivery systems. The range of prior education goes from high school dropout to PhD; and the Association of Supervision and Curriculum Development (ASCD) is a major player in the field of professional development for educators. It is a major book publisher, arranges both national and regional conferences at which its extensive staff offers courses, and of late has developed a popular online professional development program.

One could go on (a totally inclusive list easily would number in the hundreds) but the examples are perhaps representative enough to draw at least five basic conclusions. First, education and training are no longer the monopoly of the traditional historical academic providers. Second, the American need for students, workers, and citizens to know and to know more has created such a creative and enterprising alternative enterprise that in effect there are now two major education systems. Third, 3,000 colleges and universities now are paralleled by and in competition with hundreds of independent education entrepreneurs that without benefit of official accreditation, degrees, or credits often offer equally qualified and even unique opportunities for education and training. Fourth, professional development now is characteristic of virtually all organizations and sectors and in fact has become for many professions an annual requirement. Proof of continuing education credits (CEUs) must be submitted for renewal of certification. Finally, professional development now is also lifelong.

When such long-term learning is also combined with the culture of self-help, the net result is an enterprise that may dwarf all others. But these examples and conclusions, significant though they may be, do not tell the whole story. Two additional patterns though contrary are emerging. First, the two major providers appear to be on a convergent course. Second, professional development is nevertheless showing signs of becoming independent and autonomous in its own right.

First, a few typical examples of convergence or integration. ASCD has facilitated credit of all its electronic professional development courses by identifying four state universities that for a fee will grant graduate credit and thus enable teachers and administrators to receive salary step increases.

American College Association (ACE) has sent a team to review the courses offered by the Federal Leadership Institute and in effect certified them on a transcript that can be used to request transfer credit from or to graduate or doctoral university programs. The Center for Creative Leadership has arranged with the University of North Carolina in Greensboro to offer CEUs as an option to enrollees and developed a license relationship with a number of universities to disseminate their program.

Clearly, bringing together the best of both systems but maintaining independence while accessing the lingua franca of academic recognition and credits has increased both the reputation and range of professional development entrepreneurs. But it also has stirred and transformed many universities into becoming enterprising in their own right and thus considerably intensified and extended the richness of both education and professional development. Two examples of this newly emerging trend may suffice.

Cal State Fullerton through its office of University Extended Education (UEE) maintains nearly thirty partnerships with professional development organizations external to the university. Although a number support K–12 educators, the university is also involved in providing on-line instruction in oceanography, offering Spanish language training through LinguaHostel, and working with Leapfrog Corporation and Sun Computer Systems in emergent literacy. In addition, Fullerton has successfully applied for and received a number of grants that sustain other development programs such as the Geometric Thinking Institute. Moreover, UEE (mostly its director Pat Puleo) provides extensive consulting and inservice workshops to numerous school and districts annually. Finally, this extensive configuration, which in scale and quality resembles a mid-size company, is a for-profit venture of a nonprofit university.

International University of Graduate Studies (IUGS.com), which is accredited by the government of St. Kitts, according to the British Control Act offers master's and doctoral degrees. But it has no faculty and offers no courses. Nevertheless, the degree requirements—total number of credits and contact hours—are exacting and identical to traditional academic programs. Each student is responsible for building his or her own transcript. It includes documentation of all academic courses and credits taken since the last degree plus a list of all professional courses taken to date.

That latter list often lacks two academic metrics: designation of equivalent number of credits and an examination of performance. A complicated and rigorous process is followed for including the administration of a test not unlike that of credit by exam. The net result is an integration of academic courses and equivalent professional development programs until the total required number of credits and hours for the degree are met. Only then are mentors assigned to supervise a research or project assignment that serves as the basis for a final residential week of orals, discussion, and presentations. By valuing and following the traditional academic model of credits and contact hours on the one hand, but incorporating and assimilating professional development programs through an equivalency process on the other hand, IUGS has sought to create a legitimate middle ground for awarding degrees.

When all these new trends and patterns are put together, what do they portend for the future? And how are they of value to leaders and managers of learning and training? In scale and extent, long-term and lifelong professional development is a major American industry, both non- and for profit. Comparisons of the international standings of the performance of American students are probably premature and short-sighted. We are typically a country of late learners and bloomers. The distinctions between academic and professional training once histori-cally valid are beginning to fade. Professional development and training are increasingly of high quality, and often are unique and unavailable from institutions of higher education. Crossover and convergence are becoming the rule.

Each student and employee at every stage is no longer solely or only the sum of his or her official transcript or résumé. Totality requires an educational portfolio that contains a complete and composite record of acquired knowledge and skills from multiple sources—a portfolio ré-sumé as it were. That usually uncompiled portfolio needs to be assem-bled and maintained so that minimally it can serve as a basis to guide further training by employers and other educational providers, as well as provide data for composing and maintaining a lifelong résumé of pro-fessional growth and development. Training has to change to tap prior knowledge and experience as documented in the educational portfolio of each individual. In addition, to provide more targeted training, lead-ers and managers of learning in all sectors need to require greater diag-nostic testing of their employees as to their learning styles and multiple intelligences; and then to fuse that data with their learning portfolios.

Global competition joined to the American passion for learning and growth have combined to shape a rich mosaic of educational opportuni-ties and providers unique in U.S. history. In the process, parallel lines have indeed met in various credit crossovers and integration of aca-demic and professional development. The issue hopefully should not be a contest of which one is better or legal but the acceptance and even of-ficial acknowledgment of a continuum to which each contributes. Even

K–12 has been expanded to K–16. The focus of the future should be on collectively ministering to and tapping unlimited growth potential. Finally, such an integration of academic and professional development, extended lifelong, may be the best insurance we can provide not only against exporting or outsourcing work overseas, but also in creating a workforce that in size and savvy may anticipate and meet with agility and quality the global needs and aspirations of the twenty-first century.

24

LEARNING LEADERS AND MANAGERS: LEARNING ROI, CLO ACCEPTANCE, AND THE FUTURE AGENDA OF CLOS

Things do not just happen. Needs drive history and even nomenclature. Human resources is now human capital, employee evaluation is now performance improvement, work contracts have become work covenants, and so on. But perhaps the most dramatic recent change has been the emergence of Chief Learning Officers (CLOs) and its being heralded as an idea whose time has come.

The position is usually designated at a senior level and is independent of human resources, although often recommended by the VP of HR and obviously involved in presiding over and preserving the training piece. But what do CLOs do?

The examples we have to date display track records that rapidly document and dramatize their value. CLOs immediately save money on training—often as much as one half—by reviewing, condensing, and downsizing the total training curriculum. They combine and focus what is left so that it is not duplicative or nonincremental. They introduce e-learning, and thus reduce time away from work and travel costs. For those who are reluctant or unfamiliar with distance training, they combine classes with electronic experience and thus gradually bring employees into the twenty-first century. They support tuition remission programs for those relatively few employees who desire more speculative and philosophical fare. The final result is a more robust, trim, and effective training commitment and program than existed before their arrival on the scene.

Why are they able to accomplish so much in relatively so little time? Many reasons. First, they bring together under one roof what often has been parceled out to many divisions and their favorite or pet training hobby horses. Second, they are cost/benefits oriented and document course effectiveness with follow-up; third, they have made learning as much a demonstrable discipline and expertise as strategic planning, accounting, or management information systems. Fourth, their training list is clean, crisp, and cumulative. Finally, they are proactive. The training agenda always exists in the future.

What are the essential process steps CLOs employ? Catch up, line up, ratchet up, step up, and back up.

1. Catch Up
   CLOs are expert diagnosticians. They find knowledge and skill gaps and bridge them with incremental training.
2. Line Up
   CLOs take a holistic approach. They bring together macro and micro, top and bottom, and advocate alignment.
3. Ratchet Up
   Anticipating greater competition, they favor stretch goals, raising the bar, and agile interfacing.
4. Step Up
   They support next-step thinking and questioning: "OK. Where do we go from here? What is the next step? How can we push the envelope further?"
5. Back Up
   Taking both a holistic and proactive approach, they encourage backing up to see the system as a whole and in the process to recognize that the solution is often not proximate to the problem.

Unlike other senior professionals who have a prescribed job and range, that of the CLO is constantly unfinished. His or her boundaries are set only by the future. For example, CLOs are increasingly studying the linkage between learning styles and managerial styles. In addition, they relate those findings to those between learning frontiers and organizational vision.

The difference between incremental and futuristic learning is movement and positioning. Incremental learning at best is cutting edge. It extends itself and reaches for the present and the current. It brings employees to state-of-the-art boundaries. But futuristic learning is anticipatory. It leapfrogs: while we are catching up let us also get ahead. It not only pushes but is on the other side of the learning curve.

Whatever its particular focus, it is always about artificial intelligence, thinking robots, and man-machine symbioses. To nuts and bolts it routinely adds speculation, intuition, and imagination. It is selective investment. The goal is not only to get ahead but also to get there first, with the best applications, with optimum return on ROI. It is the closest thing to avant-garde learning but advanced with all the rigors of systematic research.

But perhaps the most dramatic yield of the anticipatory is the detection of not just occasional or temporary but permanent learning gaps between the present and the future. Those gulfs are born not just of general discontinuity, but of a series of continuing disconnects perhaps without end. If so, then that requires a new kind of training and leadership—that of transition training.

As transition becomes not the exception but the norm, learning and training for the future correspondingly may require more than knowledge base catch-up. It also may require managing the mercurial, reducing anxiety, and seeking temporary steady states in permanent flux. The new image may be not that of the agile manager but of the artful dodger, as Prometheus is replaced by Proteus.

When such avant-garde knowledge and training is added to all the standard offerings, it may be better understood why CLOs may offer the best ROI a company can earn from its human capital.

CLO ACCEPTANCE

Some times we have to back up in order to move forward. Or acknowledge that the future may be in the past. The recent straddling of the classroom and e-learning by Bob Mosher was a wise case in point (CLO,

January 2003). The same process perhaps needs to be applied to an idea whose time has come—CLO ism—but not all may see the revelation. Bridging and blending may be needed.

A good place to start is to question why any savvy, cutting-edge, forward-looking organization would hesitate to move in the direction or appoint a CLO in the first place? Alas, the answers may be unsettling and discomfiting, especially to the converted. A number of responses quickly surface:

1. Cost

    It is expensive. Making it a chief position immediately puts it in the top salary bracket. Then, too, there may be the not-so-hidden expenses of an accompanying staff of pricey specialists following in his wake.

2. Dislocation

    It may create internal inequities and insecurities. Will strategic planning and R&D take umbrage, become uneasy, appear threatened, even appear paranoiac? Will they rush to read his résumé to see if in any way he may be in their court? Will they perceive the appointment as an implied criticism of their performance or learning outlook (which it well might be)? In short, how many chains will be jerked?

3. Positioning

    Where does he fit in the organizational chart and chain of command? Does he have a direct line to the CEO bypassing the COO and the CFO? That may be enlightened but threatening. What is his job or task? What are his marching orders? Does he have an agenda, given or invented? Is he given free rein to roam on his own without limits or constraints?

4. Precedent

    What other organizations are going down this chancy road? In our industry? Why, and with what success? Given such concerns, it is not surprising that the prospect of a CLO may strike terror in the hearts of senior staff and lead to the following qualified recommendation (or is it kiss of death?): "Let's work toward it."

Given such misgivings, what options are available to move and advance the cause? Are there any examples or models that would be helpful in overcoming such formidable misgivings and skepticism and bringing about, if not complete implementation initially, at least a transitional arrangement? After all, half a loaf is better than none.

There are, but they may require at least three conditional and operative factors to succeed:

1. Age

   The initial transitional appointment must not threaten senior-level appointments with job displacement, on the one hand, but be their equal in years and experience to offer wise counsel, on the other hand. For example, Jack Welch recently came out of retirement to accept appointment to head up the highly visible and controversial Leadership Academy of the NYC School System. Although some would quarrel whether he is a CLO, what is certain is that he will introduce and impose the GE brand of Six Sigma as the main learning/planning salvation. (If younger aspirants are put off by this senior citizen recommendation, they need to recall that this is a transition strategy designed to open the door and prepare the way for later application.)

2. Temporary

   The appointment is to be further perceived as an experimental and rotational arrangement funded for three years. Such reassurance includes undertaking an evaluation by the middle of the third year to determine whether the arrangement should be formalized and continued and if so made permanent. The model followed would be that of the visiting professor long established for many years at universities. A variation of that model has been used by some corporations to appoint a resident futurist (Ian Wilson at GE) or organizational gadfly (Charles Handy at BP).

3. Selection

   The first appointment for the first year should not be chosen by a committee. It should be the exclusive selection of and funded by the CEO. Ideally, it should set the standards and establish the criteria for subsequent visiting or resident CLOs. Those standards should be thoroughly explained by the CEO and obviously exemplified by his choice. Later on a process of future selection can be put in place and negotiation accommodated.

The subsequent opportunity to put in the hands of managers and leaders the nomination of outstanding learning officers aside from calming fears, would clearly serve the CLO profession well. It would raise to a high level of consciousness, discussion, and debate the immense value of focusing on both professional and corporate learning, and how they can be converged.

Of course, this may seem like a less than ideal and overly elaborate and cautious way to gain acceptance. The devoted may argue that it may dilute the dedicated effort to achieve visibility for CLOs. Then, too, nominations may be so glamorous and varied so as to be inimical, and the choices so exalted that they may be not just hard but impossible acts to follow. Imagine Peter Senge being named to GM; or Steve Pinker from MIT to Paradigm Learning or Pearson Electronics; or a Nobel prize chemist being invited to Merck.

But the arguments advanced here are more than pragmatic. They also acknowledge profound change. New, different, and deviant learning dislocates. Add unlearning and that ups the ante. But in order to establish a beachhead and threshold for the dissemination of such mind-altering and organization-changing learning, CLOs need above all to be reassuring and to blend past and future. They must exhibit in fact the kind of patience, ingenuity, and savvy associated with and part of the tool kit of CLOs. In short, initially, during, and subsequently, CLOs will have to practice what they profess and not only be learning leaders, but also futurists.

THE FUTURE AGENDA OF CLOS

What invests the new role of CLO with puzzling importance is its somewhat unexpected appearance? It has emerged at a time when training generally has been downsized, minimized, and in some companies trivialized; when many HR departments have been dismantled or outsourced; when the budget line for consultants including IT specialists has been decimated or deleted entirely; and when the future of corporate universities as separate entities is being scrutinized.

But desperation sometimes can lead to enlightenment; the glass may be half full rather than half empty. CLOs may have emerged precisely because the crisis of training required not just management but leadership. Organizations were in the counterproductive stance of cutting themselves off from their future. The baby was in danger of being thrown out with the bath water. Turnaround required executive level cost containment, consolidation, and reconfiguration. No small achievements, because in tough times, saving money in the present and at the same time preserving growth in the future are precisely what top leaders are supposed to do. Due diligence and vision still remain the sign of executive expertise.

But where do CLOs go from here? After taking apart and putting Humpty Dumpty back together in a trimmer and more robust e-learning state, what are the future leadership options for CLOs? Ten areas of advocacy are rendered below in generic terms to accommodate the diversity of organizations to which they can be applied. It also assumes the subject range of CLO to be the trinity of Thinking, Learning, and Training (TLT).

The Future Leadership Agenda of CLOs

 1. Flux Management
 2. Integration
 3. Convergence
 4. Holistics
 5. Anticipation
 6. Innovation
 7. Decentralization
 8. Self-Regulation
 9. Assessment
10. Research

1. Flux Management

It will increasingly become the responsibility and focus of TLT to manage the pace and invasiveness of change. The tool kit of CLOs will employ the bridging contributions of blended learning, man-machine hybrids, and stretch-goals management. Above all, in recognition that transition may be shedding its temporary character and in the process becoming a permanent state, CLOs will offer transition training. The common goal of managing flux will be to temper future shock.

2. Integration: Linking

   TLT has to be the agent of integration on multiple levels. Minimally, it should include cross-training and cross-over training. The first is divisional, the second interdivisional. In both instances, the direction is horizontally to extend the cultural base of the work so that it becomes increasingly reciprocal, proximate, and mutual. That also may require that the traditional unidirectional focus of job satisfaction acquire an interpersonal dimension. Securing satisfaction has to involve the obligation to provide satisfaction to others. Such interactive give-and-take behaviors shift the focus from product to behavioral productivity. The goal of integration throughout is gradually to transform units into communities that face inwardly to the mutuality of cross training and outwardly to the collaborative alignment with company objectives. The glue is provided by the rationale of productivity: More gains are possible through goal alignment and between than within units.

3. Convergence

   Convergence is a higher-level version of integration. If integration applies mostly to rank and file, convergence ministers to middle- and upper-level managers. Convergence routinely includes the usual deviant and out-of-the-box thinking. But realizing the math of one plus one equaling three requires positioning in a multidisciplinary range and world of impinging parallels. Convergence requires standing on mountain tops so that apex developments in multiple fields can be perceived as they surprisingly link and converge. Such horizontal coupling has even been given a new name, the Singularity, which is projected to occur over the next twenty-five years and to bring about in that span of time the equivalent of 20,000 years of progress. The pace of convergent change may become so intense that nature and technology may fuse; machine intelligence may rival and even exceed human intelligence; and work, play, and thought relationships may be redefined. Science fiction? Perhaps, but reviewing SF reveals that two-thirds of its technology forecasts came about, a better batting average than conventional strategic planners and forecasters. Convergence in short is always the unexpected next step, the extraterrestrial solution from left field.

4. Holistics

Bumper sticker wisdom sometimes is telling. A recent one proclaimed: "It is not only the Hole we are in, but the Whole we are not." The argument is that some measure of relief or remediation comes from seeing the big picture and saying perhaps, "Oh. Now I see why we are doing what we are doing!" Increasingly, TLT needs to deliver vision and mission. It ultimately should blend the macro and the micro and be rendered as various mini-wholes of divisions and individuals. Each company has to become its own case study nested within the case studies of its industry and market. The more reflective and self-conscious nature of scenarios have to replace conventional reports and summaries. Narrative has to become the dominant form of holistic communication.

5. Anticipation

Problem solving must increasingly factor in the consequences of its solutions. It no longer can function solely in the short term. Like environmental impact statements, it must anticipate the second, third, and even fourth level of impact. Employees also need to be invited to speculate on the future nature of their jobs and in the process to identify what training may be needed to get them from here to there. Aggregated upward such findings may suggest not only the overall directions of the company's future, but also its future training agenda. The goal is to shape a workforce that is minimally future directed and optimally future driven.

6. Innovation

Innovation fuses the quantitative and the qualitative. The current gradual transformation of work to yield incremental gains of productivity needs the quantum jump of creativity. Innovation is important and different because it not only advances the present; it actually creates the future. It suddenly distances companies from each other. It lays down the ultimate gauntlet of competition. But this CLO agenda item requires finding new motivating and incentive mechanisms for stirring innovation across the board. In a recent Internet survey of the mission statements of 301 companies, the favorite operative words were "Quality," "Value," and "Service."

Only sixty-eight or less than one-fifth cited "Innovation" (Management First, 2003).

7. Decentralization

   CLO leaders have to speak out on behalf of leadership sharing. They have to move the knowledge culture of the company beyond the mindsets of centralization and hierarchy. The goal of distributed leadership is to write leadership options into every job description. Fortunately, the current commitment to teaming provides the receptive soil for planting the seeds for building such collaborative leadership. Each team should function as both a profit and quality control center. As noted earlier, an interesting variation is Robert Greenleaf's notion that teams should follow the model of the Roman legion: team leaders at best are primus inter pares—first among equals. But the position of being first is temporary and rotational. When a different expertise is required another member of the team who has that expertise becomes first. But throughout all remain equal.

8. Self-Regulation

   Control, the chief weapon of middle-level managers, is sometimes overused and always overrated. Benign abandonment also may be needed, perhaps even preferred. Research on birds, traffic jams, economic systems, and informal organizational and communication reveals the extent to which relationships and work are organized without an official organizer and coordinated without a coordinator. The cherished image of the lead bird leading his flock south turns out to be a self-selecting process requiring no official intervention. In other words, TLT needs to identify and to recognize those unofficial and informal pathways and systems that undergird organizations and provide them with their ongoing and self-organizing power. There are not one but many invisible hands and they all have to be allowed to work their magic no matter how marginal the role of indispensable control and supervision may become in the process.

9. Assessment

   Every organization increasingly must become intensely self-evaluating. Whether it is called accountability or post-Enron oversight, work, policy, and executive decisions need constant scrutiny and review. The kind of follow-up tracking designed to measure the effective implementation of training has to be applied across the board throughout the company. In the process, stretch goals have to be disaggregated into rubric levels of accomplishment. They also should be designed so that they become the do-it-yourself focus of self-assessment. Monitoring has to become at least half of every job if corrective self-management is to have its optimum effect.

10. Cognitive Science Research

Brain research or the science of knowing, thinking, and learning has to be folded into the agenda of all CLOs. In fact, cognitive science is becoming as formative to TLT as instructional design. Moreover, it is perhaps the supreme area of integrated, holistic, and convergent study. It includes computer science, artificial intelligence, behavioral psychology, linguistics and language development, neuroscience, and the like. In fact, one of the new frontiers of cognitive science is precisely the exploration of how the brain reasons about and manages uncertainty. Here is where TLT may find its new diagnostics, the sources of its training effectiveness, and innovation dynamics. Here is where CLOs will discover the future of the future.

Perhaps, the most comprehensive way to summarize the future agenda of CLOs is in the following matrix.

Agenda Category Means/Modes Goals/Outcomes

1. Flux Dynamics Transition Training Change Management
2. Integration Cross and Cross Over Training Alignment
3. Convergence Multidisciplinary Synthesis
4. Holistics Vision and Mission Big Picture Knowledge
5. Anticipation Problem-Solving Projections Future-Driven Workforce
6. Innovation Out-of-the-Box Thinking The Competitive Edge
7. Decentralization Leadership Sharing First Among Equals
8. Self-Organizing Unofficial Networks Self-Directing Systems
9. Evaluation Data Tracking Follow-up Monitoring Effectiveness
10. Cognitive Research FLT Findings FLT Applications

Another value the matrix may offer is turning it back upon itself to help define what CLOs have to be in order to implement such modes and achieve such ends. Any composite profile of the position would likely have to include minimally the following characteristics of the CLO's job description:

1. TLT Expertise

    Whatever their original area of specialization, learning has to become not only the new discipline of CLOs, but also their compulsive analytical perspective. Everything must become grist for the mill and converted into TLT challenge and opportunity.

2. Mangers of Cost-Effective Performance Improvement

    CLOs have to be supreme resource managers. Like the organizations that employ them, they have to do more with less, not just maximize but optimize programs, and constantly save money as their way of making money.

3. Documenters of Effectiveness

    CLOs have to document not so much the training but its implementation; and even then not only that it has been wired in place but that it also has made a measurable difference. Data must become the ultimate persuader. The CLO mantra should be DDD— Data Documented Difference.

4. Organizational Broker

    The integration of employee and division goals with company objectives should also include the convergence of learning and performance goals. CLOs should be the constant advocate for learning linkages as ways of bringing greater coherence and interdependence to discrete and often disparate parts. In effect, CLOs are the guardians and articulators of the Big Picture—of vision and mission.

5. New Knowledge Officers

    CLOs have to model the cutting edge. They constantly have to be alert to and knowledgeable about impactful research breakthroughs, and above all be open to future-driven innovations emerging unexpectedly from convergence. As such they have to become the information officers of future knowledge and innovation. Ideally, they should build a research-driven base into their own operations of documentation and instructional design. In short, CLOs have to function as resident futurists.

The lists given earlier in the chapter are obviously neither definitive nor prescriptive. They also are not accompanied with timetables, although clearly some might be immediate, others ongoing, and one or two long term. Their singular and/or combined value is to stir proactive debate as to what should be the future agenda of thinking, learning and training as perceived, developed, and implemented by CLOs—the new learning leaders and managers of the twenty-first century.

CONCEPTUAL FUTURES:
FUTURES THINKING AND AGENDAS

Isaac Asimov defined science fiction as "an escape to reality." That softens the threat but leaves intact the truth. But even such protective and adept trickery cannot diminish or alter a now two-way street. The fictional visions are leaving the future to become the reality of the present. Science fiction (SF) has become increasingly science fact. SF has much to recommend it. For example, its forecasting record is superior to that of strategic planning. Two-thirds of its projections have happened in one form or another. Then, too, SF's powerful alliance of imagination and technology outmatches and outperforms the standard linear analysis of think tank strategic planners. SF is invariably creative and innovation thrives on the future.

The reality presented thus always appears to be less extravagant and more acceptable, even livable. But, perhaps most important, SF is not just a powerful way of rendering and managing the future. It is also a mode of knowing. It is one of the key incarnations of futures thinking/learning (FTL).

But do futurists really think differently? Does a recurrent fixation on what is to come involve distinctive thought patterns, problem solving, image clusters, metaphors, methodologies, pattern detection, and the like? Do futurists sign their forecasts like SF authors? Are futurist

consultants sufficiently different from their less future-driven counterparts as to be understood, valued, and even preferred as such by
prospective clients? Finally, is there such a separate commodity as futurist thinking? And if so, are its benefits sufficiently generic on the
one hand and persuasive enough on the other hand to overcome
the typical resistance to looking and thinking ahead?

FTL already exists in many ways and places. It can be found in K–12
adaptations of futures labs and modules in the Rover Elementary School
in Tempe, Arizona. It also is obviously alive and well in the number of
university offerings and especially the enduring efforts of undergraduate and graduate programs like that of the University of Houston at
Clear Lake City. The contributions and impacts of resident futurists like
Ian Wilson at General Electric cannot be minimized. One even might
argue that his seminars on futures influenced the later development and
refinement of Six Sigma by GE.

But a number of new developments, applications, and trends may
impart new importance and urgency to the value of futures thinking/
learning. In the process, FTL may become not just a peripheral, bor-
rowed, or occasional mode of learning and training but a mainstream
methodology in its own right.

There are at least five major developmental areas and conditions that
needed and are more open to futures thinking and training now than
ever before: new training metrics, new strategic planning modes, corporate universities and their knowledge cultures, employee empowerment and productivity, and the future learning leaders—chief learning
officers (CLOs).

1. New Training Metrics

     How have organizations and individuals coped with even the
     less exotic versions of flux? Basically through three kinds of train-
     ing and learning: catch up, line up, and crossover.

     The thrust of catch up is incremental: bringing professionals up
     to date with the latest developments. These are usually add-ons.
     Occasionally, they may incorporate new directions but in almost all
     cases they are focused designs to bring everyone to the cutting
     edge or state of the art, together. Although future influenced, they
     are essentially present bound.

Line up involves structure not content. It is also multidirectional and requires not so much the acquisition of new knowledge or skills as their constant repositioning and prioritizing. The aim is to align individual and divisional goals with company objectives, especially if there are satellite centers, and especially if these are multinational. A key new learning complexity is managing and aligning multicultural and multigenerational diversity and values.

Crossover involves two kinds of additional learning. One is cross-training. Co-workers are trained in each others, jobs not only for obvious purposes of replacement if necessary but, more important to expand the knowledge and skills base of workers. The other crossover is more structurally ambitious—more interoperable. It involves linking the work focus of different divisions with each other to promote greater collaboration. It may link such operations as planning and customer service, marketing and auditing, purchasing and production, and so on. Employees may spend a day or week, for example, on the phone in customer service. The goal is greater integration of function and process across the board.

2. New Strategic Planning Modes

Because of increasing uncertainty and discontinuity, strategic forecasting needs futures thinking if it is to preserve its integrity as a discipline on the one hand and sustain the reality of its mid- and long-term projections on the other. The changes required reflect the degree to which the knowledge of at least three distinctive ways the future operates has been incorporated into strategic planning methodologies: in particular, patterns of escalation, degrees of knowability, and the partnership of monitoring

Responding to future discontinuity varies over reaction time and with advanced intelligence. In fact, the goal of strategic planning is to preserve decision time and store options. But FTL perceives unfolding prospects in the progressive and aggressive terms of stretch, strain, and shock. The sequence is ruled by a law of grim escalation. The first version of stretch if ignored is followed by the second; and if that in turn elicits no response, then the third dominates the scene.

If the future is an enigma it is a transparent one. It is an amalgam of the known, the unknown, and the unknowable. The obvious strategy is to move the knowledge base along that continuum. Extrapolation of present data and demographics builds the extent of the known in the present and short term. Trending converts the unknown into knowable long-term patterns. But then all stops short with the unknowable because that is in fact is what defines the final future. But the consolation is as much as two-thirds of what may come can be in hand.

Monitoring is no longer occasional and external but permanently embedded. It constitutes at least half of planning. Tracking sensors are distributed throughout to function as an early warning system to catch deviations. Monitoring requires its own plan. Usually it is a permanent overlay of data tracking equipped with its own software program, which has the capacity to adjust planning when certain parameters are exceeded and calculated.

The futuristic adjustments of strategic planning produce not only a more integrated and dynamic whole, but also—and here again is the critical point—the plan itself would be a futures thinking document. It would behave like the future.

3. Corporate Universities and Their Knowledge Cultures

The incredible growth of corporate universities, ranging from McDonald's to Ford to Disney to Toyota, bears witness to the centrality of training and learning as a major American and especially multinational investment in the future. Constantly responding to new challenges, corporate universities in the process have been involved minimally in two major future-oriented shifts: multinational acculturation and e-learning.

Acculturating new employees whose work cultures are different and may in fact be at variance from that of the desired mainstream is an increasing focus of global companies. For example, Dell employs a number of software programmers from India and recently outsourced a significant portion of their customer tech support there.

Typically, employees from India favor supervisors who tell them what to do. They find it difficult to act on their own initiative. They prefer description to opportunity. Dell, which values worker participation over obedience and nonlinear thinking over rote, employs extensive situational training to bring about a shift in values and thereby a shift in work dynamics.

The other major change is the gradual conversion to e-learning. In some cases, a blended approach has been used for older less technologically comfortable workers: Traditional f-2-f classes have been joined with e-classes. The primary motivation is cost: lower instructional costs, less time away from work, elimination of travel and per diem expenses to centralized training sites, and so on. The other gain is increased quality control through standardization of content in the three areas noted above: catch up, line up, and crossover.

To a large extent, corporate universities are themselves future entities. They embody Senge's learning organization and incorporate Toffler's knowledge workers, which when combined create unique knowledge and learning cultures. They are almost like countries in their own right. To be sure, unlike traditional academic universities, corporate universities are ideological. They promote the perpetuation of their own survival and growth, and the bottom line. They are their own lobbyists. They in effect use themselves as case studies.

But individually and collectively, they also need to be corporate global citizens by including the new ideologies of global interdependence and sustainable development. It is not enough to hail and benefit from the global economy. It also requires the unique leadership of multinationals calling for and aspiring to world stewardship of the global commons. Such a commitment requires going beyond singular ideology to embrace an interdependent ideology that commands the international respect and loyalty of all professionals. In both instances, the value of futures thinking again is thus inevitably visionary.

Finally, futures thinking would encourage convergent thinking, which raises the integration of thought and process to optimum levels of synthesis without compromising differentiation. Whether or not the Singularity occurs according to its projected timetable, what is clear is that it is born of and driven by convergence. Edward Wilson called it consilience to signify the future synergistic math of one plus one equaling three or four or five. Emily Dickinson claimed that "everything that rises converges." Discoveries or breakthroughs at the apex will in volcanic fashion reach out, touch, extend, and enrich all the other apexes to produce a total greater than the sum of its parts. In short, the visionary corrective here is that the future itself is essentially a convergent force.

4. Employee Empowerment and Productivity

The obvious goal of training and learning is to increase the holy trinity of productivity, profitability, and quality. Of the three, the first enjoys the highest priority because of the competition of the global economy. To preserve their middle-class status, American workers have had to become more productive. Often because of downsizing that also involves fewer workers doing more. Although there are many ways of increasing worker productivity, one approach that has received generally less attention and offers the option of a major application of futures learning and thinking is that of employee evaluation.

In the last five years the nomenclature has changed. Employee evaluation has become performance evaluation and then shifted to its present version of performance improvement. Employees themselves have become human capital and as such training is perceived as a way of securing return on investment (ROI). Worker agreements have in many organizations become worker contracts and finally worker covenants. The common denominator of all these changes is the increasing centrality of employee productivity and the increasing dependence of companies on the capacity of workers to constantly create or find cost-saving and creative ways of increasing productivity. There are signs that some organizations are contemplating a futures step in the performance improvement process.

Currently, the standard way to improve productivity is to encourage employees to consider how they might do their jobs differently. Many managers, especially those with seniority, have had to be retrained as coaches. They found it difficult to confer such initiatives upon the workers they supervise and to grant that those who do the job know it better than anyone else. In some instances, the inquiry into performance improvement has been pushed further in two ways: asking employees to define and evaluate the effectiveness of the interfaces between divisions and encouraging more overt interpersonal attitudes and behaviors so that receiving work satisfaction is accompanied by giving it as well to others.

The gains have been significant. Structural changes have been made and interpersonal behavior modification has improved the mutuality of work environments. Matters appear to have gone as far as they can go, in the present. Not so if one adds futures thinking/training.

The next logical step is to push inquiry into the future itself. Welcome though the changes recommended by employees on doing their jobs more productively, they are still present bound. They deal with new configurations of various kinds but they are generally incremental in nature. But endowing empowerment with more forward-looking vistas, workers can be invited to speculate on what they believe their jobs will be like in the future. Building upon their increasing competence in job review and change, workers not only may welcome such an opportunity, but also warm to the task of projecting their future roles. Such worker projections can be followed by inquiring into what kinds of training would be critical to get them from here to there. Such speculation can be a gradual rather than a one-shot process and also may be accompanied by discussion and the distribution of some basic reading materials. In any case the yields can be significant.

Individual projections of work change can be aggregated upward to generate patterns of the future that may shape that of the company itself. In addition, the same process may identify the common training needs and in effect identify the training agenda of the future. Of perhaps greater long-term importance, the process would contribute to developing a future-directed workforce. Finally, those companies supportive of such futures empowerment would have in effect created an employee-based alternative to the expert model in the form of futures learning communities. In all the aforementioned instances, the vision of the future not only brings a new dynamic to work environments, but also shapes futures learning communities of best practices.

5. The Future Learning Leaders: Chief Learning Officers (CLOs)

One of the signs of the future arriving ahead of schedule is the emergence of jobs and titles for which there is often no previous classification or formal academic preparation. The positions of chief information officer (CIO) and chief learning officer (CLO) are cases in point.

No traditional or even corporate universities offer master's programs or degrees in learning management or have retrofitted existing executive educational programs to accommodate learning leadership at an executive level. And yet professionals are being appointed to such top-level positions; and a new journal (hard copy and online), professional organization, and website have appeared devoted to the CLO.

For many the appearance of CIOs and CLOs comes out of the blue. Not so for futurists, who, in fact, routinely study and compile the emergence of new professions as reflecting the regular and most current incarnation of the future.

CONCLUSION

Stepping back in order to sum up the arguments presented here on behalf of futures thinking, the first order of business may be to summarize them visually (see figure 25.1). And similarly, perhaps the best way of expressing what futures thinking at different levels can bring to the learning challenges of the twenty-first century is to offer the display in figure 25.2.

One final observation. Over the last two decades a considerable amount of thoughtful work has been done in developing new theories of intelligence. One of the most impressive compilations is that of Howard Gardner, who identified seven kinds of intelligences. He subsequently added two more. To round it out to an even ten, I would nominate futures intel-

Current Area Futures Contribution	Future Changes	Benefits/Outcomes
1. New Training	Norms Transition Training	Optimizing Knowledge
2. New Strategic Planning	Strategic Monitoring	Optimizing Choice
3. Corporate Universities	Global Interdependence	World Citizens
4. Employee Productivity	Future Work Projections	Future Workforce
5. Learning Management	Future Learning Foci	Future Intelligence

Figure 25.1.   Futures Thinking and Learning Summary Matrix

ligence as belonging to that list of essentials, which because of its convergent power may exhibit the modest hubris of subsuming all the others.

FUTURES AGENDAS

Traditionally, organizations pursued the future. Now the future seems to be pursuing companies, in some cases into the ground. E-businesses appear and disappear with almost daily regularity. Or they are acquired, subsumed, and are no longer. Even big and traditional organizations no longer have a singular or familiar shape. They spawn incubators, new divisions, off-shore offshoots, or outsourced variations, and the like. Structurally they resemble more planets of different size and speed in a solar system than the traditional pyramidal wedding cake monolith. Young MBAs' whiz kids major in entrepreneurship.

Why does the future appear to be arriving ahead of schedule? Are we provoking it into happening prematurely by being Promethean or worse, like Daedalus, flying too close to the sun? In other words, is there the presumption, as some moralists would argue, that it is being brought about by overreaching? Or is it simply a neutral phenomenon brought about by shorter time periods between discovery and implementation? Whatever the answer, the real issue is neither blame nor innocence but understanding of the characteristics of a fast future in order to better manage it.

Historically, the future was better behaved. It waited for us to come to it. It did not have a mind or agenda of its own. It was there obediently ready to serve and to be around as an affirmation of our continuance. Often it had great political or economic value. What could not happen totally or immediately could be put off or gradualized. Of course, it also

Futures Thinking	Divergent and Convergent
Futures Problem-Solving	Innovation Methodologies
Futures Learning	Knowledge Anticipation
Futures Visioning	Paradigm Shift Anticipation
Futures Intelligence	Intuitive and Holistic Forethought

Figure 25.2. Progressive Components of Futures Responses to Steep Learning Curves

served to afflict both the faithful and the godless. After all, the second coming was always seeking a future date of incarnation. In short, as long as the future stayed in its place, it could serve a multitude of purposes and overlays. It was ultimately a servant, there to do our bidding.

But we also know that there were historical quantum jumps that opened the cage of the future and released a beast ready to pounce. Again and again stealing the fire of invention mythically and metaphorically marked one of those shifts. Eating of the tree of knowledge marked another. The printing press in preserving and releasing the past from oblivion also liberated the future. Technology in general increasingly became the midwife of major discontinuities. Science fiction appeared with Mary Shelley's *Frankenstein*. It celebrated the first of many fusions of mind and machine, intelligence and artifice.

Indeed, since that time, there has been a steady and parallel race between science fiction and the future. Sometimes the one leading, sometimes the other but the two permanently in contention or acting in collusion. Indeed, science fiction embodies such a total pursuit both of the future as well as its pursuit of us that it is difficult to determine where the one begins and the other leaves off. But in any case, science fiction may provide a key model for managing fast futures. Constantly exhorted to fight fire with fire, well then perhaps the way to engage and manage a fast future is to employ a fast future form.

Science function minimally provides three managerial guidelines: stance, scenario, and solution.

1. Stance

    The most basic stance of SF is that the future already has arrived. It is not only the key setting, but also the main protagonist. SF stands unequivocally in its midst. The future is thus not just coyly visited but intensely portrayed. Readers experience a future world in the present time and place of fiction. In addition, much of the drama may stem from the future dynamically envisioning its own future. Whether it may be glorious or disastrous, it firmly establishes that the future has a future.

    Managers and strategic planners like SF have to be time travelers. They cannot timidly and obediently stand in the present and peer out to what is to come. They must abandon their secure moorings and assumptions and allow themselves to drift into a time and place that never existed before. The only way strategic planners can withstand and understand the pursuit by the future is to inhabit and engage where the future is coming from in the first place. Although the future may still be a moving target, it now nevertheless is a tangible entity that can be examined.

2. Scenario

If God is in the details, in Zen, understanding is to be found in observing the way a wise man ties his shoes. SF is a second creation story. In SF, although it can be largely fantastic and even wild, scenario also makes the outlandish appear familiar. As Eudora Welty noted, poetry is an imaginary garden in which there is a real toad. Similarly, SF has to present a reality that offers verisimilitude, the substance and stuff of recognizable existence, and the external and internal consistency and coherency of real people and situations. In short, imagination always needs, like Antaeus, to have its feet on the ground, otherwise it loses its power and impact.

Managers mistakenly use tunnel vision to look and plan ahead. They are so preoccupied with their own special focus that the future appears monochromatic and familiar. By limiting their views to only what they believe will affect their organization, their vision invariably appears myopic, singular, and safe.

They must also examine alternative events and dimensions, which like the proverbial rock thrown into a pool, send out wider and wider ripples. In the process they may discover wider, deeper, and unexpected applications, way beyond what their more compulsively singular competitors have found. In short, inhabiting the future is not enough. It must also be a rich unexpected world, one that is dizzily strange yet logical.

3. Solutions

SF is fundamentally a problem-posing and problem-solving genre. To be sure, sometimes the solutions are terminal but given the problem that may be a logical conclusion. If well-crafted, the solution appears inevitable. In good SF, many solutions are proposed and debated. Discussions, sometimes heated, take place, the purpose of which is to eliminate options until one absolutely final solution appears as the remaining and winning contender.

Whether the ending is an unhappy or wrenching one, there is at least the consolation of all possibilities being exhausted. The work that comes to such a well-rounded end has about it the ring of inevitable truth.

The best of SF thus sets high standards for managerial solutions. Nothing cheap, trivial, or lame will pass muster. In this case, life needs to imitate art. Following the problem-solving methodology of SF, minimally every solution has to be perceived as passing five standards. First, the solution must solve the problem—the whole problem, and nothing but the problem. Second, the problem cannot be reworked or reduced in magnitude because the solution is not big enough to handle it all. Third, the solution must not become a later problem. Fourth, it must be communicable—persuasive and lifelike to secure acceptance and cooperation. Finally, it must take hold and be implementable, not in some future time and place but now in the present culture; and if not, what would it take to make it fit snugly and securely.

The SF process is exhaustively circular. The end point of future speculation must always bend back to connect to the beginning points of the present. Ultimately, they may appear one and the same with genesis becoming terminus and terminus genesis. The SF problem trajectory requires managers to take the high road of generating solutions that are robust, rigorous, and renewable. Above all, the fast future of SF compels managers to recognize that they are dealing with a rapid reality that has a mind and timetable of its own.

If one views the difference of the future as an adversary to be beaten or a competitor to be bested, that will not yield the value of transforming an enemy into an ally. A begrudging captive will not reveal as much as a liberated colleague. In short, confronting a fast future is a challenge of discontinuous growth unlike any other.

SF offers managers a model of living in the future, creating or recreating its world and laws in all their fantastic tangibility, mastering the tasking standards and circular process of higher-level problem posing and problem solving, and testing applicability with its final embodiments of communication and implementation. Finally, all managers should reread Mary Shelley's *Frankenstein* and discover that the creature snatched from the future had no name.

(26)

OPERATIONAL FUTURES: FUTURE-EMBEDDED INNOVATION METHODOLOGIES AND FUTURE RESOURCES FOR HUMAN RESOURCES

Motivational speakers prepare their audiences for a leap in thinking or behavioral change by asking the same question: "How do you eat an elephant?" And the audience responds with enthusiastic unison "One bite at a time!"

Generally it works. The audience is alerted to something big coming down the pike but manageable. Presented gradually and in digestible bites, the speaker extends a persuasively reassuring invitation to a journey of change.

Companies face the same problem. But they may not already have in hand the target and the end game. They are still busy putting together the shape of the future beast. Uncertain of what it will be, they request data, study the competition, collect trends, estimate their capacity to shift focus, and so on.

Indirectly and often unintentionally that process is diagnostic, in at least three ways. It provides an x-ray of how organizations think their way through to change, what options they characteristically identify, and finally what decision-making and planning protocols and systems they employ.

But the problem often with such complicated assessments is over-study approaching the boomerang of creating a Frankenstein. The more complex and elaborate, the more intimidating and overwhelming. Not surprisingly, refuge is sought in the form of tentative, partial, and contingent solutions. Even if luckily the bull's eye is hit, it is still accompanied and hedged by recommending further study and design. If the task were to build an ark, the floods would come and the engineers would be standing there with damp and incomplete plans in their hands and an unfinished vessel.

But the dilemma is not solely one of commission. It is also fatally a sin of omission or rather two sins. And it is not solely a failure of action but of aspiration. Two upscaling and indispensable dimensions are absent: first, requiring problem solving to also be innovation creating; second, shaping solutions that are not totally time bound but instead have at least one foot in the future. And finally, how to kill those two birds with one stone.

Solutions should always invite the creative contribution of the future. They should not only be ahead of their present time and application, but also lure the future into this world and make it more available, earlier. Competitive edge or advantage thus may be redefined as access to the future, and innovation as the future incarnate.

But easier said than done. What is called for cannot be accomplished by wild brainstorming or imaginative overleaping. What is still needed is one bite at a time; or to shift the metaphor slightly one step at a time, slightly adjusted to tap the following five methodological guidelines.

First, the solutions-innovation-future search involves not just one but many steps. How many is unknown. Second, the steps can never be hurried or skipped. The biggest failing is stopping too soon or early in the game. It is equivalent to passing off the short as the long term. Third, the temptation is to settle prematurely for small gains. Timidity always argues for early arrival. It gives the illusion of engaging the future when in reality it is only an update. In short, the enemy of innovation is "incrementalism." Fourth, the final point or step can never be known in advance. As the classic job description puts it: whatever it takes to get the job done. It is unlike the classic Japanese system of asking "why" five times until one gets to root cause because the precise number of steps is never specified. The final step is signaled by its totality and durability. It must straddle both present and future; encompass the total problem posed with no parts left out or over; and finally, be able to live in this world and to be used by real people in real time and space.

The process itself as well as its final yield must always evidence a persuasive and retroactive logic. Previous steps are never discarded but cumulatively carried forward. Its ultimate end point is startling, unavoidable, and bold. The solution stands as if it has always been there. It has an obvious and almost inevitable logic to it. It stands at the threshold of the future. Its presiding image is that of the two-faced Janus: retrospect and prospect.

How can this shift to next-step thinking/innovation best come about? The contention here is that it involves upscaling and futurizing three commitments.

1. Mission

    Innovation and learning as well as their kinship with each other have to become an integral and central part of organizational mission. Ideally, that double commitment should extend deep into the organization and embrace every employee by becoming a critical factor of employee and performance evaluation.

    Futuristic organizations in fact are characterized in two ways: first, by the inclusion of innovation in mission statements and second, by the degree to which the company is innovation and knowledge oriented, directed, or driven. Indeed, the most driven often are associated with the commitment to corporate universities and the development of unique innovation methodologies such as Six Sigma by GE.

    In a recent survey of the mission statements of 301 companies, the favorite words were "Quality," "Value," and "Service." Only 68 of the 301 listed innovation (Management First, 2003).

2. Futuristic

    Solutions-oriented cultures rather than problem-oriented cultures always live ahead of their time. Their strategy is that of leapfrogging—while we are in the process of catching up let us also get ahead. Enlightened leadership and companies also structure companywide collaboration. They especially prize the contributions of middle-level mangers to the anticipatory process. Being proactive generates the inclusive energy of forward-looking management and leadership.

3. Holistic

Companies that get there first, with the most, and the best applications always carry forward, re-create, and project the big picture. They build arks that include all constituencies and address every contingency. The classic substitution is to settle for a piece and pass it off as a whole, or opt for an early solution that makes the task more manageable in present terms rather than a solution that may be self-managing in future terms. Baby steps and obedient incrementalism limit visions and impoverish potential. In fact, it is precisely such piecemeal timidity that prematurely cuts off the present from the future, and forsakes innovation for incremental gains. Much of the power of all organizational future journeys derives precisely from the emergence of new wholes that are shaped by that future.

In short, organizations that make innovation and learning part of their mission, and are holistically proactive, generate innovations that are designed in large part by and for the future. The test of the innovation is whether it converges minimally both forecast and surviving the forecast, optimally situates and positions itself for the next convergence and the next after that. The future has to be played like a chess game in which every move prefigures and anticipates the next move and the next. Chess mastery always involves multiple positioning. The end game always exhibits the final logic of checkmate.

The following attention-getting opening line recently appeared in an ad by a major management consulting firm: "Traditional avenues to corporate growth are no longer available." To be sure, the firm, not unlike stockbrokers, then engaged in persuasive semantic bait-and-switch substitutions as a way of still staying in the game. Clients and customers were then offered new solutions uniquely available in reassuring language to tough times.

Such cosmetic shell games are unfortunate for many obvious reasons. These are tough times and that truth needs to be told. Business in many ways is facing major and real impasses. Many of the obstacles are not temporary or occasional. If there are ways out, it may require companies turning themselves inside out (perhaps again). Above all, it will compel defining deficiencies not just in present but in future terms.

Are things really that bad? The ad did not lie. Here are ten short-term trends that sum up the first issue: double-digit growth is no longer likely; there may be limits to increasing productivity; manufacturing increasingly will be shifted overseas, only offsetting American exports will be largely agricultural; short-term expedients have stripped the positioning and leveraging flexibility of many companies; mergers and acquisitions no longer attract investors; margins have become tighter; price increases often reduce market share; innovation cannot sufficiently offset glutted markets; even international expansion offers only limited opportunity and is accompanied now by higher risks; the stock market may not satisfy the search for investment; alternative sources will be sought as fewer companies show consistent probability. In short, some believe business may be encountering not only the limits to growth, but also more seriously, the limits to the future.

But many will argue that such challenges have occurred before and have been weathered. There will be a general winnowing out of too many companies and of too many inept performers. Displaced workers will find other jobs. Competition seems to be solving the teacher shortage problem; unemployed engineers are now teaching high school math and science. In other words, the hidden hand of capitalism will muddle its often painful way through, and recovery and stability will be once more restored.

Perhaps (although certainly at considerable costs of confidence and human dislocation). But the larger issue is why have faith only in the power of external cycles over which we have little control? To be sure, we are proactive in other ways. We develop long-range forecasts and strategic plans, often industry specific; compile and inventory trends; employ expert methodologies to identify probability and impact; and undertake research and education in future studies. We even have developed a slogan of synthesis: "Think Globally, Act Locally." But although it wisely combines and even occasionally aligns the macro and the micro, it omits a critical next step: "Implement internally."

What is generally lacking is the infusion of futures directly into business processes. Futures already are environmentally active outside the gates of business. The next step is to go inside—into its everyday operations. If the future of the future is to become more manageable, it has to become more operational. Nor can it remain an abstract and vague gesture of vision but needs to be wired directly into place.

Currently, the future is either an executive prerogative or enclave of strategic planning and marketing. In either case, it is generally removed from or distant to basic operations. When strategic plans are rapidly implemented without prior consultation it often encounters negative feedback and even silent mutiny. Sometimes the response that the emperor is wearing no clothes is so intense that the plan is sent back to the drawing board. The full and unexpected contributions of the future can only be tapped when it functions not solely as an external values-added supplement but an internal part of the way work is envisioned, organized, and done. Indeed, the degree to which that is embedded and granted an authentic voice defines how the future is valued.

THREE TYPES OF FUTURES BUSINESS

Organizations open to the future are of three types: mild, lukewarm, and hot.

Mild companies are just future oriented. The future is generalized; it is more of an aura than a force. It is invoked in mission statements and adorns the walls of corporate training centers. Medium or lukewarm companies are future directed. Their priorities are reflected in a mixture of detailed short-term plans ballasted and redeemed with vague midterms positioning. Strategic planning often is neither a separate division nor employs a separate staff. It is directed by the vice president of marketing and its strategies are determined predictably by market segmentation. Hot companies are future driven. The future is not an occasional but an obsessional and integral part of everything. It is not an add-on or overlay but embedded in virtually every process. As a result, it supports a companywide collective vision of collaborative and proactive leadership.

FUTURE-DRIVEN COMPANIES

How then does a company become future driven? What specific and generic business practices would benefit by being futures infused or amplified? Here is a partial list.

Basic Practices	Futures Additions	Benefits
Decision-Making	Anticipatory Perceptions	Tested in Advance
Communications	Values Advocate	Market Precision
Leadership	Decentralization	Distributed Leadership
Job Evaluation	Work Trends	Future-Focused Workforce
Strategic Planning	Employee Participation	Multiple and Diverse Forecasts
Problem-Solving	Long-Term Solutions	Scenarios and Simulations

Using the matrix as guidelines, how does one build and create a future-driven company?

Installing and incorporating futures additions is not a quick fix. In fact, it minimally involves two stages: review and refocusing. The first is total, the second aggregational.

1. Review (Total Process Analysis)

    The application of futures should lead ultimately and ideally to a 360-degree review of all basic company processes. Initially, however, the focus may be limited and selective. But no matter where one starts, the resistance to looking ahead is so regularly encountered that it becomes a given. Indeed, that is often only the tip of the proverbial iceberg when compared to how deep-seated and threatening the reluctance may be; and how surprising its causes.

    For example, the discussion with supervisors about offering employees a more proactive exercise about work futures rapidly brought to the surface their views of workers in general. The supervisors believed that most employees lacked the basic intelligence and even the self-worth to undertake such a task. Besides, they really preferred to be directed; and are happier when told what to do. The same general devaluative response came from strategic planners who raise similar objections about bottom-up planning and openly objected to what they perceived as a diminishment of their authority and the new jurisdiction and judgments of amateurs. Communications professionals withdrew from the challenge altogether. Although they concede that many decisions at all levels were poorly conceived from a communications point of view, they are hesitant when offered the opportunity to become directly involved in the decision-making process itself. Most preferred to remain outside the process. They were content to wordsmith the results.

In short, the introductory review stage though turbulent and often antagonistic can generate four key clarifying head's up guidelines. The future is one thing, futurizing is another. The former is familiar, token and generic, the latter invasive, unfamiliar, and threatening. Bringing the proactive inside the house and making it an integral part of daily work and thought is routinely dislocating. The prospect of future implementation often brings to the surface many unflattering and negative assumptions about the CEO, the company, workers, and its operations. The future functions like a magnet for dissension. Encouraging the company and its workers to project what's ahead often generates fearful future prospects. General avoidance and even denial follow, and there is a return quickly to ostrich mentality.

But far from being discouraging, the review process confirms what many have found: namely, that the most important initial value of applying futures is diagnostic. Functioning as a comprehensive probe, futures is able to identify weak process links, negative assumptions, avoidance responses, absence of trust and collaboration, and past-oriented attitudes and practices. An array of failures and problems emerge, across the board and from top to bottom. Somehow the future acts as a holistic x-ray exposing the weak links of the total organization.

2. Refocusing (Integrating the Horizontal and the Vertical)

One of the values of reviewing basic operations is that they are redundant at all levels throughout the company. A typically more popular and even glamorous approach would be to restrict attention to top leadership. But that goes counter to what the future diagnosis and reconfiguration revealed.

Leadership is no longer singular but multiple, dominating but distributed, downward but two-way. Similarly, determining the future and its training agenda are no longer the monopoly of strategic planning or human resources but becomes a collective companywide participatory and anticipatory effort. The full extent of futurizing thus requires aggregation.

To avoid piecemeal, partial, or lower levels of comprehension and achievement, it is critical that the processes that have been reconfigured with a built-in futures component be aggregated upward to help define companywide levels and optimums. What emerges are generally higher level bell curves of performance than previously achieved. The performance level of all ships rises. In addition, a shared vision of future directions and the training agenda required to get there emerges as the product of shared purpose.

By tapping horizontal process yields across the board, and directing their definition and application increasingly upward, companies can achieve a double alignment: in the present and in the future. Company needs can now be directly engaged by prioritizing and aligning current and future performance goals with current and future company goals. In addition, the company enjoys the benefits not only of a collective vision of the future, but also the reconfigured means of getting there.

Conclusion: Typically, such double gains characterize future-driven organizations. But they do not come easily or quickly. The diagnostic future is often perceived as an enemy not an ally. The refocused future threatens assured roles and invades comfort zones. CEOs and senior staff especially feel undermined by calls for collective and distributed rather than charismatic leadership.

Although the opposition may be formidable, the gains more than offset the difficulty. Beyond achieving improvements of productivity, profitability, and quality, future-driven companies also may pursue three future ideals: the transformation of organizations into communities, the renegotiation of worker contracts into worker covenants, and the redirection of futures application from external forecasts to internal reconfigurations and refocusing of basic business processes. Such a composite would then define future-driven organizations as collaborative communities of best practices designed to survive a tough present, and structured to achieve its own defined and preferred future. Turned outward that may provide just the competitive advantage business needs. Turned inward that may provide the vision to conceive of and create the workforce of the future.

FUTURE RESOURCES OF HUMAN RESOURCES: THE DEMOGRAPHICS OF WORK BEHAVIORS

Not too long ago the employee virtues that human resources (HR) extolled and recruited for were being dutiful, hardworking, trustworthy, loyal, and obedient. Those past-oriented attributes now have been supplemented by a new crop of present-focused behaviors: adaptability, involvement, agility, innovation, ownership, transformation, mutuality, alignment, morale, and empowerment.

Finally, future-driven qualities have appeared or are emerging: knowledge worker, team player, customer-advocate, technologically amplified, and distributed leader.

The range of these lists from past oriented to present focused to future driven has been structured by a thirty-year process of structural redistribution and reengineering: the gradual flattening of the organizational pyramid conferred upon managers prerogatives and responsibilities previously reserved for senior officers, and in turn employee empowerment assumed from middle-level managers more control and self-direction. In short, decentralization not concentration became the order of the day and even of the future.

The new centrality of employees proceeded from the recognition that if productivity, profitability, and creativity were to occur and to provide the competitive edge in a global marketplace, the base of the now nearly flat pyramid was where it would be found. Indeed, in some organizations teams have either replaced or made marginal their supervisors. The task of HR was to keep pace with those changes and above all to help deliver and train employees in the new elements of each ethos as they in turn were altered to minister to new challenges.

But in many ways and areas, HR needs to push the envelope of worker knowledge further by gaining more information about how workers in fact acquire knowledge. In particular, research recently has focused on the demographics of the workforce and what that reveals about the sociology and psychology of their leadership and learning preferences.

Demographics

As already noted, in a large corporation at least five typically (soon to be six) generations coexist (Adsit, 1997). The oldest were born in the fifties, the newest in the eighties. The first group probably will live until 2050, the second almost to 3000.

The past and future histories of those generations often determine their work attitudes, preferences, and behaviors. The degree to which they are willing to work together in turn affects the degree of alignment with company goals. In an e-commerce start-up, all are usually the same generation. That is why they can move so fast so far. Differentiation is not an obstacle because it is minimal. But that is also why many fail. There is no internal tension, and diversity is not sufficiently representative or had the opportunity to exhibit its checks and balances.

Targeted Behaviors

The complexity of multiple generations and behaviors has become an object for greater study. We are beginning to know much more about why employees do and do not do certain things (Ashford, 1989). The process requires keeping three targets in sight at the same time:

- Identifying targeted behaviors desired by HR and the company (usually drawn from one or a combination of those on the earlier lists).
- Determining what in the employee's demographics and background supports or opposes that change. A series of diagnostic overlays register inertia or flow.
- Identifying the bridging forces, methodologies, and strategies of coaches to win or bring them over to the desired side.

Such a process would be daunting if it had to done every time for every behavior for every employee. But the diagnostic middle piece noted earlier once done is stored in a database and can be tapped again when the targeted behaviors change. The task also has been eased by a deeper understanding of employee-manager relationships.

Employee Preferences

Flamholtz (1986) has proposed a continuum of leadership styles: autocratic, benevolent autocratic, consultative, and participative. Harrison and Stokes (1993) condensed the categories into two: directive and nondirective leadership and coaching styles, then went on to note the following characteristics of each:

Directive Versus Nondirective
Power-shift cultures vs. Achievement-oriented cultures
Role-oriented cultures vs. Support-oriented cultures

(Van Muijen and Kooperman [1994] added the following to the list)

Rules vs. Goals
Roles vs. Innovation

These researchers also have explored further how worker differences affect the perceptions of the above managerial styles. Their findings appear in the eight categories listed here. (Only those factors can be included that are relevant to job performance on the one hand and do not violate privacy on the other hand.) In effect, these factors constitute the basic demographics of all employees, but focused on identifying potential support for or obstacles to change:

Age	Tenure with organization
Gender	Functional area
Nationality	Hierarchical level
Education level	First born, middle, last born

At this point, here are Hofstede's (1997) interpretations of each factor on the list as it bears on leadership style preferences.

1. Age

    Generally older workers prefer and respond to directive managerial and coaching styles. Younger workers respond better to nondirective coaches and managers. Some high-tech start-ups where all employees are in their twenties show a high tolerance for chaos and even anarchy.

2. Gender

Males prefer directive styles, women nondirective. Typically, men are more forceful and assertive, women more cooperative and nurturing. Increasingly, however, convergence is occurring, although women may be leading the way there.

3. Nationality

National cultures shape citizens' leadership preferences. Strong and assertive national cultures want strong leaders. Other more egalitarian countries in fact distrust leaders having too much power and favor imposing constitutional limits on executive power.

4. Educational Level

Typically the higher the level of education the greater the inclination to favor the nondirective leadership style.

5. Tenure with Organization

The longer the period of employment, the greater the reliance on directive leadership; although if there have been a succession of poor or mediocre CEOs, the allegiance may be accompanied by skepticism.

6. Functional Area

Predictably, blue collar workers favor strong bosses, white collar more nondirective ones.

7. Hierarchical Level

Line personnel and managers favor what they are and increasingly want to become. Staff want an easier life associated with simply being told what to do.

8. Birth Order

First born tend to be more aggressive and insecure and more resistant to authority. Last born are more distant and harder to reach, and often capricious. The middle are usually the most reasonable, although they can lean on occasion toward the behaviors of the first and last and sometimes both at the same time.

The next step is to compile a demographic cluster, which provides guidelines as to the key perceptions and attitudes of the employee being managed or coached. Following are two sample employees. One is an older director of the transportation division whose general profile places him in a directive cluster. That is followed by a younger employee who leads a team of mostly entry-level software engineers and who falls within a nondirective cluster.

Directive Cluster
Older
Twenty-five Years' Tenure
Male Employee
Transportation Division
High School Nationality
Strong Assistant Director

Nondirective Cluster
Young
Three years
Female Employee
Marketing
College
No Declared Nationality
Team Leader

What does such clustering offer the manager-coach? The most obvious result is more data than he has ever had before. He now has a more extensive knowledge base to tap for performance evaluation sessions. He may notice, for example, instances of initiatives being taken by employees correlated with a partiality to a nondirective leadership style or a lack of initiative as a result of having to relate to a highly directive manager. The manager may find employees who prefer a nondirective style to be more open and responsive to questions about different and even more creative ways of doing their job. In contrast, the employee who prefers doing what he is told will be more reluctant to volunteer suggestions for change or improvement and prefer instead to have the coach tell him what he should be doing differently.

For companies that develop a future stance in which work performance has to be continuously improved and innovation encouraged and teaming has to become a new norm, the role of the manager coach has to become that of a stretch agent. His task is not only to coach change, but also to align and wire it in place in terms of specific job requirements and expectations on the one hand and company objectives on the other.

With an expanded demographic and knowledge base accompanied by the many clusters that it can generate and sustain, the manager-coach has a richer and more diverse and flexible set of alternative routes to take. In fact, taking the time to provide employees with an opportunity to share their histories, perspectives, values, and the overall complexities of their lives and work sets the stage often for affecting change and job improvement.

Both have a great deal to contribute and to learn from such exchanges. Such equality and mutuality hopefully generates a tangible model of what future work relationships should be all about. Turnaround of employees requires the combination of art and science. Databases and demographic clusters set up the science; the coach functions as a knowledge artist. The dynamic dialogue of partnership between equals raises the task of integrating performance and change to a new level for HR professionals. Performance evaluation, which combines the science of data and art of partnerships, may provide employees and managers with the greatest challenge each has ever faced.

An unusual but critical area that tests futurists is finding leaders with foresight, often early on before their reputations are made. Would Jack Welch or Bill Gates have been tagged when they were still young and virtually unknown? It is a particularly appropriate task for futurists because of the need to identify leaders for a different future. It thus requires always a double knowledge: an early leadership detection system coupled with scenarios of what will be required of leaders in the future.

But why is that important? For at least three reasons. Changing challenges shape the job profile. They may even prescribe a global and interdisciplinary range. It compels organizations to become increasingly self-conscious about anticipatory leadership development. (If leaders are made not born, then the company needs to study how best they can be made. If leaders are born not made, then the company needs to know what those genetic qualities are. Besides, even the born are made somewhat.) Such knowledge benefits the embryonic leader. It makes him or her more self-conscious about planning and designing his or her future professional life. Leaders have to write a career script. Their life becomes crafted. They may have to become in turn futurists.

Although knowledge about what defines a future leader can come from many sources including bibliographical ones, which are available to everyone, some employ alternative routes. As noted previously, for many years I served as an executive coach and trusted advisor to CEOs and senior staff. Not unexpectedly, the subject of the future and above all the characteristics of future leaders were a recurrent subject. Three occasions triggered dialogue: Identifying and advancing future leaders in their organization or those in their competitor's and how to lure them away; finding a successor to the throne or new member of the board or senior cabinet; conducting especially for a captive audience of senior staff an endless and open-ended seminar on the characteristics and qualities of emerging leadership. I of course attended every command performance.

As a group these CEOs were uniquely wise, cynical, egotistical, and cocksure. They believed they had a monopoly on the knowledge of the future. No one could or would contest their pontification. To their credit, however, these executives were always insightful, so much so that in my judgment their seminars were far superior than most offered at doctoral programs in business. More to the point, there was remarkable agreement as to what makes or breaks emerging leaders for a changing future. Here then are the five common denominators for identifying future leaders: vision: the big picture now and ahead; mission: leadership sharing; operations: transparent excellence and flawless execution; structure: decentralized and collaborative; and commitment to professional development: unlearning and transition training.

Before elaborating on each area, the discussion needs minimally to be framed. A futures context needs to be identified for each of the five categories. That preserves the role of the future as a partner in identifying the characteristics and qualities of leadership. Indeed, in many ways, objections might be made that these five leadership qualities do not appear very futuristic. In fact, they seem quite traditional. Not so, however, when the future bears down upon them and alters both their form and content. The following matrix provides futures equivalents for each and will be folded into the discussion of how those futures dimensions challenge, drive, and shape the emerging leader.

Leadership Qualities: Their Futures Context
Vision: Interdependent World
Mission: Collaborative and Holistic Decision Making
Operations: Horizontal Congruence and Vertical Alignment
Structure: Employee Centrality
Professional Development: Unlearning

PROFILES OF FUTURE LEADERS

1. Vision

Generally, the contemporary discussion of vision has been muted or minimized. It appears as too grandiose and belonging to an earlier time when major enterprises were launched. The days when Walt Disney could stand on a mound and look over acres of swampy land are over. No new big companies will be created. All already have been and anything new is really variations or combinations on what already existed. And so vision is disposed of and subsumed under mission especially by those hard-nosed types who do not wish to be deflected from dealing with real stuff by puffery.

But acknowledging the future in fact restores vision to the agenda. One of the functions of the future, especially a compelling and discontinuous future, is to disturb the present. Consider the projection of the two spikes alone, in technology and population. Can any organization not find its mission jarred or rendered askew? When such shocks to the system occur, only vision can serve to restate what lies ahead and how we engage it. Mission then takes its obedient second place in the pecking order.

The major new factor of vision is globalization. As a system, it is denser and more elusive than we realized. It generates strange or different partnerships: software companies subcontracting with programmers in India; manufacturers exporting the most polluting stages of their process; epidemics crossing national and even international lines; and so on. In other words, the increasing interconnectedness of the world compels a vision, which seeks to comprehend, express, and somehow master the new competence of interdependence. Moreover, in scale and daring such an effort would be not unlike the impressive one a number of year ago by Meadows in *The Limits to Growth* (1972).

Meadows and Forester were visionary futurists. Their computer simulation model while flawed (it had to be) nevertheless produced a powerful finding: There is no human goal that requires more people to achieve it. They not only studied the future but their study itself had all the impact of the future. Critics found fault with their databases, with the lines of interacting factors, with the entire computer model. Nevertheless, the impact was so great that reviewers in their discussion even changed the title from the limits to growth to the end of growth. Ideologically, for many the limits to growth meant the end of growth. And so systematically we shot (down) the messengers and gave global visionary efforts a bad name for quite a while.

Effective future leaders have to build a series of new visions of the planet, its relations to the environment and to each other (perhaps they should be the same), to sustainable growth and redistribution, and above all to the complex and often fragile ways the new globality operates. Those new leaders have to assemble and peruse a new futures bibliography, which focuses on the kind of span of Meadows and Forester and many others on the one hand, and the imaginative range of the science fictionists on the other hand.

Finally, the parameters of the vision must go beyond obvious self-interest. It should not follow the old pattern of accumulating a fortune perhaps rapaciously and then spending the twilight years dispensing wisdom as George Souras recently and interestingly has been doing or creating a foundation to dispense largesse and cleanse guilt posthumously. Rather, the vision should address not only global economics but political science so as to preserve the option that leaders may exercise as part of a larger cumulative and reinforcing effort, building a sustainable future. The future cannot be left to governments, especially dreadful ones and their notions of national security and sovereignty. A new dialogue has to include visionary leaders whose principal agenda item is always the future of the planet.

2. Mission

Ideally, each leadership characteristic should somehow resonate with all the others. The effort, however, should not compel a stifling consistency but rather demonstrate that future leadership has an interlocking range, that it is conceived, reflected on, and adjusted to be coherently whole. In this way, the most insistent dimension of the future, global interdependence, impacts on all the characteristics of leadership.

Thus, the mission of the leader is no longer a separatist entity designed to serve only those who lead. Nor is it solely limited to how the CEO can best lead his company. The future compels a new consideration: What do I do with my leadership? How do I use it? Traditionally, leadership belonged exclusively to those at the top. It was held close. It was a source of power and distinction. If it sought change, it was in the form of how to exercise more power over more holdings. Leaders of old always were empire builders and inevitably monopolists. Their goal like empire builders was to extend their rule totally.

Future leaders are not timid or myopic. They know that the top holds power and sway. But the new futures issue is how is the power of the leader leveraged? How can it be used to meet organizational change on the one hand and global change on the other? In other words, leadership has joined intellectual capital as a major factor on the asset side of the ledger. Leadership itself is on the block. How leaders use the assets of leadership determines whether the company succeeds and in fact has a future. The key mission then of futuristic leaders is leadership transfer and sharing in order to encourage and preserve the possibility that each leadership initiative could be aggregated upward and potentially be applied companywide.

3. Operations

According to nearly all leadership gurus, the overriding distinction of outstanding leaders is their decisiveness. They are able to make decisions within tight time frames, often with less than total data at their command and choose a course from among a bewildering and complex set of options. That ability alone sets apart the men from the boys, the successful leaders from the has-beens.

But leaders of and shaped by the future will need to be not only more decisive, but also technologically assisted and amplified. Increasingly, real and just-in-time data systems provide access and transparency to virtually all operations. In some cases the data will make the decision or more will be asked for such an automatic process to take place. The role of the leader will shift from content to context. Futurity and globality may be joined at the hip.

4. Structure

Currently, success or profitability is determined by productivity, quality, and customer satisfaction. The future factor is innovation.

It is the CEO's task to ensure the interlocking durability of all factors. And in the past that was exclusively perceived as in fact the responsibility of leadership, at the top and throughout the middle.

Embracing distributed leadership brought a degree of decentralization that was immediately bracing and productive. Decisions could be made quickly on the microoperational level without having to endure the time delay of ascending the chain of command. The introduction of new technology also often impacted productivity. But the global competition especially impelled by much lower wages and standards of living became crushing. To survive, leaders had once again to use or dispense their leadership in a unique way.

Gradually, over time employee productivity began to supplement technological productivity; employee centrality began to extend distributed leadership. Leadership transferred its capital once more but this time more radically and created a new governance structure, the employee collaborative.

The process was gradual, even piecemeal, because few leaders foresaw the prospect of employee leadership in totality on the one hand and because the evidence was not in that in fact it would work. But the latest and numerically the most extensive decentralization created a major supplement to distributed leadership in the form of new collaborative governance structure. Employees gradually in terms of governance were brought from the periphery to the center, from being the objects to being the subjects of productivity, from being workers to being partners. This newest investment of leadership capital was again driven by global competition, in particular the lower wages and standards of living of competitors. Technology alone could not offset the differential (in some cases it even increased it). Only employee productivity could even the odds.

Thus new structural norms began to appear: teams became the dominant form of work relationships; quality and productivity employee circles were charged with producing time and cost-saving changes; alignment teams were created across divisional lines to achieve a double alignment, horizontal and vertical, and thus to bring divisional goals and company goals in coincidence; planning and scheduling even of projected layoffs became increasingly an employee responsibility; evaluation factored in more heavily employee self-evaluation and a 360 degree to bring customers into the heart of the process; employees increasingly had input into the training agenda and even often creating unofficially employee universities when they also were asked to serve as workshop instructors; and most recently depending upon the enlightenment or desperation of the company involved, employees have been invited to be involved in futures scanning processes.

In the process of discussing this empowerment of workers as stakeholders, one older retired CEO remarked, "If we had been smart enough to do all this earlier, we might have avoided unions." That sparked a lively exchange between us that included the observation that the union take on employee centrality might be 180 degrees away from his but more to the point neither position was a leadership one. Taking the high visionary road, what set leaders apart was the degree to which they accepted the future as the determining and defining ideology. And what the future offered was the prospect of a collaborative governance structure that required not only leadership vision of its value, but also willingness to make an incredible investment of leadership capital into the hands of workers. Perhaps, the most dramatic example has occurred in the form of an employee environmental scanning process in which teams or divisions read, identify, and discuss trends and rate and record their durability and degree of impact on a monthly trending form. The forms are aggregated upward and reissued with common denominators identified. That establishes companywide commonality to identify leadership options. What more could a futuristic CEO ask?

5. Professional Development

Typically, professional development is sporadically driven by the budget and its agenda is determined by the top or supervisors. Although one of the new yields of the collaborative governance structure is the increasing acceptance of employee input, what about the professional development of leaders?

Typically, they are exempt or removed from the process. To be sure, they may decide what the training should be or serve as cheerleaders for Senge's learning organization, but generally they generate the questionable image that they are complete. They have achieved perfection otherwise they would not be where they are. But one of the telltale signs between present-occupied and future-driven leaders is that the latter model their incompleteness and the need for lifelong learning and development.

In particular futuristic leaders have to embrace and promulgate minimally three kinds of professional development: futuristics, holistics, and innovation.

As noted, future leaders need to study the future of the future. In every communication CEOs in one form or another must share news of and from the future. One CEO I know who was passionate about science fiction created an extraterrestrial newsletter.

Holistics is a critical antidote for companies too preoccupied with incremental development just as unlearning is the threshold for innovation. It falls to the leader who openly, officially, and frequently describes the ways in which unexamined past assumptions have blocked ways of thinking outside the box. That is best done, as I have witnessed it, by leaders telling stories of their own mistakes, opacity, myopia, and misplacement. They become learning leaders by paradoxically advocating unlearning.

REFERENCES

Adsit, J. D. "Crosscultural Differences." *International Journal of HR Management* 8, no. 4 (1997), 385–401.

Ashford, B. E. "Social Identity Theory." *Academy of Management Review* 14, no. 1 (1989), 20–30.

Buchen, I. H., and Zdrodowski, P. "Coaching Complexities." *PI* 41, no. 9 (2002), 27–29.

Flamholtz, E. G. *Entrepreneurship to Professionally Managed Firm*. San Francisco: Jossey-Bass, 1986.

Harrison, R., and Stokes, H. *Diagnosing Organizational Culture*. San Francisco: Jossey-Bass, 1993.

Hofstede, G. *Cultures and Organizations*. New York: McGraw-Hill, 1997.

Van Muijen, J. J., and Kooperman, P. L. "The Influence of National Cultures on Organizational Culture." *European Work and Organizational Psychologist* 4, no. 4 (1994), 367–380.

27

FUTURE EMPLOYEES: GOAL-ROLE METRICS AND EMPLOYEE MANAGERS

Although American workers are constantly on the stretch and routinely asked to do more, often with less, what is perhaps startling is that they are nevertheless succeeding. Steady increases in productivity, profitability, and quality are being achieved even with or because of downsizing. Why? Basically, two reasons are given: the sharp edge of global competition, and performance improvement training. As far as the future is concerned, all that is evidently needed is more of the same: Keep upping the ante and sustain the learning. Right? Perhaps not.

Two problems, one practical the other conceptual, exist. The workforce may encounter the law of diminishing returns. It may not be possible to continue to reach increasingly competitive goals especially with fewer employees and the thinning out of managers. In fact, the signs of a new clever desperation already are beginning to appear; companies are turning to new variables never used before.

Outsourcing abroad is only the most recent and sensational example. But the same principle was at work earlier when Circuit City replaced its entire commission-based sales force with fixed pay employees at average lower salaries. Others are following suit by replacing experienced and knowledgeable sales people with clerks capable only of writing up orders. Customers have adjusted by securing expert Internet information before entering the store.

Undoubtedly, more ingenious outsourcing and manipulative variations will surface as companies seek to remain viable and competitive. Financial experts and human resource outsourcing consultants will mount or attend conferences to display cost-saving schemes and increase the visibility of their expertise. But still there may be limits to doing more with less. A quartet reduced to a trio can still perform but not the literature of a quartet.

Can training pick up the slack and close the gap? Perhaps but only with a kind of training that is in fact shaped by the new dynamics and metrics of the workplace. One key shift already discussed is knowing more about those being trained. Thus, diagnostically driven training has surfaced—targeting training to hit the hot buttons of employees as revealed by extensive psychological and learning styles testing. Such profiles certainly will bring greater precision and efficiency to effectiveness.

But valuable though such profiles are, they are essentially inward facing and partial. They tell more about workers but not about their work. And even when the two rightly are paired, the relationship between the two is static. Column A is job description, column B is task description. A larger dynamic framework is needed whereby generic employee profiles can engage generic workforce patterns. Such interplay would recreate the dynamic give and take between employee preferences and performance objectives. The framework being proposed here involves the reexamination of the basic relationships between goals and roles.

Traditionally, goals are elaborate, roles simply stated. Goals are multiple, roles singular. Goals may alter or vary but the role remains the same. Moreover, goals and roles are not perceived as possessing a dynamic or changing relationship with each other. Rather, they are reassuring reflections of each other. Ideally, they are a mirror match. A job title or role is linked with an appropriate set of goals, which in fact essentially defines that role. Thus, for example, performance evaluation is always set against goal achievement not role change. In short, goals rule. That is where the action is. Because the focus is always on the action side of the equation, the role is regarded as a static given. It remains intact and the same.

That focus made sense in the past. Goals were manageable because they were of a piece with the given role and achievable because they were not stretched beyond the reach of that role. And even when such efforts routinely did exceed the parameters of both goals and role, no one noticed or cried foul because it was successful. There was no need to press inquiry further or employ closer scrutiny. Attaboys and congratulations were the order of the day as cheerleading managers expressed confidence of future replication.

But it can be argued that what made such achievements possible was an unexamined and even undetected dynamic between goals and roles; and that when the nature of that secret interaction is known and tapped, it can yield a model for more targeted training and performance improvement, even upgrades.

The job classification process is both clarifying and imprisoning. It follows the paradox celebrated by Robert Frost's famous "Mending Walls": "Before I build a wall/I would like to know what I am walling in/And what I am walling out." All jobs and job titles are also acts of positioning. They are sandwiched between one above and one below it. The pyramid dictates the pecking order.

The detailed list of objectives that follow and accompany each job title firmly establishes its respective role parameters. When spillover occurs and is spotted as part of the evaluation process, it is often interpreted as a basis for a promotion or reassignment of greater responsibility. But only then is role change—usually a future one not the one under examination—contemplated as part of the process of goal achievement. In other words, all attention is fixed on goals not roles and hence on goal change not role change.

But as noted, times have changed. Not surprisingly, goals bear the imprint of such changes. Although they are no longer the same, the job description preserves them in amber and gives the illusion of continuity. But an overview and analysis of the workplace and workforce reveals that goals have undergone at least five major generic transformations. They all have been stretched incrementally, even exponentially; targets have been altered while still in flight; alignment must be both vertical and horizontal; alignment must be constantly linked to structural and personnel crossovers and cross-training; and the discontinuity of innovation must be embraced.

A few words of explanation about each are needed.

1. Stretch

   Most current incremental increases are without end. They may even occur daily and subsequently not be evenly spaced. Except for their constancy, they are not predictable in scope or degree. Like computer advances, they require constant updating and sometimes abrupt shifts brought about by paradigm changes. Constantly upping the ante, incremental stretch goals have become the new norm.

2. Moving Targets

   Often even the incremental is not singular but multiple, fanlike not linear. Add-ons are affixed. Variations on threads are developed. Direction is altered. Updating and upgrading meetings are many and constant. There is little or no white space on the calendar. The pace is breathless. Head's up regularly interrupts process. Evaluation occurs every Friday, sometimes daily or tied to specific dates so as to capture the goals of the week. Flight plans or repairs have to be undertaken while enroute. All must remain in motion. Everything is in a state of transition. Multitasking is now a generic task for all. Everyone has had to become a juggler.

3. Alignment

   Individual and teamwork priorities are driven by alignment with divisional partners near and far, and with company objectives. Organizational flow systems are nested within the larger big picture of vision and mission and serve as employee road maps of coincidence. But the priorities change, routinely and regularly. For large companies, the challenge is how to rapidly change the direction and momentum of an enormous battleship. Agility is what helped Jack be nimble and quick.

4. Crossovers

   Structural reconfigurations into more open and fluid forms and functions increase and hasten cross-training and job rotation. In the process, even the lowest cog in the machine becomes many cogs. The overall shape of an organization comes to resemble more a series of rivers flowing through it than a tower of mechanical boxes. Accordingly, employee stretch goals become increasingly fluid, open-ended, and unfinished. Every job becomes a variation on a theme and every employee an artful dodger.

5. Innovation

Finally, all employees are asked to contemplate the discontinuity of job processes and functions. They are stirred to create alternative cost-saving and more productive ways of doing more with less. Every aspect of the process has to become grist for the mill of innovation. The assumption is that everything, broken or not, needs to be fixed. Creativity is no longer the monopoly of R&D.

Although at any given time not all these transformations may be operating at the same time, sooner or later they all will impact the workforce. They have to because they are driven by the unavoidable common force of competition that will not go away. To be sure, this list may be so daunting and intimidating as to require moving the conventional last phase of all job descriptions—"And do whatever is necessary to accomplish the above"—to the first position. Such a generic catch-all presented from the start would at least serve as a more accurate and appropriate warning preface of what has become increasingly undefined.

But the key obstacle to the application of this generic taxonomy is a mistaken focus on fixing or faulting only the fluxy goals. When they are not met, the predictable explanation is that the objectives exceeded the parameters of the job description as well as the skill sets required to succeed. But when success occurs, we are so delighted that we give up being defensive but still fail to ask why and how.

So it is back to basics. Every goal houses the role that requires it to accomplish it. If they are not in synch, employees regularly complain and object to being unfairly judged. So they become territorial and defensive and complain: "That is not in my job description." Currently, that disparity is ignored by hard-pressed managers who respond with, "Welcome to the new world." But what may be overlooked and lost sight of is a symptomatic mismatch. The kind of transformational-driven goal changes required cannot be accomplished without role changes. Goals still may rule, but roles trump.

The argument here is that the current achievement of changing goals can only come about by changing roles. We have been so fixed on the goal side and its measurement and training that we have failed to recognize that a secret reciprocity exists between goals and roles. Certain goal changes cannot be accomplished without role changes. Employees often unknowingly have to shift into high gear and alter behaviors and attitudes in order to reach their more demanding goals. But by failing to understand and value that new dynamic between goal and roles, managers and trainers not only have ignored acknowledging the remarkable growth potential of employees, but also been ignorant of what is deeply at work in performance improvement and its evaluation. To overcome those limits and to develop a more comprehensive and interactive basis for both training and assessment, two critical questions that need to be answered are: "What kinds of goal changes require and even compel role changes? And what kinds of role changes emerge?"

Clearly, not all goal changes stir role changes. Even some incremental ones may be different only in degree but not in kind. They thus still may be manageable and achievable and thus may not require role change. But the five cited earlier do. The task now is one of dynamic linkages, to display in the following taxonomy the matched goal-role relationships.

Taxonomy of Goal-Role Exchanges

Morphing Goals Versus Role Changes
1 Incremental Flexibility and Stretch
2 Multiple Multitask and Entrepreneurial
3 Alignment Priorities Decisions and Corrections
4 Variations Open Ended and Unfinished
5. Reconfiguration Innovation and Implementation

From these partnerships between goals and roles, two sets of conclusions may be drawn. The first describes the essential changing and reciprocal dynamics between goals and roles; the second redefines the new job descriptions driven by role performance upgrading.

GOAL-ROLE DYNAMIC

Most current training focuses on goals transformation not role changes. Most performance evaluations fail to factor in the changing relationships between morphing goals and morphing roles. Changing goals cannot be met without changing the roles required to achieve such objectives. Job descriptions create static expectations of a dynamic goal-role relationship and need to be totally redone. The ultimate and cumulative impact of goal-role metrics is the transformation of the workforce.

The correctives are clear. Training has to pair goals and roles, and link emerging roles to reach morphing goals. Performance evaluation has to mirror and reinforce the training by measuring the emergence of roles appropriate to goal attainment. Job descriptions have to be brought in line by spelling out the unfinished nature of "whatever it takes" as the highest and ruling priority. Finally, learning and human resource directors have to contemplate that given the transformation of performance goals on the one hand and the corresponding emergence of higher level roles on the other hand that the upgrading required is more a matter of kind not of degree.

When the roles listed here are reviewed, what dramatically emerges is a new workforce definition of rank-and-file workers. Here then is the second set of conclusions. The roles compelled by morphing goals are essentially managerial in nature. Employees not only have to do their work but also manage it. The level and kind of reflection and evaluation normally reserved for supervisors now has to be exercised by those in the trenches. Monitoring, scheduling, and planning, traditional preserves of middle-level managers, now are routinely carried out by rank and file. Innovations of form and/or function are not lofty interventions introduced from above but introduced and accomplishable at the basic job level. New job descriptions have to be written for the emergence of the employee-manager.

Goal-role changes have to become the new and future focus of training and evaluation. But their application has to be revised to develop not employees but employees as managers. Such a dramatic change at the base reverberates throughout the entire organization and not only alters, but also parallels the new goal-role changes of managers and leaders. Collectively, they constitute the emerging workforce of the future.

28

FUTURE MANAGERS:
THE MANAGER-LEADER HYBRID

Managers and leaders are constantly juxtaposed, Most of the time it is a lopsided comparison done not to honor the differences between the two but to preserve and elevate the distinctions of the latter. Thus, here is a typical composite put-down drawn from Rost (1993), Dumaine (1993), and Kotter (1996):

Managers	Leaders
Direction: Planning	Vision
Alignment: Controlling	Creating shared cultures
Relationships: Focus on objects	Focus on people
Role boss	Coach
Outcomes: Maintains stability	Creates change

No wonder everyone wants to be leader; and books on leadership far outnumber and outsell any on managers. In a typical three-ring circus of workers, managers, and leaders, the king of the hill always appears center stage. But aside from being a forced exercise of hype to make leaders look good at the expense of managers, there are a number of serious, pejorative, and perhaps unintended distortions.

The first is that the process of comparison and contrast fixes a rigid and myopic mind-set and lock-step upon managers that may be ultimately

embarrassing to leaders. How are those limitations to be discarded, revised, or trained out of managers on their journey to the top? Evidently,
it regularly fails because some CEOs are often criticized for behaving
more like managers than visionaries or worse, of being micromanaging
leaders. But paralleling the two roles involves a more serious distortion:
It obscures the current transformation of managerial roles.

Observation of the current actual behaviors of managers in diverse
environments yields a profile that integrates rather than separates the
two columns listed earlier:

1. *Information Gathering* Managers must scrutinize and maintain
   sources of organizational knowledge by developing information interfaces and internal networks.
2. *Market Competition* Managers must observe, be knowledgeable
   about, and communicate the behaviors and reactions of competitive firms.
3. *Holistic Strategies* The introduction of any major new system
   must be perceived and wired in place by managers. Their coordination is essential to managing the total impact on the entire organization and its decision-making process (Utunen, 2003).
4. *Strategic Monitoring* Because of fluxy environments, managerial
   monitoring has become an important ally and adjunct of strategic
   planning. Aligned, both serve as indicators not only of company direction, but also of restructuring (Lucas, 1997).
5. *Technology Supervision* Every manager is now a technology manager whose task is to link and optimize information to achieve operational success.
6. *Consumer-centric* Managers are responsible for creating, implementing, and aligning customer relationship management (CRM)
   systems and applications across divisions (Frawley and Shrum,
   2003).
7. *Resource Optimization* Managers oversee enterprise resource
   planning (ERP), which is a shared management tool used across
   the board to optimize both internal and external resources accessible at an unlimited number of points to achieve higher levels of
   productivity.

8. *Financial Thread* Managerial awareness of and contributions to financial and accounting processes is driven by cost control and cost savings (Davenport, 2000).

9. *E-Commerce* Managerial development and engineering of an e-commerce value chain is used to promote market adaptability and agility (Castells, 2001).

10. *Success Overlays* Managers need to identify and communicate industry-level knowledge of critical success factors (CSF), especially those of innovation (Ulrich, et al., 2003).

Although not all these roles are assumed by all managers at any one time, it also can be argued that some do even more. But given the historical and perhaps inevitable compulsion to glorify leaders and to minimize managers, a major corrective is thus in order. Most companies can operate (and often do) without leaders but would fall apart without the leadership of managers.

If the list of additional functions is reviewed, what emerges is the emergence of a new hybrid—the manager aggregated as a leader. The success of many companies in sustaining annual increases in productivity each year for the last fifteen has largely been brought about not by CEOs but by manager leaders.

But how did that happen? Three factors: morphing goals, emerging roles, and thereby the general restructuring of the goals-roles of managers. All three exist in tandem and require a brief reexamination of the basic nature of the relationship between goals and roles.

Not all goals are morphing in nature. Traditionally, goals were stable, stated, and enumerated in job descriptions and generally recognized as appropriate to the job title role. Above all, they were familiar and accomplishable. Besides, if anything new surfaced, that was subsumed under the last line of whatever it takes. But then gradually and sometimes precipitously, some fixed managerial goals became more mercurial and even chameleonlike. They appeared to develop an elusive life and speed of their own.

Workers and managers increasingly have become breathlessly involved in catching their own tail or constantly playing catch up. They also have become nervously accustomed to tasks being perennially incomplete and even out of reach. But the remarkable achievement is that even though all these new goals exceeded their job descriptions, they somehow got done. And because such higher productivity was thankfully accomplished, even with downsizing, we generally failed to ask why.

It is an understandable sin of analytical omission. Targets were met, quality maintained, customers satisfied, market share retained, and so on. The assumption was all would continue. All that was needed was to keep the pump primed and apply what had worked before: The pressure of competition and performance improvement training. But the argument here is that the competitive demands will increase and that if performance is to be maintained, there is a need to know the dynamics behind current success and reshape training accordingly. Specifically, learning and training have to be driven not solely by explicit and definable objectives but by goal-role reciprocity—by the dynamic interplay between task and talent.

Traditionally, the relationship between managerial goals and managerial roles was clear, static, explicit, and appropriate. Tasks were linked to roles and that was that. Spelling out such equivalents was in fact the function of job descriptions. But unknowingly, stretching and changing goals compelled role changes. Managers had to shift into high gear, regularly exceed the parameters of their job descriptions, routinely embrace and implement new systems, and above all stir and train rank and file to function in teams and even become team leaders.

This unnoticed and pervasive series of transformations stemmed from the special, dynamic, and reciprocal relationship that secretly exists between morphing goals and changing roles. All stretch and mercurial goals carry within them the embryonic roles to accomplish those goals. The goals and roles are thus like secret sharers.

Conventional goals only require conventional managers. Morphing goals require manager leaders. Managers had no other choice but to step up to the challenge, exceed their job parameters, and close the gap between emerging goals and moving targets—in short, to do whatever it takes. The gulf between knowing and doing described by Pfeffer and Sutton (2000) is being bridged by managers assuming roles previously reserved for those at the top. Managers have moved up the chain of command because of necessity not aggrandizement. The result is they now occupy and function across an enlarged and major center of the organizational chart.

In the process, hierarchy has essentially been leveled and given horizontal extent. The vision of distributed leadership of Robert Greenleaf and Charles Handy has found its realization in the emergence of manager leaders. But to be effective, traditional managerial training has to catch up and embody the dynamics and metrics of goal-role synergy. Thus, what is now needed is to train managers for their new leadership roles, rewrite their archaic job description, and finally figure out what to do with CEOs.

REFERENCES

Aber, R. "Improving Customer Relations." *Entrepreneur* XII, no. 2 (2002), 36–40.

Bourgeois, L. J. "Strategy and Environment." *Academy of Management Review* 5, no. 1 (1980), 25–39.

Castells, M. *The Internet Galaxy*. New York: Oxford University Press, 2001.

Davenport, T. H. *Mission Critical*. Boston: Harvard University Press, 2000.

Dumaine, B. "The New Non-Manager Managers." *Fortune*, February 11, 1993, 80–84.

Edelhart, M. "Various Approaches to Systems Strategic Plans." *PC Week* 4, no. 26 (June 30, 1987), 38–39.

Frawley, Mike and Bob Shrumm. "Relationship Management." *Electronic Business*. October 1, 2003.

Kotter, J. P. *Leading Change*. Boston: Harvard University Press, 1996.

Lucas, H.C. Jr. *IT for Management*. New York: McGraw-Hill, 1997.

Pfeffer, J., and Sutton, R. *The Knowing-Doing Gap*. Boston: Harvard University Press, 2000.

Rost, J. C. *Leadership for the 21st Century*. Westport, Conn.: Praeger, 1993.

Taylor, B. "From Corporate Governance to Corporate Entrepreneurship." *Journal of Change Management*, 2, no. 2 (2001), 128–148.

Ulrich, D., Goldsmith, M., Carter, L., and Smallwood, N. *The Change Champion's Field Guide*. New York: Best Practices Publications, 2003.

Utunen, P. "Identify, Measure, Visualize Your Technology Assets." *Research Technology Management* 46, no. 3 (2003), 31.

29

FUTURE LEADERS: NEW CEOS, EXECUTIVE AGENDAS, AND EXECUTIVE COMPOSITES

As everything becomes routinely crazy, big, and new, and relentlessly frequent and sudden, simplistic solutions—usually the province of politics—are acquiring currency. In particular, there is the rallying cry for new leaders and leadership, even though that call moves in a number of often contrary characteristics and directions.

The new leader, given turbulent times and permissive values, needs to be a solid, sober, and stern savior. Alas, salvation reopens the door to charisma, which in the past often has led us down the garden path. The leader also should not be a celebrity or superhero anymore. Instead, the CEO should exhibit execution, humility, and above all, post-Enron integrity. He should be almost ordinary. Finally, he should be a she; perhaps even foreign born.

The problem with all the above is not that they are mistaken or wrongheaded but that they are piecemeal. They thus totally underestimate the range and scope of the change needed. If the total complexity of new and future CEOs is to be addressed it must be recognized that the reasons for new leaders are holistically part of a total realignment of all positions and roles. The definition of the new CE neither can be isolated from the general dynamics of the emerging employee manager and the manager leader on the one hand, nor ignore the specific and different challenges of the twenty-first century on the other hand. Here then is a composite of ten descriptors of the new leader.

1. Staying Power

    The focus has shifted from getting the job to keeping it. In 2001, 25 percent of CEOs were fired. In 2002, that went up to nearly 40 percent. The dilemma is that leaders are damned if they do and damned if they don't. But being a time-server and playing it safe and close to the vest won't answer the call for major changes. Above all, CEOs who stay the course often lead companies that last. Chief executives may need to have workout gyms built next to their office and follow the Schwarzenegger training model.

2. Results-Driven

    The job itself is now intensely and constantly measured. Personality and morale-building play second fiddle to bottom-line deliverables. Executive performance will be data managed and calculated. The new CEO may have to have an IT or project management background to be knowledgeable about information management and assessment systems in general and know enough to have some say about how he is being evaluated in particular.

3. Process Decision Making

    Tracking systems increasingly using real and just-in-time information resemble internally observable medical procedures that are process invasive. Data embedding has brought new access and transparency to the dynamics of customer preferences, market fluctuations, product inventory, warehouse storage capacity—and so on—all while they are going on, not after the fact. Just as express mail providers can track and tell where a package is en route, so CEOs must make critical and data-driven decisions and midcourse corrections daily even hourly. The new CEO thus may have come up from the ranks of UPS or FedEx or at least have served as an airline traffic controller.

4. Restructuring the Organizational Chart

    The new leader must fuse vision and organization. In the process, what must occupy first place is the traditional last line of all job descriptions: "Do whatever it takes." A strong background in HR will be indispensable.

5. Learning Leader

   Senge's call for creating a learning organization has been pushed further and harder to become the design and development of learning management systems (LMSs). LMSs are increasingly delivered electronically, managed cost effectively, and implementation evaluated and affirmed. The new leader has to develop a vision of the workforce of the future and to become a tireless advocate of the training needed to get from here to there. CEO candidates unexpectedly may currently be the chief information officers (CIOs) of corporate universities or the chief learning officers (CLOs) of learning-driven companies.

6. Diagnostically Driven Empowerment and Training

   Knowledge of employees across the board (including the executive level) is approaching a science. Through brain research and extensive employee testing, it is now possible to develop precise individual and group profiles of preferred performance and learning modes. With the overlay of Gardner's Multiple Intelligences to learning styles, the focus has shifted from "How smart am I?" to "How am I smart?" The new CEO may or may not have majored in psychology but he has to be knowledgeable about the emerging field of cognition science.

7. Acknowledging and Working with a Transformed Workforce

   The new CEO cannot assume a business-as-usual attitude and expect leadership deference all along the chain of command. Even the traditional sanctuary of the executive team as already noted has been pierced and reconfigured. But most important the CEO not only must recognize, but also support the emergence of manager leaders and employee managers. He may chafe at such leadership sharing but if he seeks to lead a successful company he may have to recognize and strengthen the sources of that success. It thus may be helpful to have come from HR to the top post.

8. Innovation

   Innovation will accompany and accelerate transition. Incremental improvements of current in-house products and services will parallel and some times compete for resources to support achieving big breakthrough innovations. If the forecasters are correct, innovation increasingly will be the offspring of convergence. Current fusions like biosociology, genetic psychology, human-machine symbiotics, and the like are but the tip of the iceberg. And the speed with which such hybrids will appear may be dizzying. It is estimated that the second decade of this century will exhibit a degree of progress ten times that of the entire twentieth century. The new CEO should be an avid reader of science fiction and require his executive team to follow suit. Ideally, he should hold a few patents.

9. Globality

The new CEO must be a globalist not as an occasional but as a constant focus. He must map and display an international and interoperable electronic and marketing network of suppliers, sales reps, and customers. Overseas volatility must be added to risk management. Offshore cash flow also needs the careful tracking of money managers of fluctuations against the dollar. Multinational companies may even have to shift their currency base to maintain balance. The new CEO may come from international banking and electronic commerce. He may be Chinese with an American MBA.

10. The Future of the Future

Of all competencies, foresight tops the list. It has to. It alone encompasses the future-driven strategies for all the above: staying power, results-driven performance, process decision making, restructuring, learning empowerment, surviving transitions, championing innovation and internationalism. Of all the fusions, the most critical is that between futurity and globality that need to be paired into a seamless partnership. The new CEO will have to be a futurist and a member of the World Future Society.

Minimally, three common denominators emerge from considering why new CEOs may be needed, where they are likely to come from, and how they will be different. They are globality, futurity, and global and futuristic training. Such an integrated focus raises the prospect that the future CEO should be a combined GBO and CLO.

NEW AGENDAS

Historically, workforce components were discrete and hierarchical. The organizational chart laid out a vertically oriented structure of positioning. The top and the bottom were dramatically far apart. The middle segment filled the gap in between and differentiated the levels of managerial responsibility and functionality. Although complexly layered, organizational structure exhibited clarity and stability. Such reassurance was essentially an affirmation of both the general business environment and the particular culture of the company. Both converged to provide the ultimate yield of future continuity. Finally, all defined not only American wealth but also dominance. The Fortune 500 companies collectively summed up the triumph of capitalism and their CEOs the constellation of leadership.

But things changed. A few years after profiling the ten best companies half the list had disappeared. In 2001 25 percent of CEOs were fired. In 2002 it went up to nearly 40 percent. Downsizing, outsourcing, and now job exporting have become the new norms of maintaining solvency and profitability in the face of global competition. Financials and marketing often are in the driver's seat. Databases and MIS feed decision making. The leading and managing mantra was and still is productivity. Every level was impacted. Each one ultimately responded by altering the chain of command. A series of movements up and across began to disturb the layered clarity of organizational charts. Gradually and rapidly, the neat segments blurred into each other; and like dominoes the momentum multiplied and cascaded.

Rank and file not only had to work harder and smarter, but also had to manage their work and that of their teams. And because there were generally fewer of them around with the needed skill sets, employees had to train and supervise themselves while in flight. No down time was available. As employees became managers, managers in turn, tasked to achieve stretch and even morphing goals, moved up beyond their traditional middle ground and assumed leadership roles. Both manager leaders and employee managers thus stepped into the same presumptive breech to engage chameleon goals and to ratchet up increases in productivity necessary for survival.

What is amazing is that this essentially unacknowledged, unexamined, and undirected process of doing whatever it takes worked. Productivity gains were posted annually for the last fifteen years, quality increased, and profitability was maintained. But it also exposed and left unanswered a key question: what kind of executive leadership is now required for enterprises that consist largely of employee managers and manager leaders? Indeed, what substantive roles are left over for CEOs after subtracting the assumption of leadership by employees and managers? Does the new equation require a different kind of CEO?

Typically, three different kinds of answers surface. The favorite focuses on personality and character. The CEO is no longer celebrity or superhero. That has happily been replaced by execution, humility, and above all, post-Enron integrity. Another response stresses external challenges particularly the two-headed dragon of global interoperability and future volatility. In addition, future CEOs may be women but they also increasingly will not be American born. Finally, organizational charts and structures have to become more fluid, integrated, networked, and agile.

Like the proverbial process of defining an elephant by focusing only on a separate part, each answer is correct. The problem is that they are piecemeal and fragmented and thus encourage favoring one piece over the others and passing that one off as a whole. The hard truth is that if CEOs are to succeed and lead productive companies, they have to not only embody all three directions, but also bring them about. In other words, they have to create the conditions for their own success. And that goes far beyond asking for the resignation of all vice presidents and bringing in a new team. Such termination may ultimately be required but it needs to wait on the CEOs' new vision and structure to determine whether their support and affirmation appears or does not.

The fusion of vision and role specifically requires that future CEOs be performance driven not personality oriented; shape and put in place structures informed and guided by globality and futurity; and finally ensure that all the changes are wired in place and are so embedded that they permeate the entire organization even to the lowest rung. In addition, the future CEO must be centered on results not cronyism or nostalgia. Like Deming before him, she must be obsessed by data measurement and statistical profiles. But now the data must exist in real and just-in-time form so as to access and render transparent the immediate flow of customer transactions, market fluctuations, inventory space, and so on. The CEO needs to direct his MIS and communications personnel to craft explanations of what is being measured, why, and how. He also has to display a global matrix along a future time line so that every employee at every level knows that is the new way the world now operates. A genuine invitation should invite their suggestions of what else should be measured or differently.

Predictably, one multiple request will be for a CEO monthly report card. The CEO has to articulate performance targets (by which he is measured as well). The rallying cry is the last line of all job descriptions— "whatever it takes." Throughout, globality and futurity will become increasingly versions not alternatives of each other. Traditional American ignorance of world geography may be repaired by global business.

But perhaps the most daunting task is to find or create the right agile structure at the top with the customized kind of expertise to meet urgent and shifting global and future challenges. Typically, the executive echelon consists of three levels. The first is the CEO. The second the various other chief executive officers: chief financial officer (CFO), chief operating officer (COO), chief information officer (CIO), and two new additions, chief learning officer (CLO) and chief globalization officer (GBO). The third are the vice presidents of all divisions.

Different CEOs (and sometimes different industries) develop different consulting and decision-making relationships among the upper echelon. In addition, because of partisan politics and divisional advocacy, CEOs often bring on board their own executive coach who is unilaterally loyal and savvy and performs like a fly on the wall. But whatever the personal or industry preferences of CEOs, there is an overall need to develop a structure that minimally is both holistic and expert. In other words, it must miniaturize and represent the whole organization and its input on the one hand, and be able to bring to bear quickly and precisely the expertise needed for immediate decision making on the other hand. The first establishes representative balance; it is democracy in miniature. The second is rotational and precludes the fixed rigidity of a Maginot line; it is a meritocracy.

Perhaps, such a dualistic structure is to be found in the recommendation of Robert K. Greenleaf (cited and applied earlier to employee evaluation and team operations). Reaching back into Roman times, Greenleaf urged employing the system of the Roman legions. The head of each platoon of ten was dubbed "primus inter pares"—first among equals. In addition, the head was not permanently fixed but rotational. What determined selection was always a mix of shifting circumstances and appropriate expertise. But it was always understood that the change was temporary. When the need again changed and a different kind of leadership was required, the new one chosen to be first was as close a match as was available. In the process, what unexpectedly occurred was a double gain. Each team member developed lateral extensions of his particular expertise, and all acquired both the language and attitudinal modality of the others. If they survived battle, each team became a progressively proficient and productive series of heads leading equals.

Many CEOs might find the prospect of rotation belittling and the notion of others being equal unsettling. But the decisions and the directions to be made are so complex and the expertise needed so multiple that the CEO is the only one who can take the lead to totally reconfigure the executive level into a rotational structure. In the process, the CEO must select executive expertise that can function collectively, collaboratively, and above all integratively. Moreover, such interoperable relationships become their common performance standards and the basis of bonuses, if any. The days of the lone ranger, especially of the CEO, are over. Leadership has to be shared. There is nothing like rotation to task the egos of all alpha dogs.

Although critical, performance and structure, data and networking, are not in themselves the most engaging factors of an executive's agenda. The CEO needs to talk in more stirring terms without falling back on rhetoric or charisma. Driven by the fusion of globality and futurity, the CEO has to put forth a vision over time that brings together a new big picture and features the interrelationships of values, innovation, and learning.

Vision unfortunately has attracted more romantic heat than analytical light and excessively set CEOs apart as lonely inhabitors of mountaintops. Nothing has wrecked more companies and resulted in more executive terminations than the inability to anticipate both the near and long-term future. And nothing has been more misguided than elevating gut instinct to the level of infallibility. Forecasting and trending is hard work. Business intelligence gathering is not unlike the database assembled by the CIA and FBI. There are professional futurists with degrees in future studies and futurist consultants who have developed impressive strategies and scenarios for diverse companies. There have even been resident futurists in the past. Ian Wilson held such a position at General Electric for many years. In short, the vision needed by the CEO is to add to the executive team a CAO—a chief anticipatory officer—or to add that dimension to his own and to the job descriptions of all executives. Although it need not be someone brought in from the outside, it probably should not be a retread from within. The expertise of foresight is too critical to be entrusted to time servers.

Valuing joins such visioning in two ways. The future direction is always to make the saving of jobs and the company compatible goals. That may seem obvious but layoffs and downsizing indicate otherwise. In fact, many CEOs basically have chosen fast and dirty solutions: Save companies by eliminating jobs. They have not learned the lesson of Henry Ford who paid his workers more than others so that they could afford to buy his cars. National policy has to become corporate policy. Wherever possible, employment and company survival have to be joined at the hip; CEOs have to agonize rather than amputate.

The second dimension of valued visioning is to wed anticipatory management with participatory management. CEOs need to set up companywide input on future directions. Every employee at every level has to be reshuffled into cross-divisional teams and during brown bag breakfasts or lunches become involved in studying the future. To keep the process anchored and to forestall blue skying, the focus should initially be on the future of their job and expertise. Scenarios need to be written of what that job will be like two to five years from now and if considerably different what it will take to get from here to there.

Aside from generating and contributing grassroots perceptions of the future, this fusion of anticipation with participation will help to shape a workforce that is minimally future oriented and optimally future driven. Then too, there is no point in projecting a future if the means to get there are not made available. Employee identification of the supplemental skills they will need in the future not only makes them more receptive to change and growth, but also defines the company's training agenda. Futurizing also can lead to innovation.

Innovation creates the future. The new moves us beyond the now to the then and the there. Indeed, it can be further claimed that one of the most stimulating ways of stirring innovation across the board is to make all employees futurists. But like the figure of Janus, which faces back and forward at the same time, innovation must be applied in both directions. Current products or services already in house need to be tinkered with, reconfigured to require fewer steps, moved more rapidly across divisional lines—in short, incrementally improved. Such day-to-day improvements are small but cumulative; they add up.

As far as technological breakthroughs from the outside, that is often a wild card. Often unknown and unexpected, some are nevertheless discoverable. Futurists have been able to anticipate two-thirds of future technology but they also have missed another two-thirds. Science-fictionists may have a better track record. Companies need to maintain or outsource advance guards who monitor the edge for coming attractions. But even then the feasibility and durability of each new imminent development requires the use of an evaluative tool such as the expert Delphi.

More in hand are major innovations pursued from within and propelled by the high priority of the vision of the CEO and his role as resident futurist. But once again the CEO cannot leave to chance or tradition the structures to make it happen; and once again his executive performance standard in this case is being able to create the structures that stir big innovations.

The CEO may experiment as many companies have with separate enclaves and budgets, functioning even outside company structures, which are self-orbiting and self-centered. Or designate and shape an internal cross-divisional oasis manned by cross-functional teams. But whatever amorphous form is chosen, the structural overlay must mirror the same rotational dynamic of the executive level. Collaborative synergy is at the heart of the innovative spirit and its nature and intensity constantly has to reflect the learning curve of its collective experts if it is to exceed the present.

Finally, the CEO must be an absolute champion of learning and even unlearning. The future training agenda generated by employees has to become his agenda and that of his executive team. But they should not be exempt from being part of the training. They also should not be allowed the privilege of a special session or version; they should join their division as equals. Although training is critical to futurity and innovation, it takes employees away from their jobs and is expensive. It thus requires a new kind of executive expertise that most CEOs lack. It requires a learning leader or CLO as an addition to the executive team.

CLOs like those who head up the some fifty corporate universities nationally and internationally are expert minimally in three areas. First, they know instructional design and know therefore what works best with what subjects and what employees. In many organizations they have increased the testing of employees to discern learning styles, team compatibility, and multiple intelligences. They have shifted the focus from "How smart are we?" to "How are we smart?" The net result is diagnostically driven training.

Second, they know what makes the difference. They understand that the key is not the training but its implementation. And so adopting the same corporate focus on performance and data measurement, they design elaborate follow-up systems of evaluation. Finally, they are expert on the cost-effective delivery of training, including reducing time away from task. A mix of f-2-f, electronic, and blended learning is put together that balances diversity and costs.

The futures agenda of the CEO and the future CEO are of a piece. Ideally, they should be indistinguishable from each other. Similarly, performance goals and data measurement should be equally interoperable, seamless, and embedded. The CEO focus must always be double: globality and futurity, totality and foresight. And just as he must create the structural conditions under which he will be successfully evaluated, so he must deliver and disseminate that double focus throughout the entire organization.

Participatory management must find its match in anticipatory management. Finally, the CEO needs to project a vision that not only aligns global alignment with foresight, but also embodies the values, innovation, and learning both will require. Finally, that symbiotic fusion of vision and role not only is generated by, but also applies to and serves to evaluate CEO performance as well. She may be first but everyone else is her equal.

CLO AS CEO?

If we are compelled to think of a single solitary CEO rather than a hybrid, I recommend we look at CLOs. Why? What about them exhibits the future stuff of top leadership? Minimally five factors. They are increasingly through e-learning global in reach. They are future driven. They are experts at data-driven assessment and thus comfortable with the CEO job being now increasingly results driven and data managed. Their vision is to train and sustain the workforce of the future. Their mission is to build a learning system that supports goal and role changes and stirs innovation.

Although this list favors CLOs, it does not rule out why a CFO, COO, GBO, CHR, and so on should not be equally considered. What in short gives CLOs the edge?

Only the CLO is a learning manager and leader. Whatever else other experts may contribute to solvency and productivity—and it is often substantive—nothing matches both the immediate and long-term gains of developing a smart and agile workforce supervised and evaluated by assertive and flexible manager coaches. Indeed, it may not be an exaggeration to claim that CLOs are in fact training the workforce of the future. And that is likely to involve the development of new hybrids— employee managers and manager leaders. In other words, CLOs are already comfortable with living ahead of their time and thus having in hand at least half of the paired focus on globality and futurity.

Many, especially those involved with multinational companies and corporate universities, also have natural and often deep access to globality as well. Indeed, they are routinely much more aware of the diverse training attitudes of different cultures to the American way of doing things, especially our emphasis on individual initiative and self-reliance. They also have encountered educational mosaics and time travelers who though anchored in ancient cultures also have acquired degrees at and been acculturated by Georgia Tech. Finally, many of the candidates in their leadership development programs, especially the women and non-Americans, are likely to head up Fortune 500 companies (as some already have). Fortunately, even those CLOs limited to U.S. companies have ample access to an increasingly diverse population here.

With globality and futurity firmly in their field of vision, what other building blocks must be put in place or refocused for the progression to CEO to take place? Many other deliverables.

Embedding globality and futurity throughout the total organizational culture as a shared worldview. Encouraging experimenting with the creation of work environments and structures that are rotational and reciprocal and not hierarchically rigid. Adding the overlay of real and just-in-time data for access analysis and decision making to all performance reviews. Extending further and deeper employee testing to produce diagnostically driven training and to change the focus of the question from "How smart are we?" to "How are we smart?" Designing and following up innovation-driven training that results in incremental improvements, anticipates deus-ex-machina interventions or surprises, and finally achieves genuine and paradigm-shifting breakthroughs. A word or two of explanation about each of these.

DIFFUSION THROUGHOUT

The future CEO will have to fuse vision and role and create the conditions and performance standards on which she and her company will be judged. Toward that end, the future must not be allowed to become part of the typical abstract, knee-jerk, and exclusive rhetoric of executive speeches or visions. Instead, it must be delivered, embodied, and shaped. Performance evaluation now must include individual employee speculation about what that job is going to be like two to five years from now and what is needed to get that worker from here to there. Aside from helping to shape a future-oriented and even future-driven workforce, the aggregated recommendations of subsequent training needed may constitute the company's future training agenda.

FORESIGHT EXPERTISE

A recommendation to join the World Future Society is not facetious. Indeed, every annual conference is preceded by optional workshops on futures basics: methodologies, trending, scenario building, and so on. There and elsewhere CLOs will discover that because of volatility, monitoring has become the adjunct partner of strategic planning, and further that the function of prediction is to generate preventive early warning systems. Thus, the future is to be perceived not as a single intact entity but as a mixture of stretch, strain, and shock. The first state of stretch offers many and often happy alternatives when the writing on the wall is read. But if ignored or trivialized, a law of escalation takes over. Stretch gives way to strain. Options are still available. But if that state is rejected, we move into future shock that is often grim and ugly. In other words, CLOs seeking to become CEOs have to align the learning with forecasting curves. Indeed, they have to make them compatible training goals. And while that fusion is evolving, CLOs have to become CFOs to their company. They have to serve as Ian Wilson did for many years at GE as resident futurist.

WORK ENVIRONMENTS

CLOs are experts not only on how people learn but also how they learn collaboratively. That fundamental interactive and synergetic process should serve as the structural model of executive relationships. It should also lead and shape the reconfiguration of the executive team especially along the lines of globality and futurity.

RESULTS AND DATA DRIVEN

Current CLOs are committed to evaluating what works. Follow up and measurement of training effectiveness and thereby cost controls have become for them a norm. But to reach executive levels, CLOs have to ratchet up data gathering in three ways. First, data must be company-wide; second, it must be provided in real and just-in-time form and access; and third, in must become a deliverable. The last item is a critical commitment for the CLO-CEO. What is being measured, why, and how must not only be applied, but also communicated across the board. All need to be reassured that it is not a sinister version of big brother out to play gotcha, but a companywide reflection of the common company commitment to performance, applied to the CEO as well. One way of clinching a number of performance targets is to develop and display a generic companywide global matrix set along an extended two- to five-year time line, with provisions for individual variations to be worked out by supervisor and employee dialogue. Such metrics should make clear that this is not only the way the company but also the world now operates now and in the future.

EMPLOYEE TESTING

Happily, CLOs are already ahead of the game here and in the process have made the quantum jump to diagnostically driven training. As CEO, such employee diagnostics also should be applied to recruitment, interviewing, hiring, and orienting. Above all, profile forecasting needs to anticipate workforce needs, minimally for the next five years. Because of their close observation of the resources of human talent and potential, CLOs also are in an excellent position to identify the major managerial and leadership changes in the workforce, thus advancing and empowering the trends toward the emergence of employee managers and manager leaders.

INNOVATION

Finally, CLOs also would bring to the executive table considerable knowledge about the ways to stir creativity. Aligned with futurity, they even can claim that innovation in fact creates the future. The new moves the now into the then and the there. But they may need to differentiate applications, minimally into three stages. The first is incremental improvement of existing in-house products and services. The second is the wild card of technological and paradigm breakthroughs. The third is discontinuous innovation. The first is pretty much in hand; but if not, can be rapidly made part of the performance improvement system and added to job descriptions and expectations. The second is problematic and probably can be best handled by outsourcing to advanced guard experts, just as many firms currently do with computer and MIS developments. The last is a real challenge for the CLO-CEO but in all likelihood will follow the synergetic direction of collaborative teaming, extended perhaps by the metrics of primus inter pares.

But perhaps the most important reason for the CLO becoming the CEO is that he more than any other executive is responsible for helping to train and create the workforce of the future. Moreover, if more employees are to become mangers and more manager leaders the commitment must be at the top and must be total and unwavering.

This workforce is genuinely new and transformational. Nothing quite like it has ever existed before. It has been shaped and evolved by the convergence of globality and futurity. The CLO-CEO thus has to resist the temptation to reverse such growth by going back in time to create obedient narrowly defined jobs suitable for overseas outsourcing. This genuine brilliant American achievement must not be undone or trivialized to meet short-term and small bottom-line gains. In the long run—and that has to be the vision of the CLO-CEO—this workforce will sustain and restore American preeminence in the workplace here and globally.

EXECUTIVE COMPOSITES AND THEIR RECONSTITUTED EXECUTIVE TEAMS

Typically and even traditionally, discussions of the future of leadership in general and of CEOs in particular stress the need for new visions and goals. Although what that shall include may vary significantly with different organizational and sector priorities and urgencies, it will undoubtedly include globality, forecasting, information networks, learning management systems, and the like, and most important, the pressure to integrate all the above.

But if such projections portend a substantial and even radical change in CEOs, should not who they are, where they are coming from, and where they will be heading be as important as what they will have to do? Should not new goals be linked to new roles? Perhaps, in the process even the familiar executive acronym may be altered. Indeed, here are at least five new titles for CEO drawn from the alphabet soup of the future:

CIO
CLO
GBO
CIC/CIA
CIP

Whether or not any of these prevail over time or appear officially on the masthead, they do serve to identify and perhaps to define the new dynamics of top leaders and why the new focus on recasting goals and visions surfaced in the first place. Above all, they may demonstrate that the CEO of the future like the organization he leads will not be a singular but a multiple composite, not a lone ranger but a hybrid blend of diverse associates. In any case, exploring and examining each new pretender to the throne may tell us more about the seat of power than what only the current discussion of new goals has yielded so far.

1. CIO as CEO

This top-level position of chief information officer is the creation of information technology and systems. In some organizations the CIO is designated as CIT to signal and symbolize the degree to which all business has become e-business. Indeed, all courses in current MBA programs are officially or unofficially e-courses to dramatize the extent to which research and information sources are Web based. In some instances the Internet serves as the only current library available.

The CIO is responsible for creating, maintaining, and structuring organizational data and information flow. The extent to which that is increasingly the life blood and circulation system of companies has determined the elevation of the director of IT to CIO. What also has pushed that position forward to the executive level and even to the point of becoming the CEO is the addition of data decisions. Embedding just-in-time and real-time data in all internal and external operations has brought new transparency and precision to decision making, the key task of top-level executives.

2. CLO as CEO

The chief learning officer, whatever his initial specialization, is a generalist. His discipline and expertise is generic learning. He creates, manages, and evaluates learning management systems that operate vertically from top to bottom, horizontally cut across all divisional lines and provide e-training available 24/7/365.

The CLO is the heir apparent of Senge's learning organization. His immediate and ongoing principal task is to increase productivity, profitability, quality, customer satisfaction, and market share-margins through knowledge acquisition and management. His long-term goal is to help create and train the workforce of the future; that visionary prospect alone nominates the CLO to be a CEO.

What also reinforces that equivalency is cost-control–driven assessment. Constantly evaluate offerings to determine whether they in fact are implemented, by all, across the board, and bring about the desired degree of performance improvement. CLOs are ruled by ROI, as are in fact all CEOs.

3. GBO as CEO

The global business officer is an empire-building executive who operates in two ways and directions simultaneously. First, he creates a miniature of the whole. Depending on existing structures, it either serves as a global overlay over all operations and levels or subsumes them all under a new international imperative. Second, a GBO dramatizes the extent to which companies envision themselves and their future to be global in nature, scope, and focus. When all three combine and become the primary goal, the GBO may become the CEO.

But even as an intermediate position, the GBO is mission critical. He offers a center that is often lacking altogether or only occasional and partial: a global mind-set. The task of the GBO is to facilitate the diffusion of that new ideology throughout the entire organization and to spell out the opportunities and challenges of global markets and customers. As overseas numbers climb and reach the point of matching or exceeding national sales and/or when profit margins are greater than those of domestic operations, the prospect of a GBO becoming CEO will proportionately increase.

4. CIC/CIA as CEO

Progress is always incremental but it is not often holistic as well. Intellectual capital (IC) or intellectual assets (IA) qualify on both counts. IC was developed initially by Skandia in Sweden to bring more realistic criteria and greater precision and detail to the evaluation of company assets. Book value and annual reports not only failed to reflect critical but often intangible assets, but also in the process distorted both market capitalization investment and stock purchases.

But the correctives involved required a total conceptual over-haul not just the financials. That involved factoring in both tangi-ble and intangible assets like human capital and R&D until all the parts now summed up a new whole. As IC became the shaping structure of organizations, it seemed a natural progression for a CIC or CIA to become a CEO.

5. CIP as CEO

This title may appear initially mischievous but what is behind it is instructive. Jacob Jaskov claims to be the first chief innovation pusher. Not accidentally, Jaskov is a futurist and active member of the Copenhagen Institute of Futures Studies. Indeed, he even suggests that his role is totally future driven.

The essential thrust of his new title is innovation. Minimally, creativity will be so critical to future success that it is future creat-ing. The CIP thus will preside over a future time that will be so constantly and intensely new that as much as 90 percent of every-thing may appear different.

Reinforcing and accelerating that prospect will be the Singular-ity that is projected to produce more progress may occur in the first two decades of the twenty-first century than in all previous periods combined. Future shock may have to be redefined as fu-ture displacement. Past inventory will be replaced by future cor-nucopia. Innovation will be the front and back of change and may even become its synonym. The company that redefines change as innovation will according to Jaskov inherit the future and ulti-mately replace its CEO with a CIP.

In summary, the following matrix may exhibit the major CEO al-ternatives:

Title	Shaped/Driven by Future Goals and Gains	
CIP	Information Technology	Data-Decision Systems
CLO	Knowledge Acquisition	Future Workforce
GBA	Global Competition	Worldwide Operating Systems
CIP/CIA	Other Than Financial Assets	New Integrated Enterprises

There remains one final matter to discuss. How will all or any of this come about? Are current CEOs less egocentric than those in the past and can they therefore accept leadership sharing? Have they been differently educated or trained to recognize and be receptive to these new executive level trends and usurpations?

When was the last time a training program for CEOs was ever offered? Evidently, everyone else needs it but CEOs are finished learning or that task has been turned over to a private or invisible executive coach or trusted advisor. In other words, aside from the shock of the new and its future-driven executive titles, the comfort zone of most current CEOs would preclude wholesale adoption.

Thus once again gradualism rules the day. At least three less-dramatic and more gradual courses of action surface. The first involves the CEO as hybrid; the second an amplified CEO executive team; and the third a two-tiered executive layer, one traditional, the other transitional.

1. CEO-Hybrid

     The CEO may in fact have come from one of the key new areas and/or the changing direction of his company may have compelled his becoming a quick study. He also may be a she and also not American born or both and thus be more reflective of the demographic and market shifts of the company. In any case, current CEOs have the option to choose a new partner identity and to exist as a hybrid before circumstances force such collaboration.

2. Executive Team Reconstituted

     If the CEO prefers remaining intact, he may shift the need for change from himself to his executive team. Typically, that minimally consists of a COO and CFO, sometimes also the head of HR and the head of legal. The latter may have been elevated to that level because of mergers and acquisitions.

     To that inner circle, all five or a selection of what is listed earlier could be added. It may not an easy fit. The new may be younger, culturally more diverse, speak in technical terms or different paradigms, and behave like young and impatient Turks storming the barricades. It is thus not unlike putting two very different families together and the Brady Bunch notwithstanding it is no easy or successful task.

     The CEO may have to become involved in conflict reduction and resolution. He may have to calm the waters during the shakedown cruise as well as exploit and direct the tensions toward shake-up. But sooner or later he must forge a new diverse executive team who are all on the same page. That may require a retreat. With this polymorphous group, one every three months.

3. Two-Tiered System

The prospect of such interpersonal turbulence as well as the jockeying for power and leverage may lead the CEO to pause. If the traditional and older members have his ear they may heighten uncertainty. They may argue that these new titles and areas of expertise are unproven flashes in the pan or advanced by and for obvious self-interest and self-promotion. They may ultimately suggest that these new areas can be subsumed under traditional operations and thus not incur the additional expenses of a new executive level appointment as well as their expensive staff. But if the CEO has any vision at all, he will hearken to the directions of the future.

The CEO will move toward compromise. He will create a two-tiered executive team. One will be traditional, the other transitional. Like the choices of a Column A and a Column B, they can exist in different combinations.

The CEO has a number of options. He can make them equal, meet with them separately, and combine them for certain topics such as long-range planning. Or he can elevate one team over the other, permanently or temporarily. He even may set them at odds with one another by assigning both the same task.

But whatever variations on the theme of future leadership are played, the position of CEO itself is now beset by the same forces of change buffeting his organization. Indeed, the first order of business may be to set the executive house in order as the threshold for developing companywide future plans. The challenge now is that there are many new and eager firsts.

EPILOGUE: CLAIMS AND
MISGIVINGS AND PUTTING
FORECASTS ON TRIAL

I hope reading this book has been more of a learning journey than a wild ride. If so, it is intended to resemble a similar learning journey that managers are urged to undertake to straddle like Janus retrospect and prospect.

Similarly, the range of the book. Anchoring study in the busy ever-changing present, reaching ahead to capture emerging short-term trends, and finally leaping forward and speculating about the future reenacts respectively the threefold span of future stretch, strain, and shock. In other words, I have diabolically designed and structured the impacts of this book to simulate the impacts of the future itself.

Why? Because strange as it seems, those involved in looking ahead do not seek to shock or discomfit. In fact, their proactive aim is constantly to turn shock into stretch, and to convert crisis into choice.

Admittedly, it is difficult. When Naisbitt's *Megatrends 2000* appeared, no one believed that his sources were mostly drawn from daily newspaper items. The projections were thus not really about what might occur but rather what was already happening.

Then too, we often resist having our deeply held beliefs and hopes challenged or devalued. When Meadows et al. published their global simulation model under the title *The Limits to Growth*, so many reviewers were so upset with the notion that their cherished notion of infinite growth might no longer be available that in effect they changed the title to the end to growth. Actually, the conclusion of the book is that no genuine future goal should require more people to achieve it. Population limitation was offered by the futurist authors as leverage on a future that would restore unlimited growth. Once again intervention partners with early warning, vision with foresight.

Still, forecasters should be held accountable. How that rigorously might happen is the final item to be considered.

> A forecast should be tried by a judge and a jury, much like a criminal.

> —Future Trends (Winter 2002)

Accountability and oversight increasingly are becoming new norms. For some it is too little, too late. More seriously, too alien. The controls are add-ons not organic to the process, band-aids treating symptoms not causes. Besides, greed will likely be too creative and entrepreneurial to be content to replicate the old manipulations. But perhaps the most serious objection is questionable positioning. It is comparable to the old way of placing quality control at the end of the production line rather than as an integral part of the process at all key stages.

Would it not make more sense to be accountable beforehand and during rather than as an afterthought? And be not outside but inside the process from the start, and thus be a more anticipatory and internally involved partner so as to avoid later embarrassing and panicky external correctives?

What are some of the essential characteristics and benefits of this more invasive and internalized concept of accountability? It should be proactive, participatory, diverse (not one-size-fits-all), built into every major decision point and process, focused not only on pinpointing error or lapses, but also on improving the process itself, self-correcting, contributory to the larger process of continuous improvement. internalized, institutionalized, and integrated into each operation, and finally, seamless.

How to start? Select initially problem or fallible processes, structures, or roles. Then mercilessly put them on trial. Give each one the third degree. But make sure that the excess indicated is central and generic not peripheral or occasional. Then and only then can accountability be built in as a self-correcting agent. To illustrate how it might work, putting forecasting on trial might be particularly appropriate.

FORECASTING

It has been argued that forecasting possesses so many flaws that it may not be amenable to any sort of accountability (Mintzberg, 1994). In addition, the standard disagreements between strategic planners about theories, methodologies, and trend gathering have been around for some time now and no resolution seems in sight (Hamel and Pralahad, 1994). Such a bewildering diversity of approaches may paralyze accountability by dispersing the crime over such an extensive area that one cannot take specific forecasts or the general process to task. But repositioning the focus may accommodate accountability (de Geus, 1988). Specifically, to what extent have forecasts included assessing the capacity of the current workforce to realize such projections? More important, define the future workforce itself.

Already noted on an anticipatory and experimental basis are those companies that initially encouraged the crafting of employee mission statements (Buchen and Zdrodowski, 2001). In addition, what has been called for is a gradual replacement of worker contracts with worker covenants (Champy, 1999). Moreover, forecasts increasingly have focused on the transformation of jobs in both the short and mid term (Habbel, 2002). Most recently, Thomas W. Malone (2004) addressed The Future of Work. In short, a key way of holding forecasts accountable is to compel their addressing constantly and comprehensively workforce trends and impacts. Such a focus is both summative and precise. On the one hand, it encapsulates organizational mission, cultures, systems, and structures and renders them transparently operational. On the other hand, it captures the day-to-day drama, narrative, and cast of characters in the futures forms of scenario and simulation, the forecasters' version of science fiction.

The litmus test of futures accountability thus resides in its focus on workforce issues and its use as an insistent agent of reengineering (Hammer and Champy, 1984). Finding weak data and trend links is to be followed by positioning accountability precisely at those points to correct the flaws, failures, and excesses from occurring in the first place. In addition, such checks and balances when found, communicated, and put in place stand a better chance of being self-correcting because they are intimate and proximate to basic and recurrent processes.

Sustaining and internalizing mock trials proactively might prevent real ones; and requiring forecasts to endure the trial by fire of workforce projections and applications may forestall stillborn results. In short, any study that seeks the future range of business cannot do so until and unless it addresses the future of work and workers.

As noted at the outset, serious students of the business have no other choice but to look down the road. It is also characteristically American. When at the end of the book it looks like Huck Finn may be taken in hand and finally civilized, he chooses instead to light out for the territory ahead. There he, America, and its evolving workforce will remain forever young, resourceful, mischievous, and unfinished—like the future itself.

REFERENCES

Argyris, C. *Overcoming Organizational Defenses*. Needham, Mass.: Allyn & Bacon, 1990.

Bakken, B. *Dynamic Decisions Environments*. Diss., MIT, 1993.

Buchen, I. "Disturbing the Future." *Foresight* 22, no. 4 (August 2001).

———. "Directive and Nondirective Employees." *PI* 44, no. 2 (May 2002).

Buchen, I., and Zdrodowski, P. "Employee Mission Statements." *PI* 40, no. 6 (July 2001).

Champy, J. *Reengineering Management*. New York: HarperCollins, 1999.

de Geus, A. "Planning as Learning." *Harvard Business Review* (March/April 1988).

Habbel, R. *The Human Factor*. New York: Booz, Allen, Hamilton, 2002.

Hamel, G., and Prahalad, C. K. "Competing for the Future." *Harvard Business School Press*, 1994.

Hammer, M., and Champy, J. *Reengineering the Corporation*. New York: HarperCollins, 1995.

March, J. G. *Decisions in Organizations and Theories of Choices. Perspectives in Organizational Design*. New York: Macmillan, 1994.

Mintzberg, H. *The Rise and Fall of Strategic Planning*. New York: The Free Press, 1994.

Rosen, R., and Berger, L. *The Healthy Company*. New York: Putnam, 1993.

ABOUT THE AUTHOR

Irving Buchen is executive career consultant and senior researcher of National Executive Personnel (NEP), a member of the doctoral faculty of Capella University, and training editor for *The Futurist*, the official publication of the World Future Society.